C.G. Jung and the Sioux Traditions

C.G. Jung and the Sioux Traditions

Dreams, Visions, Nature, and the Primitive

Vine Deloria, Jr.

Philip J. Deloria and
Jerome S. Bernstein, Editors

Fulcrum Publishing
Wheat Ridge, Colorado

Library of Congress Cataloging-in-Publication Data

Names: Deloria, Vine, author. | Deloria, Philip Joseph, editor. |
    Bernstein, Jerome S., 1936- editor.
Title: C.G. Jung and the Sioux traditions : dreams, visions, nature, and
    the primitive / Vine Deloria, Jr. ; Philip J. Deloria and Jerome S.
    Bernstein, editors.
Description: Wheat Ridge, Colorado : Fulcrum Publishing, [2022] | "First
    published by Spring Journal Books, 2016"--Title page verso. | Includes
    bibliographical references and index.
Identifiers: LCCN 2021036635 | ISBN 9781682753231 (paperback)
Subjects: LCSH: Jungian psychology. | Dakota Indians--Psychology.
Classification: LCC BF173.J85 D45 2022 | DDC 150.19/54--dc23
LC record available at https://lccn.loc.gov/2021036635

Printed in the United States
0 9 8 7 6 5 4 3 2 1

Cover art by Mary Sully (Susan Mabel Deloria),
her Personality Print "John Philip Sousa"

Fulcrum Publishing
3970 Youngfield Street
Wheat Ridge, Colorado 80033
(800) 992-2908 • (303) 277-1623
fulcrumbooks.com

CONTENTS

Western science, following Roger Bacon, believed man could force nature to reveal its secrets; the Sioux simply petitioned nature for friendship.

—Vine Deloria, Jr.

A Note on the Notes

Footnotes are used for the Editors' Comments on Vine Deloria's text. They are indicated with symbols (*, **, †, and so on) and are found at the bottom of the page.

Endnotes are reserved for references citing the book's sources and, occasionally, for some supplemental information Deloria wished to provide. They are found at the end of the book.

FOREWORD

Philip J. Deloria

Some three decades ago, when I was a senior in high school, my father presented me with a copy of Carl Jung's *Memories, Dreams, Reflections* and an admonition to read it. "This is loaded with interesting stuff," he said. "It is particularly useful in thinking about families, ours included. You'll see that, like our family, Jung had a set of clergymen in his past. Like us, he sometimes wondered if he were answering questions posed by his ancestors." Equally to the point, at least as far as my father was concerned, Jung had been willing to open his mind to new ways of thinking about the world, about history, and about our human relation to it: "Be sure you meditate on that passage where he is making his way through a series of cellars deeper and deeper into the earth," he said, "and read the passage on his visit to Taos Pueblo too." My father thought that *Memories, Dreams, Reflections* was the perfect book for a young man on the edge of adulthood. So I read it, along with *Zen and the Art of Motorcycle Maintenance, Meetings with Remarkable Men, The Once and Future King, Raintree County*, and a haphazard and eclectic list of other books, most of which my father also tossed my way.

I see now that he recommended *Memories, Dreams, Reflections* to me because the book was tremendously important to him. In truth, I had not been thinking much at all about whether our family was answering questions posed by our ancestors, or how one might move deeply into psychic and developmental time. I was not really able, at that point, to consider such things, but my father surely was contemplating the possibility of both. Jung's thinking profoundly influenced his own. He began working on this book in the mid-1980s, with an intensive reading of Jung's various and copious writings. The project, in the end, spanned two decades, though no doubt it had been in his mind for longer than that. Jung's influence was critically important to my father, although such influence may not be readily visible to those more familiar with his career as a Native American activist, legal expert, writer and educator. Indeed, readers familiar with his writings

in American Indian history, law, and politics may find this book to be somewhat out of his oeuvre.

Vine Deloria Jr., (1933-2005) was born and raised in South Dakota,
the son and grandson of Dakota Sioux Indian leaders in the Episcopalian
missionary church. His aunt, Ella Deloria, had done ethnographic work
under the auspices of Franz Boas and in partnership with the first generation
of female anthropologists, and his great-grandfather, Saswe, had been an
important spiritual and political figure among the mid-nineteenth century
Yankton Dakota people. He truly did descend from a family of ministers
and spiritual leaders. Even as my father acquired a solid "Western" education at boarding schools, and later, Iowa State College (now University) and
the Augustana (now Lutheran) School of Theology, he grew up surrounded
by the stories and cultural contexts of his Lakota and Dakota Sioux Indian
people. In 1965, he began serving as the Executive Director of the National
Congress of American Indians, and he worked tirelessly to mobilize tribes
and Indian people in general toward effective participation in the American
political process. Drawing on these experiences, he wrote the 1969 bestseller
Custer Died for Your Sins: An Indian Manifesto, which used wit, humor,
and biting critique to awaken Americans of all stripes to the persistence
of American Indian people. Though he is best known for the numerous
political, legal, and historical writings that followed *Custer*, my father never
truly retreated from the questions of metaphysics and spirituality that his
family had bequeathed him, and that had sent him to the Lutheran School to
earn a degree in Divinity. His explorations of those questions took concrete
shape in books such as *God is Red* (1973) and *The Metaphysics of Modern
Existence* (1979). The present work ought properly be seen as a continua-
tion of those explorations, one that brings together the many strands of his
diverse intellectual interests, and that reflects his longstanding interest in
matters Jungian.

The task of this book, as he saw it, is to convey to readers the kinds of
influences he found in the writings of Carl Jung, and to carry them further.
In *C.G. Jung and the Sioux Traditions: Dreams, Visions, Nature and the
Primitive*, he means to establish the grounds upon which mutual influences—between Sioux traditions, practices and ways of thinking, and those
emanating from Jung and those writing in the Jungian tradition—might be
recognized and fostered. Such a dialogue did not come easily to my father.
He devoted years to a reading of Jung's entire *Collected Works* (the full set
still remains in his library in Colorado), and he reveled in the moments when

Jung seemed to be speaking the same conceptual language. At the same time, he was deeply disturbed by the seeming omnipresence of the intellectual legacies of European colonialism, naturalized in many of Jung's utterances concerning "the primitive" and the place of "primitives" in contemporary society, and in Jung's developmentalist understanding of the transformations of society, culture, and the psyche. A staunch critic of both colonialism and evolution, my father had a difficult time squaring his appreciation for Jung's cosmology with Jung's culturally-inflected discourse. Some of that difficulty inevitably shows up in these pages, as he attempts to negotiate these tensions.

My father believed deeply in the power of the spirit, and when he confronted numerous setbacks in the writing of the Jung book, he took those troubles to heart. On at least two occasions, he suffered from severe writer's block (the only time in his substantial writing career, to my knowledge, that he found himself blocked). My memory is that, in both instances, he reached the same page number, and found that he could go no further (the actual page is lost to my memory, but it was somewhere over 200). Taking the writer's block and the "coincidence" of the page number seriously, he set the book aside for significant periods of time. When he returned to it, in both instances he simply started again from the beginning. He experienced a devastating office fire in January 1994, and had to rebuild notes and files for many of his projects, including this book. He suffered from health issues later in that decade, which slowed the pace of his work. And of course he was in constant demand as a writer and lecturer, which kept him from spending large amounts of focused time on the project. Finally, he confronted a repeated disinterest on the part of publishers for a book that was not only tightly specialized and counterintuitive in relation to his larger body of work, but also a sometimes-confusing blend of critique and appreciation, and of psychology, philosophy, and ethnography.

When he died in November 2005, the book was under review with Nancy Cater and Spring Journal Books, and my father was excited about returning to it one last time. Jerome Bernstein was serving as the outside reviewer, and he had offered generous and timely comments for the next round of editorial revision. Sadly, that round of editorial dialogue never took place.

In August 2006, I met Nancy Cater and Jerome Bernstein in Santa Fe for a discussion concerning the manuscript and how we might bring it to fruition. In consultation with my mother, we agreed on a number of basic principles. First, we recognized that an editorial dialogue would have been a normal part of the process of publication, and that my father had in the past altered his writing—sometimes in significant ways—in response to such dialogue. We agreed that we needed to try to approximate that process of revision, even in his absence. Though my father was often extremely precise in his logic, many of his most striking insights were intuitive and connective, and he sometime failed to develop them as fully as one might wish. Indeed, it is fair to say that my father's excitement about this material was such that he did not always pause to translate from his "thinking language" to one more attuned to communication with a reading audience. Instead of working the material through multiple edits of a single, always-developing draft, he had simply started from scratch on three distinct manuscripts, experiencing the material in interior ways which produced inevitable leaps of logic and argumentation. As much as possible, these things needed to be addressed in order to turn the manuscript into a book.

Second, we noted that my father had not revised the manuscript in almost a decade, and that certain of his arguments and citations had fallen out of date. These needed to be revised, eliminated, or updated. Third, we agreed that any revisions had to exist in delicate balance with a commitment to preserve his words, style, and mode of argument, and that we would avoid changing his expression whenever possible. There are a number of moments in the book at which we felt that the questions of voice and style outweighed any editorial desires to make changes, and we have allowed those to stand. This book is, after all, his book; not ours. Fourth, we recognized that my father is himself already the subject of scholarship, and that future investigators may well want to read the original—or at least the final iteration to emanate from his typewriter—and so we will deposit with his papers (the final disposition of which is still uncertain at the time of this writing) the draft that he submitted to Spring in early 2005.

At our meeting in Santa Fe, we set up and modeled a number of editorial practices. At the most interventionist, we decided to collapse together two separate chapters on family dynamics, as understood by Sioux people on the one hand and by Jung and Jungians on the other. These two chapters now take form in Chapter Eight, "The Individual and Kinship." Though we discussed other large structural changes, in the end we decided against these. We went through the Introduction, working together on a line-by-line edit to give ourselves a sense what kinds of changes we were willing—and unwilling—to make. We made minor adjustments in the order of chapters and we re-named the first and last chapters as Introduction and Conclusion. From the Introduction and Chapter One, we pulled two short passages to be published as a stand-alone article in *Psyche and Nature*, a special edition of *Spring Journal*. We touched down on a number of other chapters, identifying various issues to be addressed as we moved forward. Finally, we decided to recruit Gay Bradshaw, an expert in the field, and someone who had known my father, to help with the editing of two important chapters on animals.

During 2006-2007, I went through the entire manuscript, building on some of the previous editorial suggestions offered by Jerome Bernstein. Gay Bradshaw did a marvelous job with the two animal chapters and I am extremely grateful to her for that work. I reorganized sections and some syntax, added transitional materials, and signposted and clarified arguments where necessary. Both Jerome Bernstein and I have included, in addition to my father's basic endnotes, occasional discursive footnotes offering further clarifications and interpretations. I want to offer special recognition to my mother, Barbara N. Deloria, who went through the entire body of endnotes, double-checking citations and tracking down ambiguities, and who has been a consistent and reliable sounding board throughout the editorial process.

As I've suggested, this book is consistent with both *God is Red* and *The Metaphysics of Modern Existence*. Like those books, it also makes a contribution to American Indian studies and to non-Indian awareness of the continued vitality and importance of Native peoples in the world. The book was conceived as a dialogue, in the true sense in which neither speaker is able to leave untouched; my father was suggesting that Jungians, having encountered even a basic sense of Sioux traditions, could not maintain their previous practices and beliefs without serious reevaluation. As interesting, however, was my father's willingness—and indeed, eagerness—to understand Sioux traditions in a new way, courtesy of his encounter with Jung. Undoubtedly, this book would have been stronger had my father lived to conduct a full dialogue of his own with Jerome Bernstein, Nancy Cater, Gay Bradshaw and others. It is my own hope, however, that our efforts have not been in vain, and that some of the openness of Jung and some of the strength of my father's own passion and convictions have made their way into this volume. And I hope that you, the reader, find in the text a worthwhile occasion for your own thoughts and inspirations. I know that my dad would have wanted exactly that. He was always driven to open up old ideas to probing conversation, to question dogma, and to imagine the possibilities of the new—which is what this book seeks to do.

Philip J. Deloria
Ann Arbor, Michigan
December 2008

FOREWORD

Jerome S. Bernstein

In January 1925 Carl Jung visited the Taos Pueblo, and there met with Och-wiay Biano (Mountain Lake), an elder of the tribe.* In my view, Jung was so psychologically, emotionally and intellectually affected by the impact of his visit to Taos Pueblo and his discussions with Mountain Lake, that it perme-ated his theory and work throughout his life.**

To gauge the emotional and psychological impact on Jung of this encounter with the American Indian realm, I quote from Jung's *Memories, Dreams, Reflections* regarding one engagement with Mountain Lake:

> "See," Ochwiay Biano said, "how cruel the whites look. Their lips are thin, their noses sharp, their faces furrowed and distorted by folds. Their eyes have a staring expression; they are always seeking something. What are they seeking? The whites always want something … We do not know what they want. … We think they are mad."

---

* Ochwiay Biano's given (Christian) name was Antonio Mirabal, which is consistent with the hispanic names forced upon all Pueblo Indians by the Spanish. Some accounts of Jung's encounter with Mountain Lake identify Ochwiay Biano as a Hopi elder designated by the Taos elders to represent the tribe in his two meetings with Jung. This is extremely unlikely. Taos Pueblo and the Hopi Tribe, though "cousins" in their Puebloan culture and religion, are distinct cultural and tribal groups. The language of Taos Pueblo is Tiwa; Hopi is a distinct and separate language and members of the respective tribes would not understand the language of the other without having studied it. It is difficult to imagine that elders of Taos Pueblo would appoint a member of any other tribe to represent their religion and culture.

It should also be noted that Jung believed Ochwiay Biano to be "a chief of the Taos Pueblos," a common misunderstanding on the part of Westerners. He was not a "chief," nor was there a single "chief" of the Pueblo.

** Deirdre Bair, in her biography of Jung, asserts that, "His letters make it very clear that he had long ago lost interest in everything related to Native American cultures."[1] On the contrary, Jung's works are permeated with references to Ochwiay Biano and the wisdom that he gleaned from his encounter with him, including a letter to Miguel Serrano less than a year before Jung's death, where Jung observed: "We are sorely in need of a Truth or a self-understanding similar to that … which I have found still living with the Taos Pueblos."[2]

I asked him why he thought the whites were all mad.

"They say that they think with their heads," he replied.

"Why of course. What do you think with?" I asked him in surprise.

"We think here," he said, indicating his heart.

I *fell* into a long meditation. For *the first time in my life*, so it seemed to me, someone had drawn for me a picture of the real white man. It was as though *until now* I had seen nothing but sentimental, prettified color prints. *This Indian had struck* our vulnerable spot, *unveiled a truth* to which we are blind. *I felt rising within me* like a shapeless mist something unknown and yet deeply familiar. And out of this mist, *image upon image detached itself:* first Roman legions smashing into the cities of Gaul, and the keenly incised features of Julius Caesar, Scipio Africanus, and Pompey. *I saw* the Roman eagle on the North Sea and the banks of the White Nile. Then *I saw* St. Augustine transmitting the Christian creed to the Britons on the tips of Roman lances, and Charlemagne's most glorious forced conversions of the heathen. … *With a secret stab* I realized the hollowness of that old romanticism about the Crusades. Then followed Columbus, Cortes and the other conquistadors who with fire, sword, torture, and Christianity came down upon even *these remote pueblos dreaming peacefully in the Sun*, their Father.[3]

All of the italics have been added to the above quote to highlight the degree to which Jung was impacted by this experience. If we read the above taking into *our hearts* (as well as our thoughts) what Jung is sharing with us, we can see that Jung was thrust into the unconscious by this exchange and that he was deeply penetrated ("stabbed") by this encounter with Ochwiay Biano. This was no mere intellectual encounter. Rather it was a profound emotional and psychological confrontation for Jung. Because his reaction was so strong, as evidenced by the many references to Mountain Lake throughout Jung's writings, we can realize the pronounced influence of American Indian culture and its unique psyche on Jung's work.

We can also see Jung's idealization of the life of this Indian Pueblo "dreaming peacefully in the Sun." No doubt they did dream peacefully in the Sun. But they also experienced genocide, great poverty, discrimination, and other hardships, and of course, like all cultural groups, Taos Pueblo culture had its own shadow side.

Now let us move to 1932 and Jung's essay, "Archaic Man," wherein he raises an extraordinary question:

> The question is nothing less than this: Does the psyche in general—the soul or spirit or the unconscious—originate in *us*, or is the psyche, in the early stages of conscious evolution, actually outside us in the form of arbitrary powers with intentions of their own, and does it gradually take its place within us in the course of psychic development? Were the split-off "souls"—or dissociated psychic contents, as we would call them—ever parts of the psyches of individuals, or were they from the beginning psychic entities existing in themselves according to the primitive view as ghosts, ancestral spirits, and the like? [In Navajo these so-called "split-off souls" would be the Holy People or Yei; in Hopi and Pueblo cultures, Katsinas, i.e., primordial images.] Were they only by degrees embodied in man in the course of development, so that they gradually constituted in him that world which we now call the psyche?[4]

At the end of this essay Jung says, "[While] this whole idea strikes us as dangerously paradoxical ... at bottom, it is not altogether inconceivable."[5] However, "I must leave this question unanswered."[6]

Here Jung sits between the opposites, holding the tension of this awesome question of whether psyche originates in us or actually outside of us.

Enter Vine Deloria, Jr., whose response to this question would, I think, be "Yes." *Not* "Both," but "Yes." Deloria would not have accepted the "either/or" duality in which Jung poses the question. I believe his response would be based on experience more than on thought. His experience would be "Yes."

And here, in this posthumous exchange between Jung and Deloria that I have constructed, rests the tension between these two systems—and their connection. If the reader can feel and hold the tension of "yes" and "both," then he can begin to experience what Deloria and Jung intuited.

Jung obviously intuited much of the culture and psyche of the American Indian world. But at the same time, in his own words, "We are now *surrounded* by a world that is obedient to rational laws ..."[7] [emphasis added]. That is, he knew that notwithstanding his intuition, he could not get outside of the Western rational dualistic mind-set even while experiencing something psychically profound which seemed to be to moving him beyond that mind-set.*

Vine Deloria, Jr. knew this as well about Jung. As a scholar who had immersed** himself in the study of Jung's psychology, he recognized, coming from the other pole—the other side of the rational mind-set—the connections between Jung's psychology and American Indian religion and medicine.† He saw that Jung's psychological system could serve as a functional bridge between those two worlds that existed side by side.

At the same time he was piqued and shocked by some of Jung's presumptions and seeming arrogance when observing the world of "the primitive." He determined to respond to Jung as a "primitive psyche" himself, addressing the many errors in Jung's observations and to represent the wisdom of the indigenous mind and culture as well as what he perceived to be its superior attitudes, values and practices as compared with Western psychology and culture. In his own words:

> While Jung has been thoroughly discussed by his Western peers, he has not, to my knowledge, been compared or critiqued by someone Jung would have referred to as being "a primitive." Such an analysis may help to illuminate parts of Jungian psychology that have been controversial

---

* If we are to understand what Jung was getting at, it is vital to bear in mind when reading any of Jung's essays, and particularly his writings on the "primitive psyche," that Jung was a man of his times. In this context, his visits to North Africa (1920), Taos Pueblo (1925), Kenya and Uganda (1925) were central in his formulations of a general and hierarchical theory of the psyche, ranging from the "two-million-year-old" man to aboriginal man, the American Indian, and ultimately to the Western psyche as we understand it up to the time of Jung's death in 1961. (I believe that his travel to India was more of an influence in his understanding of religion than to his understanding of what he called the "primitive psyche.")

It is also essential to remind ourselves that in the formulation of his theories, Jung was limited by the nature of the psyche itself as he came to understand it at any given point in time. He had the unique problem of trying to understand a psyche which was evolving in his midst, and at the same time being a primary agent for formulating theories to explain the very dynamics of that psyche which he was trying to understand. It does a great disservice to Jung, and the theoretical formulations he set forth, to judge them from the vantage point of our hindsight and the further evolution of the psyche and the body of research which has ensued since Jung's death. Vine Deloria, Jr. understood this well and expressed his appreciation of the seeming limitations in Jung's work in this regard.

** He had read the entire twenty volumes of the *Collected Works* of Jung, plus the additional seminars and other essays published subsequently.

† Unlike Western culture, medicine and religion typically are inseparable in many indigenous cultures. In most American Indian cultures they constitute one system.

in Western intellectual circles. Indeed, such a critique could provide additional insights and data to some Jungian concepts that are more intuitive than empirical.

Jung was very bothered by the Western psyche's split from nature which he addressed and alluded to repeatedly in his writings:

> No wonder the Western world feels uneasy, for it does not know how much it has lost through the destruction of its numinosities ... Its moral and spiritual tradition has collapsed and has left a worldwide disorientation and dissociation ... Nothing is holy any longer. Through scientific understanding our world has become dehumanized ... His immediate communication with nature is gone for ever, and the emotional energy it generated has sunk into the unconscious ... We *have been* that mind, but we have never *known* it. *We got rid of it before understanding it.**8

Deloria recognized the same deficit in the Western psyche. But unlike Jung, he did not think that loss was irretrievable. Indeed, he felt that this was one of the great gifts that the indigenous psyche still had to offer Western culture. In producing the achievements of Western culture, humans have at the same time cut themselves off from understandings of nature as a source of spiritual and psychological life. Sioux culture—and the cultures of other indigenous peoples—contain certain understandings that can help us rethink and redress this lack.

Notwithstanding disagreements with some of Jung's often erroneous pronouncements regarding the "primitive psyche," Deloria had a profound respect for Jung and his psychology. He clearly saw the latter as the only psychological lens through which the wisdom of American Indian culture could be communicated to the Western psyche, an essential compensation for a great culture that had become too one-sided in its overly rationalistic orientation to life and itself. Obviously this has great implications in terms of the perilous times into which we have moved regarding the earth's ecology.

There are some details which should be clarified for the reader with regard to Jung's understanding of American Indian psychology. Jung's contact with American Indian culture was limited to his discussions in

---

*　It is important to note that this essay was written in 1960, a year or less before his death. His concern with the Western psyche's split from nature was prominent throughout his life.

1925 with Mountain Lake at Taos Pueblo. By all accounts, this contact amounted to a few hours—not days—over a two-day period and the subsequent exchange of a few letters between Mountain Lake and Jung over the ensuing years. It was far from in-depth. Unlike some of the African cultures Jung visited, Taos Pueblo is one of the most secretive regarding its religious and healing practices. To this day, that culture is as closed-mouthed as it was in Jung's day, if not more so, even towards members of other Indian tribes. Most would fare no better than a white man today in pursuing such information. During this visit of a white European—albeit a distinguished one—most of the important cultural and religious knowledge and practices would have been withheld. Thus many of Jung's subsequent analyses and insights were necessarily intuitive.* Many were right; some were close to being right; and many were just plain inaccurate.**

Another problem was Jung's tendency to lump together all indigenous groups because he thought of them as more or less having the same "primitive" psyche. Thus he based some of his analyses of American Indian ways on his insights gained during his visits with African tribal members. One of many examples of this was his observation—not true of most American Indian culture and beliefs†—that,

> While it is perfectly understandable to us that people die of advanced age or as the result of diseases that are recognized to be fatal, this is not the case with primitive man. When old persons die, he does not believe it to be the result of age. He argues that there are persons who have lived to be much older. Likewise, no one dies as the result of disease, for there have been other people who recovered from the same disease. Or never contracted it. To him, the real explanation is always magic. Either a spirit has killed the man or it was sorcery.[9]

---

*   The reader is again reminded that Ochwiay Biano was not a "chief" of the Pueblo, nor was he a kiva chief (priest), the one who presides over religious rites. He was a wise man designated that day to meet and talk with Jung—in part probably because his English was considered good.

**   Again, it is important to note that Jung visited Taos Pueblo in 1925, a time when few outsiders had made a serious study of American Indian culture. It is important, too, to remember that Jung was a European with no indigenous culture of its own to prepare his European psyche for engagement with indigenous cultures and the indigenous psyche. For the most part, indigenous peoples were seen as an anomalous curiosity. Jung was one of the first to approach the subject with the seriousness that it deserved, notwithstanding the limited exposure he did have.

†   While a number of American Indian cultures experience witchcraft and sorcery, including the Navajo and Hopi, this belief does not constitute the basis for the death of old people.

Jung early on had an image and theory of a hierarchical evolution of the human psyche.* Thus as he was exploring and analyzing the nature of the indigenous psyche, it was in the context of a theoretical framework which he had partially formulated in his mind.** He was therefore simultaneously seeking information and data to support a theoretical frame while exploring the nature of that psyche on its own terms.

In this regard, when Jung happened upon the concept of *participation mystique* as formulated by Lucien Levy-Bruhl, wherein "the subject cannot clearly distinguish himself from the object but is bound to it by a direct relationship which amounts to partial identity ...",[11] he found a (too) convenient mechanism which would explain some aspects of the "primitive psyche" consistent with his hierarchical approach to the evolution of the human psyche. In the process he tended to see all of the American Indian's perception of life and spirituality in the "objects" of the natural world (e.g., rocks, plants, water, animals) as projection.[12] Vine Deloria, Jr., as we shall see, took particular exception to this notion that the individual's connection to objects in the natural world all emanated from projection as formulated in the concept of *participation mystique*.†

I never met Vine Deloria, Jr. in person. From 1968 to 1976, I was a consultant to the Chairman of the Navajo Tribe and the tribe's registered lobbyist on Capitol Hill in Washington, D.C. Having been involved in American Indian politics on behalf of the Navajo Nation and through many connections with Indians in the ensuing years, I have known who Vine Deloria was—as a celebrated American Indian activist, as an articulate author who challenged the authority and history of the dominant American culture, as a scholar, and as a hero figure to American Indians.

---

*   See his essays on "The Structure of the Psyche," "On the Nature of the Psyche," "Mind and Earth," "Two Kinds of Thinking," and "Archaic Man," among others.

**   "Just as the body has its evolutionary history and shows clear traces of the various evolutionary stages, so too does the psyche."[10]

†   I personally have come to side with Deloria on this issue, notwithstanding a few similar representations in my own book, *Living in the Borderland: The Evolution of Consciousness and the Challenge of Healing Trauma*, which I hope to correct in subsequent printings. This represents not only what I think, but my experience. See pp. 160-161 in *Living in the Borderland*.

So one day in 2005 when I received a manuscript authored by Deloria sent to me by Nancy Cater, Publisher of Spring Journal Books, I was both surprised and delighted. My surprise was at the title: *C. G. Jung and the Sioux Traditions.* I did know that Deloria had some knowledge of and feeling for psychology, but this Jungian connection was yet another side of Vine Deloria, Jr. I was excited to read it.

I soon realized that this was a very important document. I also began to reflect on the several passages in Jung that I had read over the years with which I disagreed and which continually niggled at me, and discovered that most of these were being addressed by Deloria. It was also clear that Deloria felt as I did—that Jung's psychology was the only system of Western thought whose theories could hold and make sense of much of American Indian religion and medicine from the Western perspective. Jung's theories of the collective unconscious, archetypes, the psychoid and the subtle body, and the Self, along with the prominence given to the role of mythology in explaining the archetypal foundations of culture and individual psychology, provided a unique lens through which to view the rich world of the American Indian. Most important of all, from my point of view, Jung's psychology remains the only school of thought that considers the religious/ spiritual domain as indispensable and integral to the understanding of the human psyche. There is no understanding of Indian culture or the individual Indian without an appreciation of their religion.

Most importantly, it was apparent that Deloria's manuscript constituted nothing less than a "primitive psyche" responding to Jung's views and interpretations of the Indian psyche more than eighty years after Jung's first encounter with the Indian world. Or perhaps I should say it a little differently. Deloria responded to Jung from the *subject position* of a "primitive psyche." No primitive himself, Deloria was well versed in Western philosophy, literature, and social science. He crafted a persona through which to engage Jung's understanding of "the primitive," one that incorporated his own frame of reference and his discursive "language," which was in fact that of the Sioux. It was the world that he knew best in a particular experiential way, though many of his observations apply to other American Indian cultures as well. In the years ensuing since Jung's meeting with Ochwiay Biano, his assertions for the most part lay unchallenged. To my knowledge, Deloria's book is the only scholarly statement that offers a direct response to Carl Jung from the position of "the primitive." It may well be that this book will remain the only written treatise of its kind.

Deloria wrote his manuscript in the 1980s. He told me that he had tried to get major publishing houses to publish his book. There were no takers. They did not get the importance of the work.

In submitting the manuscript to Nancy Cater of Spring Journal Books in 2005, Deloria told her that the one thing he wanted most before he died was to see this manuscript published. He was already quite ill due to complications following surgery and apparently had a knowingness of his impending death.

Nancy Cater asked if I would act as Spring's agent in working with Deloria, and I did. We had an initial telephone conversation about the manuscript and were making plans for me to visit him in Golden, Colorado to work on it. That was not to be. We had email exchanges about the manuscript, another phone conversation, I made some editing suggestions, and most important, he did receive a contract for the publication of his book. Sadly, he died three months after my first contact with him.

So why is this book important? After all, it is seemingly very esoteric. How many people will be interested in Jungian psychology and Sioux traditions?

For scholars of Jung, it is a major contribution to Jungian literature and thought. Jung's view of the evolution of the psyche was hierarchical and what he came to call the "primitive psyche" became an essential building block in his formulations over the years regarding the structure and dynamics of the (modern) psyche. Whether we realize it or not, Jung's views of the "primitive psyche" have come to influence all students of Jung.

Some would argue that to understand Jung's psychology, one must understand something of Carl Jung the man. To the extent this may be true, it is important then to appreciate that Jung's meeting with Mountain Lake in 1925 impacted him emotionally and intellectually and played a role in his thoughts in the remaining 36 years of Jung's life. And therein lies the importance of understanding the American Indian psyche: it played a significant role in his formative thinking about the evolution of the psyche.

Beyond even that, Deloria brings us a view into the American Indian psyche and culture on its own terms, from which we have a great deal to learn. There is a rapidly growing awareness of this need.

In one of Jung's last essays, "Healing the Split," written the year before his death, Jung laments the tragedy of Western culture's split from nature.[13]

He said that our world has become nothing less than "dehumanized." And he attributed this state of affairs to the irretrievable loss of man's "immediate communication with nature." Sadly, as reflected in this essay at the end of his life, Jung could only imagine at best a symbolic connection with nature. It was as if he could no longer hold the tension of "yes" to that critical question Jung formulated in his essay on "Archaic Man," as I proposed at the beginning of this Foreword.

It is now nearly 50 years since Jung wrote that essay. The world is in more dire straits than it was in 1960, and the place of the environment is rapidly becoming the front and center focus in the context of the survival of our species. It is clear that science and technology have a major role to play in this regard. At the same time, there is a growing recognition that science and technology alone will not be enough to save us—unless we come to the realization that psyche is an indispensable technology along with applied science in the struggle to survive ourselves.

It is my view that the unconscious will play as central a role as science and (the other) technology in this regard. Jung spoke of the evolution of the psyche,[14] and his concept of individuation through ego-Self dialogue constitutes nothing less than the description of man as a co-evolutionary partner. Jung's concern with Western man's dissociation due to his split from nature anticipated the state in which we now find ourselves.

It is my contention that nature itself has as crucial a role to play in the survival of our species, as does man's ego and science and technology. By this I mean that the collective unconscious is speaking to us through our individual and collective dreams and transrational experiences, which are becoming more and more prevalent and are addressing the ecological catastrophe we face. It is also moving the Western ego towards a re-connection with nature—not a return to a connection that once was, but a connection in the current context of collective and individual consciousness. This is being manifested in what I have come to call Borderland consciousness. (See *Living in the Borderland: The Evolution of Consciousness and the Challenge of Healing Trauma*, Part I.) It is in this realm that nature has once again begun to speak to and through the Western psyche. Our capacity to hear and take in what is being said may determine our survival as a species.

Vine Deloria's book, *C. G. Jung and the Sioux Traditions*, provides a language and a conceptual bridge, along with Jung's, for Western culture in its effort to find its way through the maze of its own making to a healthier relationship with nature, and therein a healthier relationship with the Self.

It provides a means with which to better listen to and hear nature, and even to be guided by it towards a healthier relationship between *Homo sapiens* and the rest of life. We are beginning to learn that our life as a species is not sustainable without respect for all of life.

It is not that we should begin to practice Sioux or other tribal rituals. That has already been tried (see *Playing Indian* by P.J. Deloria, New Haven: Yale University Press, 1998). I think the word that is most appropriate here is "respect." Among other meanings, as I have learned from Indian friends and medicine people, it refers to a profound feeling of appreciation, an intuitive knowing that speaks to and guides an ego open to the spirit of the sacred. That spirit, that sense which we Westerners cannot quite name, is what has attracted us to the religion and traditions of the American Indian from our very first contact. It is what Mountain Lake asked Jung about the white man: "They are always seeking something. What are they seeking? The whites always want something ... We do not know what they want. ... "

C. G. Jung and the Sioux Traditions addresses Mountain Lake's question. Jung attempted to build a conceptual and psychic bridge to that realm from which Western culture became severed. Vine Deloria, Jr. saw Jung's effort, and through this book has built a conceptual and psychic bridge from his side of the river to meet Jung's. I have an image of the two of them meeting somewhere on that span, sitting and smoking together, arguing and having one hell of a palaver, all the while appreciating and respecting what the other brings.

Jerome S. Bernstein, M.A.P.C., NCPsyA
Jungian Analyst
Santa Fe, New Mexico
June 2008

INTRODUCTION

PSYCHOLOGY & THE PSYCHE

Vine Deloria, Jr.

For several decades, I have been struck by the interest shown by some Jungians in the spiritual traditions and practices of the Plains Indians.* I have often been approached by people who have immersed themselves in Jungian thought, and then come away from that experience wanting to know more about Plains Indian religion. Their interest, it seems to me, indicates good intuitive sense; at many levels there is indeed a connection. Over two decades ago, I sought to understand that connection by tracing where this interest might originate within the Jungian system. When I found several Jungian concepts used to describe psychological states that seemed similar, if not identical, to the Sioux Indian beliefs and experiences, it seemed to me that a book discussing the possible points of agreement between Jung and the Sioux might be useful and enlightening. At the same time, however, I worried that these intriguing points of agreement had led some to believe they could move directly from a Jungian background to an immediate understanding of the ceremonial life and religious beliefs of the Plains people without any effort to translate the ideas from one context to the other.

At least three major concerns emerged as I pondered the possibility of an extensive comparison of, and dialogue between, the two cosmologies and two bodies of thought. To begin with, Jung has had his share of critics and detractors within his own culture. He has often been accused of sneaking metaphysics and superstition back into Western intellectual thought (as if that body of knowledge had absolute boundaries that could not be violated). This concern, however, also presents an opportunity. While Jung has been thoroughly discussed by his Western peers, he has not, to my knowledge,

---

*   Readers often raise the question of naming and proper word use in connection with American Indian people. There are a range of possibilities, each with its pitfalls and virtues: Native, Native American, American Indian, Indian, indigenous, aboriginal, First Nation, tribal, as well as specific names such as Sioux, Dakota, Navajo, etc. Vine Deloria's usage here was consistent with his other writings: "Indian" was his preferred marker of generic Indian identity.

been compared or critiqued by someone speaking from an American Indian culture—someone Jung would have referred to as being "a primitive." Such an analysis may help to illuminate exactly those parts of Jungian psychology that have been most controversial in Western intellectual circles. Indeed, such a critique could provide additional insights and data to some Jungian concepts that are more intuitive than empirical.

Secondly, Sioux culture and its beliefs and practices are themselves highly complex. Despite long histories of European assertions of Indian inferiority, Sioux practices do in fact meet the most rigorous standards of intellectual discourse and understanding. Though different, Sioux knowledge is equal to that of Western peoples. Demonstrating through Jungian psychology the nature of this great complexity might help people inspired to learn about the Plains Indians understand in greater detail a specific system of thought. It would, at the least, enable them to avoid errors in interpretation and help them see the kinds of personal discipline and social relationships that constituted the old traditions and enabled the Sioux to handle certain kinds of psychological problems easily.

Finally, cross-cultural exchanges, particularly in the United States, are often no more than the appropriation of concepts and beliefs of the "smaller" culture by those people of the larger one. Rarely does an idea from a less dominant culture have any effect or influence on the beliefs and practices of a more dominant one. Today, we have a great revival of traditions in many Indian tribes, and this movement has attracted people from the dominant culture who seek to find something of value. Ideas, of course, cannot be confined to any one group of people. But cross-cultural work, if it is to prove useful and ethical, should also subject the ideas of the larger culture to critique by those of the smaller in such a manner as to help create a new intellectual framework that partially transcends each culture.

In producing the achievements of Western culture, humans have at the same time cut themselves off from understandings of nature as a source of spiritual and psychological life. Sioux culture—and the cultures of other indigenous peoples—contain certain understandings that can help us rethink and redress this lack. The long history of appropriations from Indian people, however, requires us proceed with great caution. My intent here is to establish a balanced dialogue between the two cosmologies and the spiritual and psychological dynamics that derived from them.

The collected works of Jung, transcripts of his seminars, his autobiography, and the works of his first-generation disciples make Jungian thought easily available. Not so with the Indian data. Most of the material describing or illustrating the Sioux traditions must be gathered anecdote-by-anecdote from a few sources and classified according to subject matter and themes. I have relied primarily on Frances Densmore's classic work *Teton Sioux Music and Culture* in which, in addition to recording a multitude of songs, she reported extensively on the stories that explained the songs and rituals. *Teton Sioux Music* was originally printed in 1918, so the stories Densmore includes have an authenticity that more modern data lacks. As important are the works of early twentieth-century Sioux authors like Luther Standing Bear and Charles Eastman, which also give us a glimpse into the minds and emotions of the old people who grew to maturity following the old customs and beliefs. I have turned to other ethnographic sources, as well, and have also incorporated the traditions, memories, and knowledges that have been passed to me through my family and through encounters with Sioux traditionalists.

There are intrinsic problems in the task of bringing two worldviews together for comparison. Paraphrasing a prolific thinker like Jung, and giving a generalized interpretation of his thought, can often lead to misplaced emphases. This problem becomes a major stumbling block when two large bodies of knowledge are placed side by side for comparison, as I seek to do with Jung and the Sioux. Therefore I have used extensive quotations from both Jung's writings and from the stories related by Sioux medicine men so that they can, in effect, converse with one another. The selection of quotations does introduce a certain bias since neither the Sioux nor Jung anticipated this encounter. However, the old medicine men spoke of their experiences and religious discoveries in ways that provide us with a good sense of how they understood the world and themselves. More important, these old men could demonstrate special powers to heal, predict the future, find lost objects, and establish relationships with other living beings. These things must be part of any profound psychology.*

Jung was a man of his time and therefore some of his ideas and his language have a certain archaic flavor when seen in the light of contemporary

---

* Here, we point readers to the book Vine Deloria Jr. had completed and sent to his editor only days prior to his death. *The World We Used to Live In* (Fulcrum, 2006) offers a more complete treatment of accounts of the powers of Indian spiritual leaders, and serves as a useful companion to this discussion, particularly for those interested in the practices and possibilities of indigenous spirituality.

thinking. There have been significant transformations in knowledge and language since Jung produced his great corpus of psychological writings. His approach to gathering data, however, was considerably more sophisticated than most of his colleagues in psychology. In recent years, some psychologists have substituted statistical conclusions for original thought. Much psychology today tells us very little about the world or ourselves; it merely seeks quick mechanical adjustments in lifestyles. Today, Jung would undoubtedly be in the forefront of intellectual thought in such areas as near-death experiences, reincarnation, psi experiments, psychic archaeology, and geomythology. He would certainly be conversant with quantum mechanics, string theory, chaos theory and other recent advances in physics and cosmology. He might even be living with a tribe of people in Africa, the Pacific, or the western United States. Almost certainly, he would have adjusted his conception of tribal peoples, who are often described, using the language of his day, as "primitive."

Unlike some of the other members of the first generation of psychoanalysts, Carl Jung was not content with developing a psychology that spoke primarily to other professionals in the field or with restricting psychic experience to the social conventions of the time. Ranging over many periods of human history, cultures, and academic disciplines, Jung tried to bring together data that would aid in constructing a theoretical framework for understanding psychological processes in therapeutic practice. He endured much criticism from scholars in other fields who saw his omnivorous scholarship as an invasion of their territories and feared that their disciplines might become mere footnotes to psychology.

Jung boldly approached and invaded the realm of religion, for example, believing that "Religions are psychotherapeutic systems." "What are we doing," he asked, "we psychotherapists? We are trying to heal the suffering of the human mind, of the human psyche or the human soul, and religions deal with the same problem." He came to this conclusion when he realized that "Among all my patients in the second half of life—that is to say over thirty-five—there has not been one whose problem in the last resort was not that of finding a religious outlook on life."[2] Although this condition may indeed have existed in his patients, one wonders if the long tradition of ministers in Jung's background did not encourage him to see psychological problems in religious terms. That tradition may well have led him to conclude that the psyche needed the clothing of religion and could not stand naked before the secular world.

As might have been expected, some theologians, in an effort to reassert their authority over the field, accused Jung of theological naïveté. He was particularly chastised for suggesting that contemporary Roman Catholic doctrines on the Virgin Mary saved Christianity by making the Trinity into a quaternity. His response to these attacks was well reasoned. Jung carefully drew boundaries that he knew he could easily defend. "Psychology, as a science," he argued,

> observes religious ideas from the standpoint of their psychic phenomenology without intruding on their theological content. It puts the dogmatic images into the category of psychic contents, because this constitutes its field of research.[3]

This explanation is a clever way of saying that theology, but for its doctrinal formulas, is itself a psychology. Psychology, according to Jung, did not try to explain psychic processes in theological terms but merely sought to illuminate religious images by relating them to similar images in the psyche. Left unsaid was the obvious retort that dogmatic images themselves had to originate in the human psyche and not in external events, and in the last analysis, archetypes could be understood as "the equivalents of religious dogmas."[4]

Nevertheless, Jung maintained the distinction between psychology and theology, graciously giving theologians more credit than they probably deserved. "Psychology is very definitely not a theology," he wrote,

> it is a natural science that seeks to describe experienceable psychic phenomena. In doing so it takes account of the way in which theology conceives and names them, because this hangs together with the phenomenology of the contents under discussion.[5]

He further added that psychology did not have the capacity or the competence to pass on questions of truth and value since this was the province of theology. One might call him polite. But there was no question in Jung's mind that psychology had replaced theology. Indeed, he believed that twentieth-century man had devised a psychology precisely because theology no longer provided any explanation of the world or any comfort for the soul.

Jung employed a similar critique when considering philosophy, for it, like the established religions, suffered an inability to respond to humanity's deepest questions in a satisfactory manner. Jung felt that psychotherapy was replacing philosophy as the living discipline that helped our species formulate answers to its deepest and most important questions. Explaining this position, he observed that,

> whenever a science begins to grow beyond its narrow specialist boundaries, the need for fundamental principles is forced upon it, and with this it moves into the sovereign sphere of philosophy. If the science happens to be psychology, a confrontation with philosophy is unavoidable for the very reason that it had been a philosophic discipline from the beginning, resolutely breaking away from philosophy only in quite recent times, when it established itself within the philosophical and the medical faculties as an independent empirical science with mechanistic techniques.[6]

Therefore he concluded: "I can hardly draw a veil over the fact that we psychotherapists ought really to be philosophers or philosophic doctors—or rather that we already are so."[7] Psychology then for Jung could transcend philosophy quite easily because it had a practical application as a medical technique. As a science based on experience, psychology offered an individual more than a static, externalized and remote picture of life.

In contrast to his predecessors, including Freud, Jung explicitly sought to place his psychology midway between theology and philosophy by creating intimate relationships with both, and by offering a psychological interpretation of phenomena once regarded as exclusive property by these older traditional fields. While at the same time pointing out disciplinary overlap, Jung distinguished psychology as a discipline that sought to understand the world that we experience through an examination of the human mind and emotions in a scientific manner. Psychology, therefore, built on what had preceded it in the European past, which by inference included Western religion and philosophy. "What we call 'psychology' today," Jung said, "is a science that can be pursued only on the basis of certain historical and moral premises laid down by Christian education during the last two thousand years."[8]

In the final analysis, Jung was seeking to supplant the history, religion, philosophy and educational traditions of the West with a new synthesis, with psychology as its focus and psychological analysis as its methodological tool. This ambitious goal—creating a new synthesis of knowledge—is precisely what makes Jungian psychology, with its wide-ranging breadth and its openness to experience, the best candidate for a comparison and dialogue with American Indian beliefs and practices. What will become striking as we proceed is the curious nature of the comparison, for there are points at which the two cosmologies seem surprisingly similar, as they approach deep knowledge from distinct traditions. At the same time, however, those traditions will also remain radically different, with a huge gulf between their foundations and premises.

Unlike Western thinkers, for example, the Sioux did not separate their thoughts into categories and disciplines.* Everything was practical, economic, political and religious all at once. Indeed, they had a word to describe this totality, *wounicage*, which simply meant "our way of doing things." They accorded other people the right to have their own ways also. Although Sioux people did not develop "disciplines" as ways of sorting knowledge and inquiry, they nonetheless had an observational and analytical approach that generated knowledge of the world. Their view of life was holistic. All experiences were carefully analyzed and remembered, and beliefs always had an empirical referent. Approaching the comparison from the Sioux position, we can see that its consistently empirical base readily speaks to that of psychology, which sought to use empiricism to transcend theology and philosophy. We can look, then, for similarities and matches in treatments of experience, understanding and interpretation.

The distinctions between psychology, religion and philosophy occurred in the West because each discipline addressed a distinct audience and claimed primacy for its conclusions. Once a new synthesis had been achieved by Jungian psychology, however, the psychology could then communicate more easily with non-Western cultures that had not subdivided their understanding of the world into specialty fields. Recognizing that he had devised a framework that could speak to different human traditions,

---

*   Readers may wonder which Sioux people are under discussion and at what point in time. Vine Deloria's comments on Frances Densmore suggest that he was conceptualizing the old ways in terms of the cultural developments of the late eighteenth and early nineteenth centuries, prior to the attacks on Sioux culture that characterized the American policies of the mid- to late-nineteenth and early twentieth centuries, many of which aimed specifically at the social and cultural fabric of Sioux people. "Sioux" itself is a word marking the large communities of people ranging, at this time from what is now Minnesota west across South Dakota, North Dakota, and Nebraska, and into Wyoming and Montana. "Sioux" encompasses eastern (Dakota) and western (Lakota) language dialects, and a range of band, kinship, and now tribal social and political structures.

Jung felt perfectly at home borrowing symbols and techniques from other cultures. This openness was possible because of the manner in which Jung conceived the psyche and his belief that all human psychological structures were basically the same.

We can, then, look briefly at some of the hallmarks of the Jungian system, beginning with the term "psyche." In the appendix of *Memories, Dreams, Reflections*, Jung's autobiography, there is a glossary covering the major technical terms used in his psychology. This listing suggests that Jung feared later interpreters might bicker over the meaning of many of the concepts of his psychology so he needed to express his preference for certain definitions. In that glossary we do *not* find the word "psyche"—the basic concept that must underlie any psychology and certainly the primary concept in Jungian psychology. Left to our own devices, we might assume that "psyche" is a general term for whatever constitutes the great reservoir of organic emotion and behavior. Since the psyche forms the subject matter for psychology, we tend to think of it not in terms of matter and energy or the material and spiritual but, as a mysterious, non-physical thing or, to establish a parallel with thinking in modern quantum physics, as a set of possibilities.

Through the systematic analysis of the hysterical behavior, traumatic dreams, and "Freudian slips" of their patients, the psychologists of the early twentieth century posited the existence of two major areas (or functions) of the human psyche: the conscious and the unconscious. The conscious consisted of those bits of information, feelings, experiences and memories which could be easily and quickly retrieved by the willful act of individuals. The unconscious, on the other hand, was an entirely different creature. It could range from a simple repository of repressed memories to a highly complex interlocking set of instinctual responses and physical energy drives expressed in basic survival patterns. For Jung it also consisted of energetic archetypes that both constituted the experiential world and made it possible. In this sense, the psyche was something that everyone shared.

Jung eagerly accepted the division of the psyche into unconscious and conscious, and he used their apparent interaction to build his system of thought. He took the broadest possible approach to the unconscious, avoiding the admonitions of Freud that it contained only the repressed memories of childhood, and suggested instead that it was the substrate of the physical world. The unconscious was the ultimate repository of all of the experiences of organisms on this planet, of the imprints of ancient learned patterns of survival, of the collective memories of our species, and of the historical remembrances of the many societies as well as the ancestral family traits inherited by the individual and, of course, his or her set of repressed memories. As time passed, the unconscious expanded to incorporate new experiences of the biosphere. It was, in other words, a capacious reservoir.

We need not discuss the possible contents of the unconscious as Jung came to know them. Rather, our immediate concern is to understand Jung's thinking in the area where he wished to have a profound impact—the connecting of psychology with the other sciences through a more metaphysical and philosophical definition of the unconscious. After many years of practice in which his patients provided him with increasingly strange dreams and patterns of energy distribution, Jung came to believe that the psyche and the atom could be understood as essentially the same thing and he saw a need for a proper exposition of their similarity.

This insight led Jung to make overtures to physics, and he sought to identify areas and energies of the psyche that might find a place in the vision of the physical world then being advocated by that discipline. Initially, he suggested that

> sooner or later nuclear physics and the psychology of the unconscious will draw closer together as both of them, independently of one another and from opposite directions, push forward into transcendental territory, the one with the concept of the atom, the other with that of the archetype.[9]

This belief rested on the correspondences Jung discovered in two areas: the relationship between psyche and matter that allowed interactions between them, and the processes that both the psyche and matter seemed to manifest when under investigation by scientists.

Regarding the interaction of psyche and matter, a nasty problem avoided by most psychologists and philosophers, Jung focused on relations and interconnections:

> Psyche cannot be totally different from matter, for how otherwise could it move matter? And matter cannot be alien to psyche, for how else could matter produce psyche? Psyche and matter exist in one and the same world, and each partakes of the other, otherwise any reciprocal action would be impossible. If research could

only advance far enough, therefore, we should arrive at an ultimate agreement between physical and psychological concepts. [10]

Here, he thought that through refinement of terms, psychology and physics could announce a joint discovery linking mind and matter in a simple expression of cosmic unity. Such an admission would make the physical world predominantly mental or spiritual, a conclusion recently advocated by some physicists as well. Jung may well have anticipated this admission.

Unfortunately, Jung could not conceive how either psychology or physics could establish the basis for an experiment that would confirm the identity, let alone the similarity, of psyche and matter. The hard sciences demanded an experiment in which most factors could be measured with some degree of precision and which could then be duplicated by others. The social sciences relied on observation and interpretation rather than experiment and therefore had a degree of subjectivity that prohibited many critics from admitting the validity of its results. A merger of the results of observation and controlled experimentation was not possible then—and may not be possible now, although some quantum theorists might interpret their explanation of their methodology as such an identity. Some quantum physicists today maintain that the indeterminate methodology in subatomic physics is itself evidence of such a unity, a unity that might easily include the psyche in its open and indeterminate frame.

Jung conceived of the psyche in terms of mind and matter, then, which led him to an exploration of physics. He also defined psyche, however, in relation to the developmentalist arguments of his day, which led him to characterize it in another way—as the product of evolutionary process. "The psyche is not of today," he wrote. "Its ancestry goes back many millions of years. Individual consciousness is only the flower and the fruit of a season." [11] Thus Jung would claim that, "the lowest layers of our psyche still have an animal character. Hence it is highly probable that animals have similar or even the same archetypes." [12]

So far, it has become apparent that our comparison will need to consider the cosmologies implicit in both Sioux and Jungian conceptions, particularly as these cosmologies place the psyche in relation to the very large of the universe and the very small of the atomic and subatomic. In both cosmologies, as I will argue in Chapters Six and Seven, animals offer us an opportunity to explore particular aspects of the psyche. Animals were, and are, crucial neighbors, partners, and spiritual figures for the Sioux; for

Jung, they open up questions about the ancestry and depth of the psyche, particularly as that depth takes shape in archetypes, one of the great key concepts of Jung's psychology.

The glossary in *Memories, Dreams, Reflections* provides three different definitions of the archetype. Two of them are appropriate to this inquiry. In "Psychological Aspects of the Mother Archetype," Jung says that the form of the archetype "might perhaps be compared to the axial system of a crystal, which, as it were, preforms the crystalline structure in the mother liquid, although it has no material existence of its own."[13] Jung also says that "it seems to me probable that the real nature of the archetype is not capable of being made conscious, that it is transcendent, on which account I call it psychoid."[14] Both definitions suggest a kind of Platonic psychological world in which pre-existing categories or structures for sorting information exist. But these are Jung's matured considerations, and it may be useful to look back in his writings for practical working definitions that might enlighten us on the manner in which the idea originated.

It may be helpful, for instance, to consider an earlier statement: "the inborn mode of *acting* has long been known as *instinct* and for the inborn mode of psychic apprehension I have proposed the term *archetype*."[15] Jung always insisted that he had discovered the archetypes when certain familiar patterns in patient behavior matched the story lines and images of well-known myths. The opposition of archetype and instinct seems to suggest rather that he needed a methodological working concept to account for actions other than instinctual, a concept that balanced the influence of instincts and represented some measured degree of rational thought and mental deliberation.

This interpretation is supported by a common sense observation on the way we experience the world. "Although the changing situations of life must appear infinitely various to our way of thinking," Jung noted,

> their possible number never exceeds certain natural limits; they fall into more or less typical patterns that repeat themselves over and over again. The archetypal structure of the unconscious corresponds to the average run of events.[16]

The idea of the archetype therefore must have arisen after some years of his therapeutic experience, when it became obvious that diverse patients had produced similar problems, symbols, dreams, and solutions. Jung concluded that certain kinds of situations produced predictable kinds of responses, and that growth patterns proceeded in ways that could be anticipated.

Archetypes and instincts can manifest themselves so similarly that the distinction between them can seem more theoretical than real. "To the extent that the archetypes intervene in the shaping of conscious contents by regulating, modifying, and motivating them," Jung says, "they act like instincts."[17] Presumably the therapist can determine whether the intervention is archetypal or instinctual. But how does he or she know? If we refer to Jung's idea of the development of consciousness, we might well argue that a completely primitive or original unconscious could not distinguish archetype from instinct. There would be no consciousness with which archetypes could react. If archetypes eventually emerge as co-equals of instincts in the governance of the psyche, how do they do so? Would they not always be the same thing?

For Jung, however, instincts and archetypes did not seem to be co-equal. He described the response of the organism to the world around it as initially instinctive—although he gave no good illustration of what instinct was. Most probably, we are talking about a spontaneous response to the world that ensures survival of the organism, but apparent non-rational behavior by an organism may also imply some "higher" control mechanism. For organisms that have developed a coherent relationship with their environment, the archetype must give them additional assistance in making sense of the world. "Instinct is not an isolated thing, nor can it be isolated in practice," Jung said. "It always brings in its train archetypal contents of a spiritual nature which are at once its foundation and its limitation."[18] Instinct must therefore be a prior condition of the archetype and in important situations the archetype must transcend instinct in the same way that an overdrive gear assumes control of the speed of an automobile for a brief time. We do not know, however, whether the archetype is a "given," an *a priori* element of the psyche, or whether it arises over the passage of time as the learned responses of an organism to its environment.

Jung seemed to believe that archetypes came into existence as a result of the cumulative experiences of organic life. He said that the

archetypes whose innermost nature is inaccessible to experience, are the precipitate of the psychic functioning of the whole ancestral line; the accumulated experiences of organic life in general, a million times repeated, and condensed into types.[19]

He suggested, as well, that in the archetypes

> all experiences are represented which have happened on this planet
> since primeval times. The more frequent and the more intense they
> were, the more clearly focussed they become in the archetype.[20]

One thinks, for instance, of stalagmites in a cavern that simply accumulate material until they become something specific in form and substance. This accumulation would make archetypes minimally a product of
the passage of time. But were there originally "forms"—like the crystalline
structure of Jung's analogy—that attracted and sorted experiences to form
individual archetypal patterns?[21]

We never get a clear answer from Jung, and so archetypes, because they
transcend the individual psyche yet appear as its product, have become one
of the most controversial ideas in modern psychology. Since people undergoing Jungian analysis seem to have more colorful and symbolic dreams
with longer storylines than other dreamers, a suspicion exists that the form
of therapy induces or produces the archetypal patterns. Certainly many psychotherapists have found it unnecessary to use archetypes when describing
psychic disorders; some theorists reject the notion out of hand. But many
people have found the archetypes useful and interesting enough to ensure
them a place in the higher levels of twentieth-century thought. They surely
matter to our comparison and dialogue, for they are critical in thinking
about dreams and visions, animals and the primordial, family structure,
and communications with the unconscious and with other dimensions, all
of which will serve as points of entry for our discussion, and indeed, make
up the chapter structure of this book.

Where Jungian psychology has a hierarchy of archetypal forms that
appear as symbols in dreams or manifest themselves in strange behaviors, the
Sioux developed sets of relationships with other entities that they believed
shared the same status. Sioux people expected that through living inter-
mediaries, such as stones, animals, plants and birds, they would be led to
an understanding of their world and lives. There is no symbolism or hierarchy here in the Jungian sense. Instead, spirits, sometimes human, sometimes not, sometimes birds and animals, appeared physically before them
in visions and befriended them. With the assistance of these entities and
through their strength, individuals were able to exercise useful powers and
to live constructively. Jung might have suggested that the appearance of

other creatures was merely symbolic of archetypal realities, that the unconscious was manifesting itself to individuals. The Sioux would not agree,
observing perhaps that there is a great difference between simply dreaming
of a bird or animal—having a strictly symbolic encounter—and being able
thereafter to be successful in calling it to show itself physically, to produce
actions in the material world. Sioux philosophy rested, not simply on the
dream, but on the empirical evidence produced by such demonstrations.

Sioux people understood that *Wakan Tanka*—a word that defies easy
definition but reflects the "great mysterious"—is in everything, so that there
was no doubt that humans shared certain elements with all other creatures.
As we probe more deeply into the mystery of life, we come to learn how
closely related we are to other creatures. It is almost as if, looking down from
a distance, we can watch as Sioux, Jungian, and scientific cosmologies draw
close. Language differs, of course, because the perspectives are different.
Where Jung would say, "Theoretically it should be possible to 'peel' away
the collective unconscious, layer by layer, until we came to the psychology
of the worm, and even of the amoeba,"[22] the Sioux would simply say that
such a demonstration proves we are related to all life and that possibility is
self-evident. As the psyche is the world, so too is the Great Mystery.

And at times, even the language draws together. We might suspect that,
at one point, Carl Jung came exceptionally close to conceiving the psyche in
something approximating the Sioux Indian way:

> Since the collective unconscious, through the archetypes, sets the
> task, it is often called "the grandfather" directly. The primitives
> use that term. They call those powers that make people do the
> particular things, "grandfathers."[23]

This term is precisely what the Sioux, and many other Indian tribes, use
when they describe experiences in which *Wakan Tanka*, the Great Mystery, has become personified. The classic Sioux narrative, *Black Elk Speaks*,
is filled with references to the Six Grandfathers, who represent the directions and powers of the universe. One might add that the Grandfathers are
always represented as ancient but also human figures, invoking somewhat
obliquely the "wise Old Man" archetype so favored by Jung.

Jung achieved his understanding of the psyche through decades of
practice, and his method was one of probing deeply into the psychological makeup of his patients, watching as certain kinds of patterns emerged

with a sufficient frequency to enable him to identify psychic processes. The development of a psychic structure with its mediating archetypes suggests that, indeed, Jung was constructing a philosophy based on psychological data that laid a claim to some form of empiricism. Philosophy, one might suggest, covers considerably more ground than does a specific psychology, for it must deal with the nature of the world as a whole. When we seek to compare the beliefs and practices of the Sioux Indians with those of Jung, we are necessarily opposing philosophy to philosophy. Sioux philosophy approached problems by initially looking outward, empirically, before then looking inward. If we take Jung seriously and admit the psyche as equivalent to the world, we can then arrange our dialogue properly. Jung is examining the world via the psyche, while creating a psychologically-based philosophy; the Sioux examine the world with empirical observations, also creating a natural philosophy/theology.

This book seeks to explore the convergences and differences that exist between these two philosophies, and it does so by moving from a consideration of history, language and representation to an examination of the universes of the Sioux and of Jung, to a set of explorations of discrete themes. Chapters One, Two, and Three will set a historical backdrop. First, we will look closely at Carl Jung's encounters with Indian people at Taos Pueblo, his use of Indians as examples, and his dissections of them as symbolic images. Then, we will turn to the positive and negative ways in which Indian representations reveal not only Jung's own cultural limitations, but also critical developments in his thought. In Chapters Four and Five, we will explore the Jungian universe and that of the Sioux, before turning, in subsequent chapters to more focused treatments of evocative comparisons and convergences. In Chapters Six and Seven, we will examine the critical importance of animals in both systems of thought. Chapter Eight will look at the family, Chapter Nine the nature of dreams and visions, and Chapter Ten the mysterious call of "the voice," which can establish communication with the psyche, with animals, and with other worlds and spirits. Returning to some of the large issues raised here, the Conclusion will offer some thoughts on the results of this dialogue and comparison.

Can parallels be drawn and dialogues established between these two bodies of knowledge? This book will argue that they can. Jung's development of concepts of the unconscious and of psychological experiences in a framework that accommodates religious, philosophical, psychological and physical knowledge allows us to find similarities and tangent points.

The difficulty in opening this dialogue comes from a point of significant difference: the Sioux saw everything as a matter of personal relationships even between and among sacred powers that stood as equals to each other; Jung, following a scientific format, used words that conveyed the sense of objectivity required of scientists. Only in his autobiography did he begin to admit that many of the apparently neutral words of his psychology are really identifiable figures of intense personality. If we can escape these barriers of culture and language, however, Jungian thought and Sioux traditions may well turn out to be compatible, for there are many evocative points at which we can explore the convergences and the differences.

CHAPTER ONE

JUNG AND THE INDIANS

In 1920 Carl Jung visited Algeria and Tunisia. He sensed immediately that he was in a radically different social and physical environment, one that did not always mesh with a narrow European psychology. His perceptions broadened, and he began to reflect on what other cultures might represent and teach him:

> When I contemplated for the first time the European spectacle from the Sahara, surrounded by a civilization which has more or less the same relationship to ours as Roman antiquity has to modern times, I became aware of how completely, even in America, I was still caught up and imprisoned in the cultural consciousness of the white man. The desire then grew in me to carry the historical comparisons still farther by descending to a still lower cultural level. [1]

So in the winter of 1924-25, Jung came to America, and as part of his tour visited the Indians of Taos Pueblo in New Mexico.

At the time, Taos was the playground for a kind of 1920s version of the Beatniks, the counterculture, or the New Agers. Mabel Dodge Luhan was the unofficial hostess of the town, sponsoring important visitors and trying to duplicate her earlier salon success in Greenwich Village. D. H. Lawrence was Taos' resident intellectual and mystic, the Taos school of painting was well under way, and members of the cultural avant garde seemed obliged to make a journey to northern New Mexico as part of their personal quests for spirituality and authenticity. Mabel Dodge Luhan seized the opportunity of Jung's trip to the United States to have the famous psychoanalyst visit her domain, and so a hasty side trip to New Mexico from Chicago was arranged. During this visit, Jung was able to visit Taos Pueblo and hold long conversations with some of the Pueblo elders and representatives. In *Memories, Dreams, Reflections,* Jung included a few pages of an unpublished manuscript on the Pueblo Indians that reflected on his trip and experiences. Those pages reveal a man profoundly changed in his view of the history of Europe and the West. Jung seems to have seen for the first time the dark shadow of what was commonly seen as "progress" and "civilization."*

The landscape of Taos is itself haunting and magnificent, and gives visitors a more realistic perspective about themselves than they typically experience in everyday life: we are but dust compared to the mountain and rivers of that plateau. Jung, too, was similarly affected and he remembered both the mountains and the physical setting of the pueblo:

> Behind us a clear stream purled past the houses, and on its opposite bank stood a second pueblo of reddish adobe houses, built one atop the other toward the center of the settlement, thus strangely anticipating the perspective of an American metropolis with its skyscrapers in the center.[2]

He would later pose a rhetorical question in "The Complications of American Psychology":

> Have you ever compared the skyline of New York or any great American city with that of a pueblo like Taos? And did you see how the houses pile up to towers towards the centre? Without conscious imitation the American unconsciously fills out the spectral outline of the Red Man's mind and temperament.[3]

Here, at Taos, appeared a psychic apprehension he had not anticipated, an experience that challenged his psychology in new ways.

Jung's American experiences made a deep impression and would always stay with him. These reflections suggest that the psychological impact of the Indian was emotionally significant, something that transcended his critical and scholarly analysis. At one level, Jung was impressed by how the American unconscious had been influenced by Indians and was projected onto its landscapes. Jung decided that the Indians, with their multi-storied pueblos, had anticipated the later creation of large cities with massive buildings, so that the whites were unconsciously fulfilling ideas first generated by the

---

* It is important to note that the material in *Memories, Dreams, Reflections* (247-249) does not represent Jung's full statement on Taos. Among those unpublished writings to which we do not have access are apparently other reflections on Taos and Jung's trip.

Indians. Undoubtedly he had seen adobe villages in Algeria and Tunisia that closely resembled the pueblos of New Mexico, so the idea of piling rooms on top of each other was not novel. Yet because it was American Indians who had built this structure, it seemed to offer him a different opportunity to examine a particularly American unconscious, one that linked immigrant non-Indians with indigenous psyche and culture. In this chapter, we will examine that opportunity, looking more closely at Jung's interactions with Indian people, his sense of Indians in relation to his theoretical speculations, and his observations about the symbolic import of the Indian.

Jung's stay in Taos, although brief, greatly affected the psychoanalyst, and he alluded to his experiences there several times in his seminars, particularly when he wished to describe and illustrate psychological maturity and stability. Upon reflection he remembered,

> It was astonishing to me to see how the Indian's emotions change when he speaks of his religious ideas. In ordinary life he shows a degree of self-control and dignity that borders on fatalistic equanimity. But when he speaks of things that pertain to his mysteries, he is in the grip of a surprising emotion which he cannot conceal—a fact that greatly helped to satisfy my curiosity.[4]

The apprehension of a calm yet intense religious feeling made a deep impression on him and he sought to get the Indians to explain their deepest religious beliefs to him.

Jung's host for the occasion was Ochwiay Biano (Mountain Lake), a man designated by the Pueblo elders to represent them before the famous psychologist. As a typical non-Indian, Jung mistakenly believed Biano to be the head chief of the Pueblo and always thereafter referred to him as his friend "the Chief." The two men played a cat and mouse game with each other. When Jung would comment on some phase of Pueblo life, he would watch Biano's face, seeking to interpret the Indian's reaction to his observations. If a hint of emotion showed, Jung believed that he had raised an important question and counted the topic as one to be pursued. But Biano was no amateur, being the person designated by the elders to deal with outsiders, and he rarely offered to explain his beliefs or responses. Instead he spoke to Jung primarily about the sun and how it was the father of us all. This belief explained why the many men of Taos sat on the roofs of their homes at sunrise. Biano said they were giving their personal energy to the sun, helping it begin to move across the sky. The idea was preposterous to non-Indians learned in celestial mechanics, but Jung, approaching this devotional setting from a psychoanalytical perspective, quickly saw the connection.

Jung later recalled:

> Never before had I run into such an atmosphere of secrecy; the religions of civilized nations today are all accessible; their sacraments have long ago ceased to be mysteries. Here, however, the air was filled with a secret known to all the communicants, but to which whites could gain no access.[5]

He needn't have fretted about his exclusion; at Taos no outsider is allowed to know anything about the religious practices of the Pueblo. Exclusion, however, was a new experience for Jung and he continued to attempt to uncover the Pueblo's religious secrets. In a letter to Biano in October 1932, seven years after his visit, Jung was still trying to discern the inner core of Taos religious life:

> I wish you would write to me once, what your religious customs are in order to secure a good harvest. Have you got corn dances, or other ways by which you make the wheat and corn grow? Are your young men still worshipping the Father Sun? Are you also making occasionally sand-paintings like the Navajos? Any information you can give me about your religious life is always welcome to me. I shall keep all that information to myself, but it is most helpful to me, as I am busy exploring the truth in which Indians believe.[6]

While Jung was at Taos, he experienced a fleeting moment that might have helped him in his efforts to gain psychological knowledge of the Indians. Unfortunately, Jung missed the point and tended to pass the incident off as a joke. As a matter of courtesy he was allowed to climb on the roofs and watch the men greeting the rising sun. When he began to climb down, like the typical outsider, Jung turned around and climbed down facing the ladder. The Pueblos walk down the ladder as if it was a stairs. Jung's everyday European behavior presented a humorous spectacle to the people of Taos:

> The Pueblo Indians declared in a matter-of-fact way that I belonged to the Bear Totem—in other words I was a bear—because I did not come

down a ladder standing up like a man, but bunched up on all fours like a bear. If anyone in Europe said I had a bearish nature this would amount to the same thing, but with a rather different shade of meaning.[7]

The characterization of individuals in relation to the traits of an animal served as an Indian way of classifying and understanding strangers. And in Jung's case it was accurate, not only in terms of his performance on the ladder but in terms of his physical body and his own character as a powerful healer. A further exploration of this linked characterization might have allowed Jung to open up a new line of inquiry into the religious life he so wanted to understand.

Still, there is inferential evidence that Jung left Taos believing that he had acquired knowledge of the essential elements of the American Indian psyche sufficient to use in the practice of comparative scholarship. Many of his statements concerning Indians and "other primitives" carry a sweeping, all-knowing style and an authority he had not necessarily earned through close study over a long period of time. Without question, however, the Taos experience clearly haunted Jung and remained with him all his life. Writing to Miguel Serrano in 1960 as a feeble old man, a year before his death, Jung wistfully reflected: "We are sorely in need of a Truth or a self-understanding similar to that of Ancient Egypt, which I have found still living with the Taos Pueblo."[8] Remembering how brief and accidental his visit to Taos was 35 years previous, we can but marvel at the impact that American Indians made on him. His visits to Algeria, Kenya, and India, while providing him with insights into different cultures, did not seem to have the same impact as his brief time at Taos. Thus comparing the Jungian psychological system with American Indian traditions has a basis in Jung's own emotional experiences.

We can easily chart the Indian influence on Carl Jung after his American visit. In a lecture in his Visions Seminars, held in the fall of 1930, Jung argued that, "the realization of Indian values by an American is an asset, not a liability. The Red Indian has great qualities despite the fact that he is a primitive."[9] Jung made many comments like this during the course of his life, and they encapsulate the complications inherent in his relation to Indians. On the one hand, the Taos experience had been transformative, giving him a sense of the possibilities to be understood in terms of Indian people. On the other hand, Jung was part of the intellectual discourse of his moment, which emphasized a social evolutionary framework in which the concept of "the primitive" had intellectual explanatory power. "Primitives"—such as Indian people—were the living examples of earlier stages in evolution. Jung's own sense of social and cultural development over time was complex, but it is not surprising that he would adopt the word "primitive." These contradictory positions—encapsulated here in the space of a single sentence ("The Red Indian has great qualities despite the fact that he is a primitive.")—form a consistent thread in Jung's thought, as they did in much intellectual discourse of the period. Indian values are offered to Americans: emulate these people and you will develop great qualities. But always remember that the Red Indian is a primitive. Here was a contradiction that haunted many people besides Carl Jung: How do you explain the presence of great qualities in a person or society that has not moved up the cultural evolutionary incline? Jung never answered this question, which had already played itself out over two centuries of American history.

In effect, Jung was giving gratuitous advice to an audience already obsessed with Indian myth. Americans had long since begun to devour Indians in a genocidal policy of land confiscation, while simultaneously applauding their virtues. The iconography of the American Revolution—the nation's founding gesture—was laced through with Indians, made to represent the indigenous qualities of the rebellious colonists. In 1833, young American men founded the Improved Order of Red Man, a group based upon a number of earlier "Indian" organizations and societies. The organization was devoted to American Indian values and beliefs, although no one with Indian blood was eligible for membership because it was, after all, an effort to improve what Indians themselves had accomplished. It must strike students of the unconscious as ironic that concurrent with the popularity of Indian virtues, Congress passed in 1830 the Indian Removal Act, which forced the Indians of the eastern United States to sell their lands and move across the Mississippi into the Great Plains because they were savages and not fit for civilized living. This belief prevailed even though the Cherokees, for example, had already devised a syllabary for written communications and had established a written constitution. Before most of the continent's eastern Indians could even begin their journey into exile, whites were already organizing a society to celebrate their virtues. Clearly, the psychological achievements of the Indian were far more appealing than real Indians in the flesh with whom one had to share the neighborhood.[10]

In the late 1920s, almost coincident with Jung's seminar, the Improved Order of Red Men organization reached its peak membership of 500,000. Members were adopting fake Indian names such as "Running Deer" and

"Pale Moon," dressing in outlandish brown canvas costumes decorated as if they were buckskins, and engaging in a host of made-up Indian "ceremonies." The organization went into decline during the 1920s and 1930s when fraternal orders of this type lost membership across the country. Or perhaps people had discovered that no matter how hard they tried, they really were not Indians—nor were they much of an improvement.

Another organization espousing the same goals as the Red Men had seemingly better results. On February 8th, 1910, the Boy Scouts, founded by William Boyce and Dan Beard, received a charter in the District of Columbia, and parents were urged to enroll their sons so they could learn the manly virtues of the Indian. The organization expanded with the founding of the Girl Scouts in 1912. There has been steady growth in these groups ever since their founding, perhaps because Indian values are cherished for young people. Even in today's political climate and in spite of conservative Boy Scout practices, membership runs into the millions. Other organizations such as the YMCA (with its Indian Guides program) and the Camp Fire Girls joined in the imitation movement and also began applauding the values and virtues of the Indian. Just how much money was squandered on these pale imitations while real Indians were starving on reservations is unpleasant to contemplate. The fact that countless Americans grow up participating in these organizations reflects the continuing idealization of the American Indian.

Jung perhaps missed that he was joining the long parade of people who claimed to find enduring values by "honoring" and emulating the American Indian. He differed from many others who wrote about the American Indian, however, in that Indians for him possessed an understanding of deep psychological truths that he could find nowhere else. [11] Scattered throughout his collected works, seminars, and lectures are any number of statements on Indians, some derogatory, some back-handed compliments, some clearly extolling their virtues, but always, it seemed, casual and spontaneous references as if the Indians had affected him at the deepest psychological level.

A recounting of Jung's actual encounters with Indian people is critical to our understanding of the possibilities of dialogue and comparison. So too are the representations of Indian people—both positive and negative—in Jung's own theoretical corpus, representations that we will take up in the next two chapters. It is also the case, however, that we need to understand some of the ways Indian images made their way into symbolic expressions and into the richer and more subtle depths of the collective unconscious.

What are some of the ways that Jung saw Indians appearing in the utterances of his patients, and in American and European culture in general? Jung often remarked that he had become aware of American Indians in therapy in the dreams and fantasies of his American patients. "I have found in my American patients," he wrote,

> that their hero-figure possesses traits derived from the religion of the Indians. The most important figure in their religion is the shaman,* the medicine man or conjurer of spirits. The first American discovery in this field—since taken up in Europe—was spiritualism, and the second was Christian Science and other forms of mental healing.[12]

Spiritualism and Christian Science were movements that emphasized self-reliance in healing, and that saw the individual as capable of drawing from hidden sources of energy and spirit within the universe without the intercession of others. Like the skyscrapers that evoked Pueblo architecture, Christian Science and spiritualism may have refigured Indian spiritual practices at a deep, unconscious level, reflecting Jung's developing ideas concerning the collective unconscious. He perceived that these traits of American Indian religions and practices were echoed in the newly founded American religions and in the revival practices of established American churches.

Jung's perceptions did not coalesce just because Indians appeared in the dreams of a few American patients. He recognized a number of additional phenomena, pointing out, for example, that the American unconscious

> chooses the Indian as its symbol, just as certain coins of the Union bear an Indian-head. This is a tribute to the once-hated Indian, but it also testifies to the fact that the American hero-motif chooses the Indian as an ideal figure.[13]

Although startling, it does not take much reflection to appreciate the profound effect Indians had on white settlers. Indians had confronted the United States as a powerful indigenous presence since its founding and

---

*   It is worth noting here that the label "shamanic," often applied to American Indian spiritual and healing practices, is something of a misnomer, a generalized term in popular and anthropological literature that has become a category in its own right. Deloria tried to avoid the terms shaman and shamanic as not exactly appropriate to the North American context.

provided more than enough reason to be included in the American cultural pantheon. Indeed, Indians are everywhere in American cultural expression, from the dome of the United States capital to its money to its literary fiction.

It is worth noting that the Indian on the penny, modeled in an eastern Indian headdress, was later replaced by the buffalo nickel, which featured a western Indian profile with different feathers on one side of the coin and a buffalo on the other. Had Jung known something of the Sioux Indians he might have smiled. Curiously, this coin suggests symbolically the Sioux Indians' belief that in a higher cosmic dimension they and the buffalo are one spirit, split into two separate entities upon taking physical form. The particular figuring of this coin might be seen to reflect Jung's ideas concerning the significant effects of Indians at a deep level of the collective American psyche, as well as the psyches of its citizens.

Jung made a wide range of similar comparisons. Thoroughly accustomed to the civilized manner in which Europeans engaged in sport, for example (before the soccer riots of recent times), Jung recoiled at the way in which Americans ferociously pursued athletic excellence. "The American conception of sport goes far beyond the notion of the easy-going European," Jung observed, adding, "Only the Indian rites of initiation can compare with the ruthlessness and savagery of a rigorous American training." He also suggested that in the much-praised American "can do" pioneer spirit and tenacity, we are really catching a glimpse of the Indian. "His [the American's] extraordinary concentration on a particular goal, his tenacity of purpose, his unflinching endurance of the greatest hardships—in all this the *legendary virtues of the Indian find full expression*"[14] [emphasis added]. While many might credit the experience of the frontier as the primary source of American inspiration, Jung understood American virtue at its deepest level as an expression of rigorous discipline and a profound willpower that was best seen in American Indians.

He was also fascinated by the idea that particular areas of the earth seemed compatible with one people and not another. He warned that invaders or intruders of any land would find themselves vulnerable to its power and that that power would change them to resemble its aboriginal peoples. "The mystery of the earth is no joke and no paradox," he warned.

One only needs to see how in America the skull and pelvis measurements of all the European races begin to indianize themselves in the second generation of immigrants. That is the mystery of the American earth.[15]

Franz Boas, the noted American anthropologist, had done some studies of first and second-generation immigrants that suggested that these physical changes were actually occurring. Though the studies are now regarded as highly questionable, Jung seized on them as evidence that Americans were undergoing a unique change—although no one recognized what was happening to them.[16] Boas himself was operating out of the framework of environmental determinism, but it may be that Jung was also seeing such changes in terms of the power of the earth, and the resonance that he had formed with American Indian religions in the development of his own ideas.[17] Indeed, as important as the prospect of physical bodily changes, he saw the immigrant psyche changing as it gradually adopted the psychology of the aboriginal peoples. Despite the best efforts of American whites, fragments of an American Indian soul were constantly appearing in their dreams and fantasies. "The American presents a strange picture," Jung said, "a European with Negro behavior and an Indian soul. He shares the fate of all usurpers of foreign soil."[18]

Barbara Hannah recalls that Jung believed that the European possessed a safe and predictable unconscious, which he described by analogy as the cellar in a comfortable old home that could be safely explored. In psychoanalysis the therapist opened the cellar door and helped the patient proceed systematically down the steps, sequentially recounting the historical experiences of the Europeans. But it was not so with the Americans. "When the American opens a similar door in his psychology," Jung used to say,

> there is a dangerous open gap, dropping hundreds of feet, and in those cases where he can negotiate the drop, he will then be faced with an Indian or Negro shadow, whereas the European finds a shadow of his own race.[19]

Jung accurately perceived significant and complex psychological differences between the native, the enslaved, and the transplanted white European, all of which have found frequent expression in American culture.

Sometimes, however, Jung's comparisons came up short. When Paul Radin published his study of Winnebago (Ho-Chunk, in contemporary usage) mythology, The Trickster, Carl Jung and Karl Kerényi were asked to do commentaries on the trickster image to be included at the end of the book.[20] Given this opportunity to discuss the knowledge and experiences that had so affected him, Jung readily agreed. His commentary illustrates his profound interest in American Indians but also reveals the pitfalls to be found in such comparative work, which can easily take shape in incorrect inferences and cultural biases. Jung immediately drew a parallel to European Christian ideas, identifying the Indian figure of the trickster, found in many tribes as the Spider or the Coyote, with the devil figure found in the medieval carnivals of Europe. In those carnivals the order of things was reversed, the devil becoming the "ape of god," a sly figure wholly unpredictable and capable of mischievous pranks. Jung's European background was evident in his selection of such a figure as the most appropriate point of comparison, a choice that led to a number of regrettable errors.

His initial analytical response was to describe the trickster as a "psychologem," an archetypal psychic structure of extreme antiquity: "In his clearest manifestations he [the trickster] is a faithful reflection of an absolutely undifferentiated human consciousness, corresponding to a psyche that has hardly left the animal level."[21] Looking at the Ho-Chunk traditions, as described by Paul Radin, as well as the beliefs of other Indian tribes, we do see much of the clever—and perhaps archaic—animal in the figure. But many Indian people believe that the trickster figure primarily represents the arbitrary side of natural events, those often near-coincidental happenings that demonstrate the fickle side of an individual's fate, the ironic unpredictable situations that arise in spite of ourselves. The figure is cosmic, but since we watch his machinations he does not touch us except when we remember his failures.

Without hesitating, Jung moved into areas of theology that had no useful correlation with any Indian tradition. "The Trickster," Jung argued,

> is a primitive "cosmic" being of divine-animal nature, on the one hand superior to man because of his superhuman qualities, and on the other hand inferior to him because of his unreason and unconsciousness.... He is no match for the animals either, because of his extraordinary clumsiness and lack of instinct.[22]

Here, his European roots led him to an unjustified comparison. Indian people generally do not stress divinity because it does not make sense to them. A "mixture" of divine and animal qualities would be absurd in the Indian context because all entities have this mixture as a matter of course. While there are many spirits found in the Indian experience, divinity in the Western sense is glaringly absent. Indeed, animal spirits have powers and knowledge in and of themselves and help humans in a practical manner that is not found in any other tradition. The trickster may be an exceptional figure among Indian people, but its exceptionalism does not come from the "mixture" of animal and divine—an idea so common as to be unremarkable.

In evoking the figures of the devil and the divine, Jung interpreted the trickster figure in comparative terms that made sense to European psychologists and scholars, but which had little to do with American Indians. His misreading should caution us about the dangers of this kind of comparative work. Indeed, having laid this base in Western theology, Jung found it hard to stop, and he found himself arguing that the trickster is:

> a forerunner of the saviour, and, like him, God, man and animal at once. He is both subhuman and superhuman, a bestial *and* divine being, whose chief and most alarming characteristic is his unconsciousness.[23]

One would be hard pressed to find in any American Indian religious tradition the concept of, or the need for, a savior. This concept is important primarily to the Middle Eastern peoples who derive the need for a savior from the Hebrew concept of the redeemer—the person in the family who steps forward and rescues the family land when it is likely to go outside of family hands because of pressing financial difficulties. There is no question that this kinship figure was gradually transformed by political events in Jewish history as the Jews were battered by the large empires of ancient times. By the end of the first century C.E., the idea of a redeemer took on a cosmic connotation and became the central figure in the mystery religions.

The linkage of the redeemer to apocalyptic catastrophe by Jung further complicates his interpretation of the trickster:

> If, at the end of the trickster myth, the saviour is hinted at, this comforting premonition or hope means that some calamity or other has happened and been consciously understood. Only out of disaster can the longing for the saviour arise—in other words, the recognition and unavoidable integration of the shadow create such a harrowing situation that nobody but a saviour can undo the tangled web of fate.[24]

Catastrophes in American Indian traditions occur when the various "ages" or "suns" collapse or come to an abrupt end, when the world becomes chaotic and a new earth and sky are created. Certainly no one anticipates a

redeemer figure to emerge out of the catastrophic conditions of these particular "last days," and while people may attribute evildoing and bad morals
as the reason for the destruction of the world, there is no idea that one's present personality will survive the end and thrive in a wholly unrealistic setting.
Fate is an acceptable factor in human life in Indian terms. Even under the
most trying of circumstances, in 1890 when the Plains Indians embraced
the Ghost Dance to gain the salvation of their people, they believed that the
whole earth would be changed, the white man would be destroyed, and the
buffalo would return, but there was never a hint of a savior figure directing
this radical change. As a rule, Indians look for cosmic physical change, not
for a political adjustment through the mediation of a savior. In short, Jung
misidentified key points of comparison, and built upon them a chain of
suppositions that carried him a long way from an accurate sense of the real
power of the trickster figure in Indian cultures.

The slippery slope down which Jung slid in this instance can be seen
in terms of his use of partially-informed comparison, but it may also be the
case that he was reflecting as well his experience at Taos. Like so many others,
Jung seems to have believed that he understood Indians and was therefore
able to speculate freely on the meaning of their beliefs. We can see a similar
overconfidence in other instances in the development of Jung's thought.
Prior to Jung's encounter with primitives in Africa and in New Mexico, for
example, he had written *Symbols of Transformation,* one of his major works
dealing with work he had done with a patient, which became popularly
known as the Miller fantasies. Originally published in 1912, it was revised in
1950 and released in its new version in 1952. In the new edition Jung hypoth-
esized that there were two kinds of thinking:

1)   directed thinking, which represented the conscious individual;

2)   dreams or fantasy thinking, which came in symbols from the
unconscious.

As one aspect of the analysis, Jung discovered that the woman under
analysis believed she had been influenced by Henry Wadsworth Longfellow's poem about American Indians. Jung admitted:

> I had never read *Hiawatha* until I came to this point in my inquiry.
> This poetical compilation of Indian myths proved to my satisfaction
> how justified were all my previous reflections, since it is unusually rich
> in mythological motifs. . . . It therefore behooves us to examine the
> contents of this epic more closely.[25]

Jung then proceeded to move comprehensively through Longfellow's poem, relating images and action sequences to a bewildering variety of motifs and symbols of other cultures. Without missing a beat he moved from Hiawatha to Siegfried, Brunhilde and Wotan, as if he were dealing with a simple continuous epic narrative in its original form.

Again, in assuming a confident knowledge of Indian people, and in adopting the comparative method, Jung missed out on critical details that may have advanced his work further. From where did the motifs in *Hiawatha* emerge? From Longfellow, who knew virtually nothing about Indians, but who had drawn from several Indian sources to create his own version of an American Indian myth? There is, to be sure, much "Indian" material in the poem, and it has certain symbols and personalities that can be found in some woodland traditions. It begs credulity, however, to think that Longfellow understood the Indian material that he used or that he had the same psychological insights and truths that made the individual myths important for Indians. Perhaps the motifs emerged from the Finnish epic, the *Kalevala*, which served as another primary inspiration for Longfellow, both in narrative form and poetic language? Or perhaps the wildly popular Indian poem was beloved precisely because its motifs spoke evocatively to American longings and anxieties, which, as Jung had already postulated, had much to do with an Indian underpinning being expressed in national culture? In other words, *Hiawatha's* mythological motifs likely had complex and blended origins, which demanded more from Jung in the way of analysis. From an Indian perspective, it is fair to say that the poem is roughly equivalent to the truths about Indians promulgated by the Boy Scouts.

Much closer to Indian realities was Jung's effort to interpret the Hopi Snake Dance, though here too, interpretation primarily served his own needs:

> In their ritual dance, they even put the snakes in their mouths. We have a picture in the Club of a Hopi Snake dance, where one of them has a rattlesnake in his mouth. That is very near the symbolism here. Also keep in mind that the snake represents the chthonic mana of ancestors that have gone underground; the snakes bring it up, and taking the snakes in their mouths means they are eating the mana, one could say. It is a communion with the mana, the power left by the ancestors. It is at bottom of course a magic fertility ritual, for the purpose of increasing the fertility of the earth as well as the fertility or power of man.[26]

Here too, we can sense the authority that Jung claimed over this material, as well as the ways he molded it to produce and support his own theoretical positions. Of course the exotic aspect, dancing with poisonous reptiles, has always been the main attraction for non-Hopis. And a variety of scholars have given theological interpretations that vary according to their own religious background. As I've suggested in terms of these other instances, however, one has to make an effort to understand the full context of the ceremony in order to judge Jung's interpretation.

The dance is sponsored by the Antelope and Snake clans, the Antelopes taking precedence over the Snakes. It is necessary to complete the harvest, that is to say, to ensure adequate water at the concluding phase of the corn-growing season, to see that the plants achieve full maturity and produce good crops. Explaining the dancing with the snakes as eating the mana of ancestors can only be useful in the abstract, and it largely avoids the obvious practical goal of bringing rain to desert crops in August, when the corn might fail completely without help from humans. The dance itself comes from an ancient pact between the Hopi and a young boy who could transform himself into a snake. He moved back and forth between humans and serpents and brought the ceremony to the Hopi as a gift from the Snakes. Jung's analysis, in other words, while productive of his own theory, might have been strengthened substantially had he developed a richer understanding of the sacred history of the Hopi and the long history of the Snake and Antelope clans. At the same time, we can also recognize that Jung was not an ethnographer. He was making comparative speculations, which tend to function best at an abstract level, and which were directed to the development of his own ideas.

What, then, can we conclude about Jung's relationship to American Indians? After an initial cultural shock in Algeria and Tunisia in which he was forced to recognize his narrow European perspective, Jung determined to make the acquaintance of the so-called primitive peoples. There was no question that he initially regarded tribal/primitive peoples as culturally and psychologically inferior to the Europeans. When the opportunity suddenly presented itself in the winter of 1924-25, he journeyed to Taos Pueblo. While there he experienced a different way of life, with a highly developed sense of religious commitment that transcended his European experiences. He remembered that difference the rest of his life. On the occasions when he mentioned Taos thereafter, it was always with great admiration. When he wanted, in his lectures and seminars, to use a living example of a mature personality, Jung always cited Biano, the spokesman of the Pueblo whom he had mistaken for a chief. Indians made their way into Jung's writings on a number of occasions. Sometimes, that meant looking at the symbolic uses of Indians. On other occasions, it meant citing and interpreting Indian practices in relation to those of other cultures, most particularly the European traditions he knew from the inside. What seems reasonably clear is that Indians—if not always perfectly conceived or understood—played a significant role in his emotional sense of the world and in the development of his thought.

Jung's quest to Indian country has been duplicated by succeeding generations of his followers. Some people familiar with Jungian writings look to Indian reservations and communities in search of spiritual enlightenment since they are influenced by Jung's admiration for Indians and the intuitive insights that he thought could inform and enlighten psychology. A few casual remarks by Jung about Taos or *Hiawatha* would not ordinarily trigger this kind of sustained desire to experience Indians as part of the missing element of Jungian psychology. That widespread desire suggests the power of the insight that underlies this particular comparative dialogue: there must be a great kinship between Jungian psychology and the American Indian traditions. That kinship has been emerging, will continue to develop, and is worth our time and energy. At the same time, however, our own acknowledgement of Jung's imperfections in utilizing his understandings of Indians should serve as a cautionary note for our efforts at comparison and dialogue. We are all culture-bound, to one degree or another, and all prisoners of the languages and concepts we use to make sense of the world. Jung was no different, of course, and it is to one of the key concepts in his vocabulary—"the primitive"—that we must now turn, exploring its negative, culture-bound uses, as well as the ways Jung utilized the concept in a positive, productive manner that proved critical to his psychology.

CHAPTER TWO

THE NEGATIVE
PRIMITIVE

The idea of "the primitive" is scattered throughout Carl Jung's writings, speeches, interviews and seminars, but the concept, as important as it is, was never systematically or clearly articulated in any single article or book. Jung's comments often come in the form of casual remarks and on-the-spot reflections rather than well-considered arguments. They are usually made to illustrate a particular point involving a specific problem in therapy or to suggest unexpected developments in the process of individuation. In most of these statements, "the primitive" refers specifically to a human primitive, and the primitive's mind is variously described as the condition from which mankind emerged or as the psychological disaster into which the patient is possibly falling. In certain instances, the primitive psyche can even be regarded as the beginning of some psychological problem. "Primitive," in other words, could refer to a range of possible meanings, from collective social and cultural evolution, to diagnoses of individual pathologies, to comparative theoretical possibilities.

In an article, "A Review of the Complex Theory,"* Jung disclaimed any intent of holding a derogatory concept of the primitive, averring:

> I would like to take this opportunity to remark that I use the term "primitive" in the sense of the "primordial" and that I do not imply any kind of value judgment.[1]

---

* The inaugural lecture of this paper was given on May 5, 1934. It is clear from the manuscript that Vine Deloria regarded the concept of the primitive to be a term so consistently problematic that it might be placed in "scare quotes" at each usage. We have chosen not to mark the word in this way throughout the text, trusting that readers will recognize (even in the moments when primitive seemed to be naturalized in the text) that it is always a vexed term, used to refer to abstract meanings, Jung's contextual senses of its meaning, the actual people perceived under its sign, and the tribal peoples to whom Deloria points in his comparison.

Indeed, on other occasions, Jung considers the possibility that primitives might have something to contribute to the development of a comprehensive psychological system that has as its goal the process of personal growth and maturation. American Indians are part of the general category of "primitives" in the Jungian system, and so we are required to examine this word and its meanings in close detail. For if Jung hoped to avoid attaching value to "primitive," the word proved too useful, in too many circumstances, for him to maintain neutrality.

In view of the difficulties in determining precisely how Jung saw primitives, I will examine this subject under two headings: the negative primitive and the positive primitive. The negative primitive consists of the detrimental, derogatory, or condescending views that Jung expressed about primitives. Many of these statements occurred early in Jung's writings and may not reflect his mature view of the subject. Nevertheless, as Jung matured and sought to extend the influence of his psychology to a broader field, such views may have remained, as part of the foundation upon which his later thoughts were grounded. That he could occasionally lapse into derogatory remarks in his seminars shows that while he may have had an increasing appreciation of primitives after visiting Africa and Taos Pueblo, he could slip into the negative connotations of the word "primitive" when in the heat of conversation or in making a specific point.*

At the same time, however (and as we have seen previously), Jung was equally able to highlight the strengths of primitive psychology or to use "primitives" as examples of a psychological state from which "modern" humans might profitably learn. Frequently, these remarks were equally casual, made to emphasize a particular point. The nebulous idea of the primitive often emerged when Jung attempted to point out some aspect of

---

*   Deloria is trying to be sensitive to, and mindful of, the historical, psychological and cultural context in which Jung's observations, judgments, and conclusions were written. And, for the current reader of this chapter, it is important to hold in mind that Deloria was writing his treatise in the wake of genocidal and colonial oppression by the dominant culture that had directly affected individuals he had known in his lifetime. In short, Jung would likely have said that his own observations were impersonal and empirical. Deloria, while taking and addressing Jung's empiricism seriously, also had some feeling reactions which do come through in his writing. Deloria's perspective had advanced and developed considerably since Jung's visit to Taos Pueblo at least fifty years earlier—in no small measure due to the influence of analytical psychology. One can see his struggle to separate his pique from his own empirical attitude, as well as his desire to be fair to a scholar for whom he had profound respect.

psychological experience that he knew intuitively, but could not yet articulate clearly. This fluidity can make Jungian psychology both attractive and frustrating to tribal peoples. At times, Jung almost connects with some of the important parts of the American Indian experience, but he seems always to retrieve his European propriety and his scientific persona.

In addition to the negative and positive uses of the primitive, Jung frequently combines these ideas with other terms, particularly "modern." He might, for instance, bring real consternation to his readers by implying that modern man has not, in any fundamental sense, moved very far from the primitive responses to phenomena. Or he might suggest that modern man has lost certain instinctive qualities or surrendered certain kinds of primitive behavior that would be of inestimable help in solving modern individual psychological problems. Taken together, Jung's statements—negative, positive, and occasionally comparative—help us form a picture of the primitive, a concept that could refer to a state of being, a position on an evolutionary hierarchy, a way of perceiving and making sense of the world, and a category of human beings. In this chapter, I will look at the rough edges of that picture—Jung's varied understandings of a primitive that was underdeveloped and insufficient. In the next chapter, we will turn to his equally revealing sense of a primitive that might be worth emulating.

We can begin by noting that Jung's actual contact with peoples he regarded as primitives was limited. He made two trips to Africa where he had some contact with one of the tribes in a British protectorate, and he made several trips to the United States, during one of which he made his hurried visit to the Taos Pueblo. Neither experience could be said to be sufficient to make Jung anything more than a tourist with respect to the tribal peoples he visited. In Africa he was unquestionably seen as part of the white man's establishment, and therefore his contact with the African natives must necessarily be filtered through his perceived status; our understanding should reflect the artificial posture that the African natives would have adopted to deal with him. He could not have been much more than another visiting fireman although, admittedly, a perceptive one.

Following established conventions concerning race, Jung also seemed to claim an acquaintance with primitives based on his visits to some mental health clinics in the United States where he met African American patients. Although he did not see them materially differing from the white majority, he thought he could understand their problems: "Insane Negroes," Jung said, very black Negroes whom I have analysed in the United States, had Greek myths in their dreams—Ixion on the wheel, for instance. It is only illusion when you think they are far apart; the Negro has the same kind of unconscious as the one that produced those symbols in Greece or anywhere else.[2]

This strange comment belies other statements concerning the very different ways American blacks haunted the psyche of the American white man.

As we have seen, when he dealt with materials he had gotten directly from peoples he regarded as primitive, Jung sometimes lapsed into reductionist forms of comparison. How else can we read the assertion made in his seminar on dream analysis?

I analysed the dreams of Somali Negroes as if they were people of Zurich, with the exception of certain differences of languages and images. Where the primitives dream of crocodiles, pythons, buffaloes, and rhinoceroses, we dream of being run over by trains, and automobiles. Both have the same voice, really; our modern cities sound like a primeval forest. What we express by the banker the Somali expresses by the python. The surface language is different yet the underlying facts are just the same.[3]

No one would argue the metaphorical similarities between the banker and the python, but I seriously doubt that "the underlying facts are just the same." Here, we can draw a line between the world of civilized man, which is wholly artificial in that it has been constructed by us, and the "primitive world," a natural arena in which every animal, bird, and reptile has a certain personality and power—in addition to whatever they may happen to symbolize in a particular context. One definition of "the primitive," then, can be seen to focus on the distinction between a natural world in which animals, plants, and objects function, not simply symbolically, but in real interactional terms, and a human-built world in which these real relationships no longer hold sway. What will matter most is the ways in which we use this primitive—as an Eden to regret, or as a primordial state to transcend—and the ways we conceive of the people occupying this sort of world.

Jung's ideas about primitive people seemed to be derived primarily from *How Natives Think* by Lucien Levy-Bruhl. Invariably, when discussing the primitive's psychological make up, Jung cited the concept of *participation mystique* articulated by Levy-Bruhl. *Participation mystique* is the idea that a strong, merged, almost strangulating psychic bond exists between primitive peoples and various objects in nature. In its best sense it is a highly spiritual communication; at its worst it seems to suggest that primitives are unable to distinguish themselves from their natural environment. In considering the question of epistemology, Levy-Bruhl devised an evolutionary scheme in which primitive man, weary of his incessant involvement with nature *à la participation mystique,* began to transform his experiences into an objective, abstract knowledge, which in turn eventually became transformed into scientific thinking as it became increasingly generalized. In this sense, "primitive" refers to an early, undeveloped position in an evolutionary trajectory.

But a simple, informed comparison might suggest the ways in which Levy-Bruhl's abstract formulation fails to capture the practices of individual societies. A Sioux response, for example, might look something like this: It is not simply that primitives "believed" in the forces of nature; they *experienced* a personal power in nature. When they ignored their relationships with this power, visible misfortune came upon them. How would such primitives have developed the kind of emotional attitude or intellectual perspective that would enable them to deny every experience they had? How could they accept a view of the world that denied the energy and intelligence of the life around them and reduced the world to a meaningless dashing of atoms arranged in a progressively complex ways? Cultural and epistemological evolution to "Western" objectivity seems an unlikely outcome for the Sioux—and by extension, for many other peoples.

Levy-Bruhl failed on this point because he saw himself providing the theoretical basis for understanding modern scientific thinking in its embryo state. He participated in a popular format in which earlier peoples are scorned because they did not achieve the technological success that we see today. They were, therefore, merely superstitious in comparison with "our" science. But we might take this distinction as the occasion to recognize that the knowledge of the primitives was *specific* knowledge derived from concrete experiences, whereas science as we know it today is often merely a set of general statements and beliefs whose categories of classification cannot always contain precise empirical knowledge, which is thus framed as anomalous. The accepted view of early people has them devising a system of astronomy so they could predict the planting seasons, and developing mathematics so they could mark the boundaries of their river-bottom lands after the spring flood had erased them. We see them as helpless before the forces of nature. In reality, it is the experience and memory of the particulars that enables the farmer to judge when to plant, not the precession of the equinox or the rising of certain stars. Mathematics or not, finding boundaries after a flash flood is more often guesswork than geometry.

Jung does not elaborate on this unlikely evolution of the thinking process, but rather accepts Levy-Bruhl's arguments at face value. Here, we can enlarge our sense of Jung's own definition of the primitive. Engaging Levy-Bruhl, Jung asserts that the primitive is lacking in development and maturity in three major areas of psychological makeup: 1) in the use and availability of functions of perception, thinking, feeling, sensation and intuition; 2) in the relative degree of, or ratio between, consciousness and unconsciousness; and 3) in the development and exercise of will. In each of these areas, Jung suggests, primitive man—the inhabitant of the primitive world of undifferentiated nature—might be seen as deficient in comparison with modern humans. At worst, such deficiencies lead those of the "modern" and the "civilized" to conceive of primitives not simply as lesser people, but as subhuman organisms for which one can have only abhorrence and pity. The existence of these negative portrayals in Jung's theory was possible in large part because they were prevalent in the broader culture of the historical moment; such attitudes surely contributed to the often-horrific treatment of humans designated "primitive." And those horrific treatments neces-sarily reinforced the common-sense understanding of primitive inferiority. Let us examine in turn each of Jung's three arguments for the psychological underdevelopment of the primitive.

In the Jungian scheme of things, each human being has four functions of perception.

> *Sensation* establishes what is actually present, *thinking* enables us to rec-ognize its meaning, *feeling* tells us its value, and *intuition* points to the possibilities as to whence it came and wither it is going in a given situa-tion.[4] [emphasis added]

Well and good. What sense we would make of our experiences if we lacked one of these basic ways of perception? How we would have originally func-tioned and survived in the physical world? Yet Jung, in discussing the primi-tive, suggested that "the primitive man possesses only one function, he is only capable of one thing, so three are unconscious."[5] Like Levy-Bruhl, he described an original scenario of transformation: primitive man emerged from the thick cloud of general unconsciousness, and it was only by tearing loose one of the functions that he was enabled to become detached. How that was brought about I don't know; it is a peculiar quality in the psychological structure of man; animals have not that ability to free themselves from the original psyche.[6]

The idea that there must have existed an original psychological state in which our species found itself is a necessary belief only if we are devoted to the problematic concept of social evolution. Nor should we regard such statements as nothing more than abstract theorizing. Almost inevitably, such a hypothetical state of primitive development has been attributed to living, non-Western tribal peoples, which we must admit is unfair and unscientific. But let us remain in the notion that Jung is really describing a psychological condition. We can imagine this if we accept his idea that

> the one function which is conscious would be very weak (not in modern man but in the man of two to four thousand years ago) and therefore he would feel inferior and sinful, his unconscious would be more efficient than he.[7]

Here, Jung moves toward describing a psychological condition that would be a prerequisite to the origin of religion, mythology, customs, and taboos—in a word, society. But again, primitive peoples are used in a hypothetical, as the explanation for the creation of modern society itself. Ironically, actual tribal peoples, if we were to take them as models of the primitive, have no more guilt (and often much less) than do civilized peoples. They may feel shame at having disappointed the clan, family or community, but guilt is more often a creation of civilized institutions. More to the point, however, we might wonder *which* function was the best candidate for such a tearing loose from the unconscious.

In *Psychological Types,* Jung takes a different approach to the problem, one that links ontological with phylogenetic development. Here, he argues that primitives really do have a developed function, and that it is *sensation*:

> Sensation is strongly developed in children and primitives, since in both cases it predominates over thinking and feeling, though not necessarily over intuition. I regard sensation as conscious, and intuition as unconscious perception.[8]

Jung elaborates on this hypothesis, suggesting that

> primitive thinking and feeling are entirely concretistic; they are always related to sensation. The thought of the primitive has no detached independence but clings to material phenomena. It rises at most to the level of analogy. Primitive feeling is equally bound to material phenomena. Both of them depend on sensation and are only slightly differentiated from it.[9]

One might suggest, then, that primitives are different in the *way* they gather data, in the *kind* of data they gather, and in the *interpretations* they create. This does not require us to assert that they are less psychologically developed than civilized people; they have simply developed a different psychological function. At best, however, the picture Jung paints is of a primitive with deficits in the development of functions, and thus in consciousness itself.

Indeed, the second area in which Jung considered these issues of development and evolution—with a corresponding use of the primitive—lies in the relative degree of consciousness, with civilized man having considerably more consciousness than the primitive, hence being more fully psychologically developed. "Primitive man's perception of objects is conditioned only partly by the objective behaviour of the things themselves," Jung argued,

> whereas a much greater part is often played by intra-psychic facts which are not related to the external objects except by way of projection. This is due to the simple fact that the primitive has not yet experienced that ascetic discipline of mind known to us as the critique of knowledge. To him the world is a more or less fluid phenomenon within the stream of his own fantasy, where subject and object are undifferentiated and in a state of mutual interpenetration.*[10]

Is primitive man unable to differentiate between subject and object? Jung seemed to think so. In a letter to Marie Ramondt in 1950, Jung wrote,

---

*   What appears to bother Deloria here is Jung's projection of the primitive's mental make-up and emphasis on "*fantasy,*" a purely internal experience. Deloria is contending that what Jung is projecting as "fantasy" is a different dimension of *experience* with the world around him.

for the primitive, the unconscious coalesces with the external world, as can plainly be seen from the numerous projections of the primitive consciousness. Here one can hardly speak of an ego–world relationship, since the ego, as we understand it barely exists. The primitive consciousness is an immersion in a stream of events in which the outer and inner world are not differentiated, or very indistinctly so.*[11]

At his most imaginative, Jung painted a picture of almost continuous hallucinations when he described the primitive conscious/unconscious. "If you could put yourselves back into the primitive world," he suggested,

> there would be so much outside yourselves and so little inside that anything could happen, all the world would begin to act in a queer way, trees to talk, animals to do strange things, ghosts to appear. Now, increase your consciousness and these phenomena will all vanish, they were only expressing to you what you yourself thought. The trees will no longer talk, and no ghosts will walk.[12]

Jung thought the power to speculate broke the hold which the unconscious held over us:

Just as Jung asserts that the primitive "has not yet experienced that ascetic discipline of mind known … as the critique of knowledge," i.e., the left-brain dominated education characteristic of Western culture, Deloria is asserting that Jung is projecting as fantasy what for the primitive is right-brain experience (what contemporary brain researchers call "implicit memory") from which the Western mind has become split.

* Interestingly, Jung begins his response to Frau Ramondt by acknowledging her apparent assertion, quoted by Jung himself, that "primitive material cannot be interpreted because it is not just a statement of the psyche *but also a statement—and an important one—of the surrounding world*" (p. 548, § 2, emphasis added by editor). Apparently Frau Ramondt is making the kind of assertion that Deloria himself is contending: that the primitive psyche is connected with the world around it as *experience,* not fantasy, as Jung would have it, and that it has a different experience of consciousness than that of the Western ego—not better, not worse, just different. Deloria is bothered here because Jung seems to be projecting fantasy where psychic reality is the fact. The former is an unconscious intra-psychic process with self; whereas the primitive has a direct psychic relationship with the world around him. And it is Deloria's contention that if Jung (and others) were to allow that the primitive psyche has a different, yet whole, psychic experience of self and world, that such realization would broaden Jung's scope and depth of understanding (and that of other Western scholars), which ultimately would contribute a great deal to Jung's own psychology, as Deloria demonstrates in Chapter Four, "The Positive Primitive." (We know nothing of Frau Ramondt except that she apparently was a professional of her day, and that the piece that she wrote appeared in a publication of the Royal Dutch Academy of Sciences.)

... the moment man reached the point where he could ask himself: "How would it be if?" his thoughts became detached, he was liberated from *participation mystique,* and he began to experiment.* Civilization is the result of this process of detachment in the development of individual consciousness, and the process is still going on.[13]

We might think of it this way: minds can be trained to filter out experiences that would otherwise give testimony about the realities of the world that we do not wish to acknowledge. Of course, one can use any of the four functions to increase one's consciousness; it is not simply by becoming more rational that you become more conscious.** And, in point of fact, we might argue that "primitive" humans must speculate even more than those placed in the category "civilized." Accustomed to the regularity of natural processes around him, primitive man is immediately alert to sudden changes in the environment, is struck by the unusual behavior of animals, carefully watches the weather, and pays attention to his dreams. He must quickly speculate on the meaning of every new event or unusual happening, reach a conclusion and take action—his life may depend upon the correct answer.

The last major area in which Jung noted distinctions and seemed to find civilized man superior to the primitive was "will," which he defined as "a certain amount of energy freely disposable by the psyche."[14] "We have control of our will power," Jung said, "but the primitive has not. Complicated exercises are needed if he is to pull himself together for any activity

---

*   Jung uses the word "detachment," which is probably correct in terms of psychic development over the millennia. In the modern era the question has arisen as to whether that original "detachment" has become dissociative and pathological. (See *Living in the Borderland,* Part I.)

**   Here Deloria is distinguishing between cultural differences as well as psychic differences, the one deriving from and reinforcing the other. He is also differentiating between (in today's language emerging from brain research) *implicit memory* (characterized more by the primitive psyche) and *explicit memory* (narrative memory and history more characteristic of the Western ego). These exist as distinct but very different dimensions of *experience.* The former has a more fluid relationship to the collective unconscious than the latter, but both represent a way of apprehending reality. Although these two dimensions of experience have been represented and related to as *separate* dimensions of experience, current clinical and neuropsychological research tends to support Deloria's assertion in this regard. [In Part I of his book, *Living in the Borderland,* Jerome Bernstein asserts that the Western ego is being reconnected with its psychic roots in nature from which it became psychically split more than two thousand years ago—that these two parallel dimensions of psychic experience are directly influencing each other. This process is changing the nature of the Western ego construct itself. (See the work of J. Bernstein (2005), A. N. Schore (1994, 2003), D. Siegel (1999), and others.)]

that is conscious and intentional and not just emotional and instinctive."[15] Accordingly Jung noted, "we have learnt to do our work efficiently without having recourse to chanting and drumming to hypnotize us into the state of doing."[16] Again:

> ... with us a word is enough to release an accumulation of forces, but with primitives an elaborate pantomime is needed, with all manner of embellishments which are calculated to put the man into the right mood for acting.[17]

As we have seen with his analyses of the trickster and Longfellow's *Hiawatha*, this sort of speculative interpretation of primitive man's supposed absence of will reveals large gaps in Jung's knowledge about even the tribal people he took as examples of the primitive. It is surely not a lack of will power that makes dances and rituals possible or necessary. These activities are efforts to gain an advantage over the opponent, or in relation to a challenge, by enlisting the powers of superior and helpful spirits. If an individual is going hunting, going to war, or planting or harvesting a crop, he or she needs to maximize the chances for success. Recognizing that everything in nature is alive with intelligent life energy and that he is simply a part of it, primitive man reduces the odds of failure by making his venture a cooperative one. He could simply go out and do the task, taking his chances, or reduce the odds by enhancing his capability with the assistance of helpful spirits.

Primitive and tribal peoples have in fact shown incredible demonstrations of will, accomplishing feats that modern people can duplicate only with great difficulty. The Sioux and other Plains tribes, for example, performed a "vision quest" in early adolescence. This ritual involved fasting for four days, without food or water, on a remote hill or butte, spending the time engaged in praying and singing songs of supplication to the spirits, asking them to have pity and to help. This ordeal, one might argue, required an expenditure of will far surpassing what the modern person in his or her best moments could accomplish. Luther Standing Bear, commenting on the Sioux man observed:

> Not only was he a man of brawn, but a man of will. In the distribution of food, this quality was uppermost. When food was brought into the village, the sharing must be equal for old, young, sick, disabled, and for those who did not or could not hunt as well as those who hunted.[18]

There are plenty of examples of extraordinary willpower among Sioux people; indeed, stoicism—one of the common attributes Europeans assigned to Indian people in general—is often tied directly to the power of the will.

And what of civilized humanity? Modern men can, of course, hunt deer with a spear but they do not do so. They usually take along elaborate hunting outfits that include tents, lights, telescopic sights, and so forth. These things can hardly be said to detract from the exercise of will. The use of will is defined in terms of the initial decision to hunt, which is hardly a significant point of differentiation between modern and primitive. Jung might well have noted that all this modern equipment serves as the physical counterpart to the ritual and ceremonial tools mobilized by the primitive. Nor should this gesture toward comparison be limited to something like hunting. One might argue, for instance, that routine "modern" work, such as assembly line or industrial agricultural labor, requires such an exercise of will that "civilized Americans" (and here we realize how much this term relies upon race and class distinctions) rely heavily on immigrant workers, many of whom continue to be seen in terms of the category of "the primitive."

Jung's interest in developmentalism helped lead him to these kinds of distinctions between modern and primitive:

> It cannot be denied that there has been a notable development of consciousness and its functions. Above all, there has been a tremendous extension of consciousness in the form of knowledge. Not only have the individual functions become differentiated, but to a larger extent they have been brought under the control of the ego—in other words, man's will has developed. This is particularly striking when we compare our mentality with that of primitives.[19]

And yet, even on Jung's own terms, the lines between modern and primitive willpower are not so clear. In order to mobilize for a major task, civilized man needs parades, songs, and morale speeches just as much as the primitive needs ceremonies and rituals. In fact, civilized man forms himself into a herd much more quickly than the primitive when concerted effort is needed to undertake some venture. And, from diets to daily labor, we find plenty of evidence of the lack of will in contemporary society.

Carl Jung's engagement with the primitive produced a number of comparisons and formulations that are indeed pejorative. At one point, Jung goes so far as to portray primitive life as a state of mental illness:

If the natural state were really the ideal one, then the primitive would be leading an enviable existence. But that is by no means so, for aside from all other sorrows and hardship of human life the primitive is tormented by superstitions, fears, and compulsions to such a degree that, if he lived in our civilization, he could not be described as other than profoundly neurotic, if not mad. [20]

At another point, in his seminar on *Nietzsche's Zarathustra*, he remarked: "It is a curious feeling to move among primitives who live as you lived when you were six years old; they are like children, with no continuity whatsoever." [21]* We can, quite properly, critique Jung on such statements, even as we note the ways that they helped him produce his theoretical frameworks. Many of the distinctions he draws between civilized and primitive man take the form of gross generalizations or ill-informed distortions that can only be characterized as unscientific stereotyping.

There are a number of reasons why it is important for us to explore this breed of remark. In their social dimension, we need to understand that such negative images are not restricted to abstract musings concerning a hypothetical aboriginal time when our species began to distinguish itself from the other forms of life. Far too frequently, Western people take such descriptions as indicative of valid scientific knowledge about contemporary tribal peoples and act accordingly. In terms of the development of Jung's psychology, we need to understand the ways in which the underdeveloped primitive formed the baseline for any and all arguments concerning the evolution of consciousness, from the idea of the functions, to that of will, and of consciousness. Since these arguments are crucial to Jungian psychology, we need to recognize that a critical understanding of "the primitive" offers the occasion—and indeed the invitation—to revisit such arguments. Finally, in such revisiting, we need also to recognize that for every negative, retrograde rendition of the primitive, we can also find a positive portrayal, and indeed, such positive understandings of the primitive reveal the complexities of Jung's thought, while laying the groundwork for further comparison and dialogue. For if Jung's ill-informed, negative connotations make us want simply to dismiss the word "primitive" from our vocabularies, his positive uses of the term were equally productive of his psychology. We turn now to a consideration of these other uses.

---

*   Given on November 6, 1935.

CHAPTER THREE

THE POSITIVE PRIMITIVE

Jung's failure to articulate a systematic conception of the primitive poses the same problems for describing a "positive" primitive as it did for assessing the "negative" consequences of the concept. Taking into account the life-changing nature of his experience at Taos, it makes sense that many of Jung's statements on the primitive would be of a positive nature. His examples of maturity and good psychological health were often drawn from his slight knowledge of and experiences with the so-called tribal primitive peoples. Indeed, in the record there are so many positive articulations concerning the primitive that Jung himself might have been surprised, were they arranged in a coherent framework. The positive comments, which often come in the form of casual admissions, suggest that he understood that there was more to the psychology of the primitive than anyone had suspected. At the same time, we should also recognize that many of Jung's positive comments come—as is so often the case—as critiques of his own society. Our own examination, then, will move from the complexities and contradictions inherent in these multiple possible meanings and uses, to a tracing of Jung's positives when read through an American Indian critique. We may be surprised to find productive theoretical insights in both positive and negative views.

The goal of Jungian psychology, as it must be with all psychologies, was to produce mature individuals who had or could fulfill their potential. Part of the negative view of the primitive, as we have seen in the previous chapter, was that the individual was not able, according to both Jung and Lucien Levy-Bruhl, to emerge from the fatal embrace of the *participation mystique* and consequently remained an undeveloped mind with infantile responses to phenomena. These ideas—common in Jung's intellectual milieu—were never critically examined, nor were real life examples given for verification of these abstract claims.

In his *Seminar on Dream Analysis*, however, Jung often took a different and more positive view of primitives, although one that sometimes continued to place them at the dawn of some evolutionary framework. In the seminar, he saw them as achieving a rare form of individuality and maturity. He suggested, for example, that primitives are:

> ... more individual and less so. They are like animals. A complete thing, unhampered, simply what it is, identical with the laws of their species. That is my idea of the complete individual, not perfect, but individual. Complete in their virtues and in their vices. Fulfilling the meaning of the species, utterly collective, and at the same time individual. I say that you cannot be a really collective being without being completely individual, because only when you are humbly the thing that nature intended you to be, fulfilling decently the experiment nature is trying to make, only then are you a decent member of society.[1]

This complicated statement may be read as a radical admission that, far from being hampered by *participation mystique,* the "primitive" is able to achieve individuality by remaining a part of the group and simply being him or herself. Jung's comment might be regarded as an effort to sketch out two different kinds of individualism: 1) the natural product of an unquestioning but sophisticated adjustment to the environment; and 2) the highly educated, prosperous, intellectually active, civilized human who was the subject of his psychology. Although in Jung's sense of *participation mystique,* the primitive was believed to live under an extreme handicap, we have seen that even this condition was not necessarily distinct from civilized man (an argument also made by Levy-Bruhl). Indeed, Jung not only suggested that primitives are able to rise above the sense of the group and become individuals, he also believed that the primitive

> is by no means that strange being from whom the civilized man is separated by a gulf that cannot be bridged. The fundamental difference between them is *not a difference in mental functioning,* but rather in *the premises upon which the functioning is based.*[2] [emphasis added]

Did Jung really mean that primitive and civilized minds function in the same manner, with only premises, beliefs, or conclusions that differ?

What are the premises that might define the difference between these two types of people? Jung observes, in "Symbols and the Interpretation of Dreams," that a realistic picture of the human mind [here I take it he means the modern civilized mind] reveals many primitive traits and survivals, which are still playing their roles just as if nothing had happened during the last five hundred years. The man of today is a curious mixture of characteristics acquired over the long ages of his mental development.[3]

The premises that distinguish the primitive from the civilized are therefore hardly formidable barriers; they appear to be based primarily on the reservoir of objective scientific information that has been available to educated Europeans since the Renaissance. But this body of knowledge is hardly comprehensive; it is simply a collection of empirical observations placed in generalized doctrines and dogmas. One might argue that primitive folklore serves the same function.

On the other hand, one might also argue that primitive folklore does in fact use different premises and conclusions, those of a world more directly encountered and less mediated by the distancing effect of modern industrial and post-industrial technology. Different premises must necessarily produce different contents within consciousness since they wholly determine what information is regarded as important, what data is gathered, how it is arranged, and how reasoning links related fragments of knowledge together to produce larger explanatory concepts. Most of Jung's negative assessments suggest that modern civilized man has a greater conscious content than does primitive man and thus is quantitatively superior. But is it not quantity but the kinds of data collected that matters? As to the quality of insights and observations gathered and retained, Jung believed that primitive man actually had a richer life:

> In the primitive's world, things do not have the same sharp boundaries they do in ours. What we call psychic identity or *participation mystique* has been stripped off our world of things. It is exactly this halo, or "fringe of consciousness," as William James calls it, which gives a colourful and fantastic aspect to the primitive's world. We have lost it to such a degree that we do not recognize it when we meet it again, and are baffled at its incomprehensibility. With us such things are kept below the threshold; and when they occasionally reappear, we are convinced that something is wrong.[4]

What are the "sharp boundaries" possessed by civilized man, and how does stripping away *participation mystique* produce such boundaries? We can assume that Jung means that entities in our field of observation are stripped of various qualities, reduced to objects, and therefore appear stark and clear in our minds and observations as "facts." Jung here seems to be unwittingly reviving the conflict begun by Galileo and finally concluded by the British empiricists regarding primary and secondary qualities of objects. Today, of course, the possibility of such clarity seems hopelessly out of date. Literary theorists have long since demonstrated the ways in which "facts" are made through practices of selection and the constitution of narrative authority. And our most sophisticated modern sciences tell us that nothing is clear and sharp; our minds and teachings make our beliefs appear to be clear. Our conception of subatomic physical activities, for instance, is wholly indeterminate and our best efforts to explain nature are but highly educated guesses. Again, the line between primitive and modern seems untenable, at least in psychological terms.

If we accept Jung's idea of the influence of training as definitive in establishing the boundary between the conscious and unconscious, then we must seek the origins of the social order before we venture to explain the psychology of the individual. Even as it defines the relation between primitive and modern, our social order (and that of Carl Jung) provides the context in which the process of establishing the boundaries of the conscious and unconscious originates. We learn from watching others. Social behavior is passed from generation to generation and modified by the historical experiences of each generation. No matter how tenuous the tie that binds people to one another or how horrific the circumstance, we never find an individual without some form of social-family context surrounding him or her.

When Jung observes that some primitive traits continue to exist in civilized man, even after five hundred years of secular scientific training, he seems to suggest that consciousness and "reason"—that defining element of the Western social order—should have wiped the slate clean. But reason is neither influential nor sophisticated. "Human reason," according to Jung,

> is nothing other than the expression of man's adaptability to average occurrences, which have gradually become deposited in firmly established complexes of ideas that constitute our objective values.[5]

Reason is thus a surprisingly simplistic function of the sorting of experiences into familiar categories, which then become naturalized within social and cultural contexts. Jung himself elaborates on this idea:

what we call "rational" is everything that seems "fitting" to the man in the street, and the question then arises whether this "fitness" may not in the end prove to be "irrational" in the bad sense of the word. Sometimes, even with the best intentions, this dilemma cannot be solved. This is the moment when the primitive trusts himself to a higher authority and to a decision beyond his comprehension.[6]

Thinking, then, has its limits, although when we are trained to believe in reason we often do not recognize those limits. The primitive seems to know when the problem is insoluble; the civilized man does not. The highly efficient reasoning process attributed to civilized man, in other words, does not necessitate any particular superiority over the primitive, as Jung himself admits that the rational solution may well be irrational.

Primitive perceptions of the world, rather than being unreliable because of the refusal or inability to depart from the context of the *participation mystique,* are not only as adequate as civilized man's, but may be considerably better. Following this "positive" line of thought, Jung observed that:

> Primitive man's belief in an arbitrary power does not arise out of thin air, as was always supposed, but is grounded in experience. The grouping of chance occurrences justifies what we call his superstition, for there is a real measure of probability that unusual events will coincide in time and place. We must not forget that our experience is apt to leave us in the lurch here. Our observation is inadequate because our point of view leads us to overlook these matters.[7]

Here, Jung largely abandons the idea that primitives are less capable than civilized people. The many so-called superstitions of the primitive appear to be simply apprehensions created by the encounter with a kind of perceived reality significantly different than that experienced by modern man.

Another issue lurks in this examination of primitive and modern observation. To be able to perceive "chance occurrences," primitives would need to have an equally keen perceptual sense of the *regularity* of natural processes. In what manner this perception would differ from rationality—that is, reason expressing itself in the apprehension of average occurrences—escapes me. These two ways of speaking (reason, on the one hand; perception, on the other) are in fact describing the same process of observation using words that imply but do not support a distinction. Jung might have maintained that civilized people are better at observing activities and events, and include more occurrences when figuring their averages, thereby providing "better" knowledge. Such an argument would be hard to sustain, however, since it is accepted by scholars that human observational powers are developed in relation to the specific contexts and environments in which people grow up, and in which they conduct their lives.

The most important observations that primitives could make would be of the environment around them. "Generally," Jung suggested,

> it is one of the shrewdest and wiliest men of the tribe who is entrusted with the observation of meteorological events. His knowledge must suffice to explain all unusual occurrences, and his art to combat them.[8]

The survival of primitive peoples over thousands of years without modern technology testifies to the adequacy of their observations. Instead of being lost in the environment or mystified by nature, Jung suggested that tribal people, in designating a tribal weatherman, were similar to civilized people in allocating responsibilities and using individual talents for the benefit of the group. Substitute the modern weatherman with his scientific training for the experienced elder and his decades of experience and you have the same kind of specialist performing the same functions, although using distinct premises, contexts, and perceptions.

No one today seriously argues that civilized people are "better" at making, ordering, and remembering observations than primitives—which is not quite the same thing as saying that there are not important distinctions. Jung, in many utterances, does not cling tenaciously to this value judgment either, and in fact tends as often to admiration:

> His [primitive man's] powers of observation can be trusted. ... What seems to us wholly senseless heaping-up of single, haphazard occurrences—because we pay attention only to single events and their particular causes—is for the primitive a completely logical sequence of omens and of happenings indicated by them. It is a fatal outbreak of demonic power showing itself in a thoroughly consistent way.[9]

Now, we cannot say that Jung's perception of primitive difference is wholly without foundation. If civilized man concentrates on the single event, and misses the relationships that surely exist among and between objects, could not the primitive perceive differently, intuiting sets of activities that can only be apprehended with a larger vision? Could one argue, for instance, that intuition serves, in many contexts, as a more powerful way of understanding things than reason? It is perhaps the form of expression that the primitive uses that is objectionable to Western observers.

Turning this question back to Jung, we find him observing that,

> people who live exposed to natural conditions use intuition a great deal, and people who risk something in an unknown field, who are pioneers of some sort, will use intuition. Inventors will use it and judges will use it. Whenever you have to deal with strange conditions where you have no established values or established concepts, you will depend upon that faculty of intuition. [10]

The primitive is thus included with the more creative and productive members of civilized society, those whose primary talent for gathering and interpreting information is intuition. To my knowledge, Jung did not question whether a continual use of intuition instead of the thinking function was a handicap. If we turn our analysis around, then, and stress for a moment the value of intuition over reason, we might argue that, apart from the occasional intuitive genius, civilized people have been injured by the intense concentration on thinking, and are handicapped in leading a balanced creative life. They are, however, unsurpassed in performing routine functions.

The thinking function—let us return to the word "rationality"—implies and requires a highly developed set of concepts through which thinking occurs. At the very least, we are talking about a vocabulary sufficient to express both abstract thoughts and precise descriptions. Here, too, a comparative move between primitive and modern is revealing. As a rule, "primitive" peoples have much more comprehensive languages than those of the "civilized," with many nuances available, different senses of time, space, and becoming, and complicated descriptive phrases indicating motion and emotion. Jung is quite frank when describing primitives and language:

> We have all these abstract concepts, and in a way they are misleading, or rather, not informing. We can say a man or a woman or, even more indefinite, a person wants to speak to you, and how little we know—whether he or she is outside, inside, standing up, alive or dead. A primitive telling you the same thing by the very nature of his language would inform you,

for instance, that an alive, erect man was standing outside your door. *There are no words in their language for a man without an almost complete description.*[11] [emphasis added]

The primitive, one might argue, has at hand the linguistic tools to formulate ideas, think complex thoughts, and describe phenomena with more precision than can the civilized person—and one presumes that those tools exist in the language because they are used on an everyday basis.

We never find a society, no matter how primitive, that does not have a language adequate to express everything its members wish to say. It might be argued that real abstractions—mathematics and physics, for example—are beyond the capability of the primitive. But what do these abstractions tell us? Unless we have been extensively trained in mathematics so that it is a specialty and we have mastered its language, most of us are equally helpless in the face of its symbols. How many people in civilized society really comprehend the doctrines of science? No matter how complex the idea, it inevitably has to be described in common language to make sense—and even the common sense language and concepts of civilized man may prove inadequate when compared to those of the primitive.

Part of the precision of primitive language comes from the manner in which primitives observe the world, and this perspective is a result of their method of education. Primitives teach their children by example and by doing, which (according to Jung)

can proceed wholly unconsciously and is therefore the oldest and perhaps the most effective form of all. It is aided by the fact that the child is psychologically more or less identical with its environment, and especially with its parents. This peculiarity is one of the most conspicuous features of the primitive psyche, for which the French anthropologist Levy-Bruhl coined the term *participation mystique.*[12]

(We will discuss the family and environment in a later chapter. For now, it is sufficient to note that, in this instance, *participation mystique* has a positive value in an effective education). As we have seen in the previous chapter, Jung interpreted *participation mystique* as a kind of curse upon primitive humans, one that denied them the possibility of reaching a significant level of consciousness. Rather than a curse, however, we might also see it as enabling the primitive to do things in a manner far different than the civilized society. Jung, for example, was stunned at the way that the Africans were able to keep track of cattle with no apparent effort to count them according to European procedures:

> The primitive counts from the figures things make. He makes an aesthetic distinction because he counts without counting. For example, an old chief knew whether all of his six hundred head of cattle were in the kraal, although he could not count more than six. He knew them all individually by name, so that he could tell if little Fritz hadn't come in yet. The count is made by the extent of the ground covered by the cattle, and the way the ground is checkered by them: it is a vision of the ensemble.[13]

We are not talking about complex mathematical expressions here, but a talent highly developed to work in the manner in which it will be employed. This ability is not superior to civilized mathematics as the average citizen uses it, but it is as useful and accurate because it comprehends complex relationships rather than simply measuring quantities. In the context in which this intuitive way of counting is used, however, it is superior to civilized mathematics. The civilized man, loving complexity, might count the animals' legs and divide by four.

The picture of the primitive that emerges from Jung's positive observations is hardly the ignorant, superstitious savage cringing before the processes of nature that we saw in the previous chapter. In most respects, this primitive is the equal of, or is superior to modern civilized man. The differences that do exist, according to Jung, consistently point to different views of the world derived from different means of gathering and interpreting information. Since the differences are partially created by the emphasis of the thinking function by civilized man and the intuitive function by the primitive, can we then imagine the possibility that, in the Jungian system, there might be four entirely different ways of gathering and processing observational data? If we say that primitives focus on sensation and intuition, how would we describe other societies that emphasize a combination of two other functions?

The psychological development of the primitive with an emphasis on the intuitive function is entirely adequate to deal with the environment in which he finds himself because the environment is almost wholly natural —primitive man, for the most part, did not make it, he only adjusted to it. Civilized man, on the other hand, in taking the thinking approach to his world now confronts an almost wholly artificial environment, a manufactured construct. It is a world created by thought that in turn nurtures further thought to the exclusion of the other functions. The creation of an artificial world, and our reliance on it, is a dangerous proposition. Jung suggested a similar critique, observing that

> the psyche of civilized man is no longer a self-regulating system but could rather be compared to a machine whose speed-regulation is so insensitive that it can continue to function to the point of self-injury, while on the other hand it is subject to the arbitrary manipulations of a one-sided will.[14]

The emphasis on thinking, the development of "will," heralded in Jungian writings as the supreme achievement of civilized man, hides from civilized man the reality of the natural physical world within which this artificial world rests. The danger in this narrow perspective is that one never knows when the real natural world is going to disrupt the artificial world with dire consequences. Indeed, earthquakes, floods, typhoons and tornados, blizzards and other natural catastrophes are always just a few days away. We are usually ill prepared when these natural disasters strike, and in severe crises we gather together with an attitude that evokes the *participation mystique,* in which we feel a hint of undifferentiated commonality as we work for the general good. Far too often we are treated to television interviews with survivors of disasters who cannot believe that they do not have immunity from the ravages of nature but who nevertheless glory in the experience of a common humanity.

Perhaps the most off-handed compliment paid by Jung to the primitive was in his discussion of ghosts in his Visions Seminars:

> It is generally supposed by the red Indians, that in a wood at night they can talk to the ghosts; and it is assumed that in the initiations people will hear voices when they fast and remain alone for a long time. This general expectation shows that to be a very frequent phenomenon. *As a matter of fact, under certain strained conditions people frequently do hear or see queer things.*[15] [emphasis added]

Now if these things do happen (according to Jung), why should knowledge of them be merely a supposition? From the perspective of Indian people, would these empirical experiences not be as valid a set of expectations as those offered by any scientific experiment? Jung, of course, would describe this phenomenon as a projection from the unconscious. As we shall see later, it is not the actual hearing of the voice that is important; it is the content of the message received. Civilized people might describe such experience as demonic, whereas primitives might see it as an enhancement of their powers through spiritual assistance.

I question whether we can discern "demonic" forces in nature without having a sense of human moral and ethical standards already in place. If we reflect carefully, we will see that the alleged superstitions of primitives are all connected to their perception of a superior morality inherent in the physical world. Their world becomes unbalanced because of their *own* moral failure to respond properly in specific situations. Thinking cannot discover the moral sense of life that underlies the physical world—although by logical analyses we can conclude that morality is necessary. Rather, the moral sense is an essential component of the natural world, whether it is clearly evident to civilized people or not. In trying to sort this question out, Jung noted that

> Primitive man appears to have a much better developed sense of the reality of evil than we supposedly civilized people, which enables him to recognize the deep, malevolent, intractable, and immortal propensity for wrongdoing at the root of every trickster's dissocial acts. [16]

Here again, we find ourselves confronted with the problems of similarity and difference between primitive and modern. Evil, when primitives perceive it, is attached to specific acts and events; it is far less metaphysical than it is for civilized people. This may well mean that primitives have a better sense of the reality of evil. But it also means that evil does not struggle with good or simply sit somewhere waiting to intervene in the lives of people.

Recognizing or experiencing evil as a real and powerful presence in the natural world, although perhaps unaware of its abstract potential, the primitive is forced to confront disorder through the development of customs, taboos, and laws. According to Jung, the primitive

> not only has a moral code but one which in the severity of its demands is often considerably more exacting than our civilized morality. It makes no difference if good and evil mean one thing for the primitive and another for us; his naturalism leads to law giving—that is the chief point. [17]

The apprehension of evil, the perception of morality, the creation of law, custom, and taboo would all seem to require determined acts of the will which complicate—and even negate—Jung's other remarks concerning the utter lack of will among the primitives. Law is the tangible expression of a society's consensus and will. A society with many taboos and rigid enforcement of customs demonstrates discipline, not only of the individual self, but also of families, clans, and other increasingly large groupings of people.

I fail to see anywhere in Jung's writings where we can find a moral dimension in the natural world that would identify evil as an identifiable principle of reality itself. Looking at the natural world, we see animals devour each other as part of the food chain of being. We see virtually helpless animals, the grazers and browsers who are apparently designed either by a deity or evolution to be eaten by predators. We observe that prey-predator ratios suggest that this condition is essential to the functioning of the organic world. We occasionally glimpse morality in the animals—primarily in the mating for life among some species and the sacrifice of the mother to protect the young. Very old animals may abandon the herd and make room for others, and virile adult animals may fight to protect the helpless in their group. Buffalo and elephants try to comfort wounded members of their herds. (We might well learn something of morality by observing animal behavior. In many ways, some species are considerably more moral than humans.)

The defects in civilized rationality, insofar as it enables individuals to fulfill their destiny, were apparent to Jung, and his criticism often took the form of casual, perhaps unintended compliments paid to the so-called primitive people. On too many occasions, however, he and his followers failed to exploit these insights. We have identified a number of these occasions above, although there are certainly others. Bemoaning the marriage problems of civilized man, for example, Jung observed:

> If only we could, like the primitives, leave the unconscious to look after this whole psychological development which marriages entails, these transformations could be worked out more completely and without too much friction. So often among the so-called "primitives" one comes across spiritual personalities who immediately inspire respect, as though they were fully matured products of an undisturbed fate.[18]

Who then, according to Jung, has a superior understanding of the nature of the marriage problem and a better solution? And yet, we can ask fairly why he did not work with such insights in more sustained ways—and we can imagine possibilities for future work emerging from this comparative dialogue.

The difference between the negative and positive portraits of the primitive is considerable and fundamental, and it begs further explanation. When Jung tried to describe the probable structure and functioning of the psyche, he sometimes used terms and concepts loosely. "Archetype," "instinct," "unconscious," "conscious," "civilized," "primitive," and other concepts often lack systematic definition. At the time of any single utterance, he may have had some specific behavior in mind that these words adequately described. Over the long run, however, the definitions became mixed and confused. Today, we struggle to find the words that most closely represent Jung's view of things. We do so at our peril, however, as is abundantly clear in the case of the word "primitive," which constantly threatens to overflow with an array of extant, socially determined meanings. We forget also that Jung's thought was always in process and that, as new data arrived, he classified it under concepts that he had developed initially to describe a limited range of phenomena. As content changed, so did the application of old concepts to the new material, creating a range of definitional possibilities within Jung's own writings.

"Primitive" became first a technical word within his scientific vocabulary that indicated the starting point of an evolutionary process of continual incremental change and improvement. This process of the incremental development of objective knowledge eventually produced the consciousness of modern civilized man. Recall, for example, his insistence, in "A Review of the Complex Theory," that "I use the term 'primitive' in the sense of 'primordial,' and that I do not imply any kind of value judgment."[19] Originally, the idea of "primitive," as used by Jung, described the theoretical beginning condition of the psyche. It was therefore a wholly abstract concept having no relationship to living persons—and probably not to our ancestors either. Yet we saw in the previous chapter a condescending attitude toward modern primitive/tribal peoples that belied his disclaimer. Undoubtedly, this attitude had some part of classic European arrogance. But it also reflects the ways the concept has migrated across social, intellectual, and linguistic categories over time, even within Jung's own writings.

The framework of cultural evolution then developing in the social sciences dictated that non-Western tribal peoples be seen and understood as representing a lower form of human social life and cultural and technical achievement. Primitive/tribal peoples were believed to represent early man—that was the reason for studying them so intensely. They would give scholars clues about how human society evolved. Jung and others of his generation needed some real-life references to use to make their psychologies demonstrable in the real world and applicable to all human societies and psychological problems. So as Jung began to develop theoretical ideas about the undeveloped psyche, he looked for examples still living in the world—the non-Western peoples. He projected abstract doctrines onto contemporary non-Western peoples, playing on the stereotypes that then existed among educated people regarding these groups.

Jung became one of the many scientific voices that helped to perpetuate and intensify the oppression of peoples who merely thought differently and saw the world differently than European peoples. Even as he offered his disclaimer, Jung made numerous statements that use the word "primitive," and are directed to a readership that would easily connect them with tribal peoples in Africa, Asia and the Americas. If Jung meant primordial, he should have always said primordial. He did not, and as a result, many of his readers have themselves applied the ideas associated with the primitive unconscious to the lives and behaviors of living tribal peoples, an application that can often lead to unpleasant results.

The negative portrait of the primitive derives largely from Jung's sometimes uncritical acceptance of social science truisms, and his ill-considered efforts to provide some reference system for his students. He would not be as quick to adopt derogatory descriptions of primitives today, at a time when social science has begun to ease away from its colonial roots. The positive image of the primitive, on the other hand, arises as a result of Jung's spur-of-the-moment need to give vivid practical examples of positive psychological moods or conditions. In almost every instance, Jung's positive remarks deal with very specific points and come from his experiences with representatives of the so-called primitive peoples he met in Africa and the United States. Counting cattle, for instance, is a fairly specific example of the way that non-Western people do things, and something that Jung himself had seen. Compare this first-hand knowledge with Jung's theoretical speculation that the primitive has only one psychological function—intuition—a speculation that was necessary if Jung was going to maintain his larger theoretical argument: that as a result of an evolutionary process, modern civilized people had developed their consciousness more than primitives, and that the modern psyche had developed four functions.

A number of later Jungians have explored the nature of the primitive in ways that build upon, and even transcend, the possibilities introduced by Jung. Jolande Jacobi, in *The Way of Individuation,* for example, argues that primitive puberty rites "present useful analogies" for understanding the first phase of individuation:

> In contrast to an individuation process extending over the whole span of life, these rites occur in a compressed form and only during a fixed period, and are an event in which the neophytes participate collectively. *The underlying ideas and aims are nevertheless similar to those of the individuation process and are often actually identical.*[20] [emphasis added]

Jacobi carries through the comparison, finding that there are also important parallels with the second phase of individuation:

> This would mean establishing relations with the numinous powers of the collective unconscious, the archetypes, which dwell in the psychic background of all members of the tribe. In the case of the single individual, it would mean the realization of a relation to the Self. In this way, perhaps owing to the relative shortness of the primitive's life the most important step in the second phase of individuation is anticipated.[21]

(Of course, the life expectancy of tribal or primitive peoples was not always what civilization imagined. There are many instances of tribal people living well past the century mark.) Jacobi is handicapped by the Jungian theoretical understanding that numinous experiences must be understood as the psychic projections of the unconscious. As we will see, an American Indian critique would suggest instead that it is the outside world that changes. Far from being an internal projection, such encounters may move objects, produce materials from nowhere, cause changes in plant and animal behavior, and foretell the future.

The Jungian practitioner most sympathetic to the primitive tradition, and who appears to understand it best, is Joseph Henderson. He draws the correct linkage when he admits

> although no Jungian analyst would call himself a shaman, there is a parallel between depth analysis and shamanic healing that we cannot fail to respect and value when it has been called to our attention.[22]

And he recognizes the unknown reservoir of psychic reality toward which religious leaders of primitive groups work:

> However well we may have analyzed our patients for personality disorders or assisted in separating them from the ill effects of parental influences in childhood, there remains the unknown source of psychic conditioning in the region of the primal Self to be tapped wherever we can find it. The shamanic model offers the best opportunity for understanding the nature of this activity.[23]

We will discuss this idea more completely when we discuss the Sioux rituals that seek to define personal vocations. It is sufficient that we note that the tendency of some Jungians has been *to move toward rather than away* from the primitive, and they give primitive understandings and practices the credibility and respect they deserve.

Our discussion of the positive primitive has centered on the several admissions that Jung made that illustrate the value and substance of primitive psychological understanding. The Jungians who now emphasize these positive qualities are helping to explain and objectify insights which Jung might have intuited or experienced, but which he did not explain, exploit, or adequately understand. Yet many of Jung's insights go well beyond the simple description of the primitive as proto-civilized man and it is important to examine them in the present context because they point toward the kinds of realities that primitive peoples confront and try to understand.

These comments center on an indefinable cosmic dimension of reality that we all hope to experience. "Whenever we touch nature we get clean," Jung said.

> Savages are not dirty—only we are dirty. Domesticated animals are dirty, but never wild animals. Matter in the wrong place is dirt. People who have got dirty through too much civilization take a walk in the woods, or a bath in the sea. They may rationalize it in this way or that way, but they shake off the fetters and allow nature to touch them.[24]

Ultimately Jung realized that civilization, for all its virtues, also came with its curses, and that the remedy at hand was an intimate relationship with the natural world—in other words, living in some measure the psychological life of the primitive. In that sense, of course, Jung's notion of a healing primitive nature was part of a broader twentieth-century understanding that remains with us today. Yet Jung's sketching of a positive primitive enables us to ask a basic question that really should be at the foundation of all modern psychology. The ultimate goal of individuation and therapy is to achieve the kind of psychological condition that primitives seem to possess "naturally." What has happened to one part of the human species, civilized humanity, that we have been forced to take a long detour to arrive at a place that is naturally available to everyone?

Traditionally we look at primitives and demand that they fall into step with civilization, which we believe is the norm. We seek excuses or reasons why the so-called primitive has not "progressed" along the same paths as civilized people. These Jungian insights enable us to ask the opposite question. What has happened to Western civilization to move it away from a more unmediated natural life and into the callous, restrictive perspectives it presently takes as natural? The positive primitive offers a formidable critical position, rich with insights into many things that have been suppressed during the journey of our species toward the industrial state. We need now to spread the blanket of primitive psychology over questions that modern psychology purports to explain—family life, symbolism, spiritual calling, cosmology—and see where the two ways of experiencing life differ and where they coincide.

CHAPTER FOUR

THE JUNGIAN
UNIVERSE

We have examined in some detail—and often in critical terms—the liabilities, contradictions, and productive thinking generated by Carl Jung around the idea of "the primitive." The same discussion, however, also makes clear the wide-ranging, adventurous nature of Jung's thought. He sought a place for his psychology in a larger intellectual world inhabited not simply by anthropology or sociology, but by physics and philosophy as well. Where many disciplinary thinkers fail to draw parallels between their conclusions and the findings of other disciplines, Jung frequently invaded other areas with his speculations, hoping to suggest a means of unifying psychology with, for example, physics, eventually achieving a powerful synthesis of knowledge. The fruits of Jung's intellectual ambitions are clear: of the various Western psychologies, Jungian thinking has perhaps the greatest potential to contribute to a unification of knowledge and a deeper understanding of the world.

Jung's work with patients brought him to the realization that the psyche was, in some way or another, the universe observing itself. Since this idea is not far from what tribal/primitive peoples have also believed, it is important that we examine Jung's thinking on matters that originate in psychology, but that have implications for philosophy. Nor can we stop there. In our present conception of the physical world as we receive it from quantum physics, the Jungian archetypes might be favorably compared to the intelligent energy fields or "mind" that some thinkers believe constitute our cosmos. Certain key questions arising from physics and philosophy, then, necessarily make up the substance of the following two chapters, in which I offer a comparative sketch of the Jungian universe and that of the Sioux. What are the natures of, and relations between, time and space? Between causality and the larger patterns that may underpin acausal phenomenon? Between the very small and the very large? Between psyche and spirit? As was the case with the "primitive," Jung did not systematically define and elaborate a cosmology, and we are left, once again, to frame our own discussion from the fragmentary insights mentioned casually in Jung's lectures or introduced as digressions in the course of his writing about other topics.

Space and time are important concepts in every culture, since as humans we cannot help but appreciate long distances or recognize the passage of time. In *The Critique of Pure Reason,* Immanuel Kant advanced powerful arguments suggesting that space and time had no independent standing apart from our particular modes of perception. We may continue to speak of space and time as if they were absolute entities in the universe, but philosophically we know that this proposition is impossible to support. That space and time had an existence of their own was popularized by Newtonian physics, which needed a set of absolute concepts to support its formulas dealing with motion. The dominance of relativity and quantum theories in the 20th century largely eliminated the freestanding status of space and time. They have been reduced to descriptive elements of the experimental situation: at both subatomic and galactic levels, space and time must be linked together as a partial unity in order for us to interpret the results of an experiment with any degree of coherence. In practical terms, of course, we all remain Newtonians in our daily lives.

Jung approached the question whether or not space and time had an independent, absolute existence as he often did, by going back to a hypothetical beginning featuring a fictionalized "primitive" man. "In man's original view of the world, as we find it among primitives," he said,

> ... space and time have a very precarious existence. They become "fixed" concepts only in the course of his mental development, thanks largely to the introduction of measurement. In themselves, space and time consist of nothing. They are hypostasized concepts born of the discriminating activity of the conscious mind, and they form the indispensable coordinates for describing the behaviour of bodies in motion. [1]

If we remember that *fixed* is a learned and preferred framework for interpretation of experience (and suffers from what Alfred North Whitehead called "misplaced concreteness"—that is, in believing these invented concepts to be absolute), then we might say that the "precarious existence" that space and time had in the primitive mind may indeed be a natural and original way of perceiving the external world. Space and time as concepts became critically important for a limited intellectual operation known as "science" because they permit us to make arbitrary measurements of the physical world.

When this "misplaced concreteness" came to define popular conceptions of the universe, it raised an immense barrier to human understanding, because it limited our view of reality to whatever could be measured. Materialist analysis became orthodoxy for some cultures—notably the West—but not others. Jung's explanation of psychic processes helped to restore what we might take as these "primordial" perceptions and status of space and time to the arena of public discussion:

> The most we can know is that under certain psychic conditions time and space reveal a certain elastic quality, i.e., a psychic relativity, where they begin to behave as if they were dependent upon the psyche… From this fact I conclude that the human psyche (and presumably the animal psyche too) has a non-spatial and a non-temporal quality, i.e., a relative power to make time and space non-existent. This would speak in favour of a relative immortality, as only in time can something come to an absolute end, but in relative time it can only come to a relative end. Concerning space we would come to the conclusion that the psyche is only to be located relatively. In other words, the whereabouts or the extension of the psyche in space is relatively uncertain.[2]

What is Jung saying? He readily discards the notion of an absolute reality of space and time, arguing that these are relative terms in certain *psychic* situations. He appears to be gesturing "back" to the conditions he described as typical of the so-called primitive man, though offering no examples of a specific psychic situation to illustrate his point. The point, however, is important—the psyche has the power to make space and time relative or non-existent. We do not experience absolute space and time ever—except in our intellectual imagination—so the sense of contingency which psychic space and time invoke in us must actually be a fundamental part of our existence. From that realization, human beings have sought, through mystical experiences and ceremonies, to explore the boundaries of psychic space and time. These psychic explorers have often told us that the space-time phenomenal world of our thinking and experience is in fact not the ultimate expression of reality in the universe. They have also suggested that a movement into this contingent state of being should be the natural direction of our consciousness during the course of our lives. But of course we *cannot* live in a contingent physical world, so we are always caught between a vision or remembrance of a different kind of existence and the practical requirements in living in the flesh in a harsh and limited physical world in which time and space do matter.

Jung saw that, logically, viewing space and time as relative would also require an alternative to the idea of causality that has traditionally dominated scientific explanations. "As the relativity of time and space includes the relativity of causality," Jung remarked, "and as the psyche partakes of relative time-space, it also relativizes causality and therefore enjoys, in so far as it is microphysical, an at least relative independence of absolute causality."[3] One might argue that we do not even need to relativize causality because it is at best a convenience for interpreting the crude actions and motions of brute physical existence. We say that one thing "causes" another in large part because we arrange them in a temporal sequence of before and after. We simply need to become more critical of the application of causality in those circumstances where it is not useful, as modern physicists have done, instead of forcing causality to interpret everything, as most materialists do.*

Modern physics has proposed that causality be abandoned at subatomic levels, and it may one day abandon causality in galactic-sized events also. Meanwhile, stranded in the middle between macro and micro worlds, we accept causality so we can orient ourselves to the world around us. We should remember, however, that "acausal" events can indeed occur, even in our world, since causality is more a statistical expression than an absolute value. In this sense, much of Western science is not forging new metaphysical paths so much as it is struggling to overcome the prejudices and misplaced concreteness of previous generations of scientists. In psychological terms we can reduce our reliance on causality by pointing out that we deal here with the psyche, which is *a field with its own relationships* and not with sets of individual entities that have been arranged in a sequence.

----

* Although at first glance, Vine Deloria seems to be confronting the historian's fallacy *post hoc ergo propter hoc*, he is in fact arguing far beyond the simple avoidance of that fallacy in causal interpretation. Any historian who has named a "cause" in relation to an action is deeply aware of the problematic of such an attribution. Even with what seems like clear-cut evidence, the actual cause(s) of an event remain largely, or potentially, unknown. Even in its most materialistic, rationalistic practice, history confesses to its inadequacies in this regard. Science, in Deloria's view, would do well to make the same confession, which is exactly what he has seemed to find in the work of contemporary physics.

And yet Carl Jung did not take this direct path in explaining his ideas about the psyche. Instead he strove to derive from the unique experiences of life a parcel of evidence that would transcend ordinary experiences and suggest the existence of something more permanent. Such transcendent moments were assumed to be particularly revealing. At one point, he wrote:

> The limitation of consciousness in space and time is such an overwhelming reality that every occasion when this fundamental truth is broken through must rank as an event of the highest theoretical significance, for it would prove that the space-time barrier can be annulled. The annulling factor would then be the psyche, since space-time would attach to it at most as a relative and conditioned quality. Under certain conditions it could even break through the barriers of space and time precisely because of a quality essential to it, that is, its relatively trans-spatial and trans-temporal nature.[4]

Thus did Jung lay the groundwork to examine the anecdotal evidence that is a crucial part of therapy, and that does not obey the statistical laws of causality.

What are the space-time barriers to be annulled? Our emotions and experiences tell us of *duration*, the passage of time during which things unfold, and of *distance*, whether personal or geographical, both of which assure us of our individuality. Space and time can easily be subsumed in the idea of growth without the necessity of positing a space-time barrier, a barrier that some experiences transcend and others do not. Quite possibly the idea of "trans" spatial and temporal dimensions means that we intuit or experience our sense of space and time from emotions and feelings, not from our physical existence. We have the deep intuitive suspicion that there is more to the world than meets the eye.* We even feel that we "take up space," creating a sense of our own subjective reality. How this idea originated cannot be determined, but it remains one of our fundamental convictions. We share this feeling with other animals, and whether we call it social distance or psychic distance, it seems to be a characteristic of life on our level of existence. The barrier, then, seems to be that which we impose

---

* One could say, in the context and lexicon of modern neuropsychological research, that these are "right brain" apprehensions and experience that do not exactly fit linear, "left brain" cause and effect structure, and for which there is no explicit language (in English).

on our minds to explain experiments and justify measurements, and which we then take as "real."

In reflecting on his therapy work, Jung mused,

> I have often encountered motifs which made me think that the uncon-
> scious must be the world of the infinitesimally small. Such an idea could
> be derived rationalistically from the obscure feeling that in all these
> visions we are dealing with something endopsychic, the inference being
> that a thing must be exceedingly small in order to fit inside the head.

But he disclaimed such reasoning, stating:

> I am no friend of any such "rational" conjectures, though I would not
> say that they are all beside the mark. It seems to me more probable that
> this liking for diminutives on the one hand and for superlatives—giants
> etc.—on the other is connected with the queer uncertainty of spatial
> and temporal relations within the unconscious.[2]

At this point the best we can infer is that the unconscious is real in our experience at every level, but that it is flexible, defining its own mode of existence and expression so that it can expand, contract, and otherwise participate in unique situations.

We can, however, move a bit further into Jung's concept of space by noting his comment that "the psyche could be regarded as a mathematical point and at the same time as a universe of fixed stars."[6] This idea is very Kantian but it also relates easily to the idea that the center of the universe is wherever the person stands or where an event occurs (this concept resonates as well with the universe we see in quantum theory). For the purposes of determining meanings, then, space is a function of the framework in which an event occurs and meaning issues forth. This idea, we will discover later, is central to the practice of ceremonials among the tribal/ primitive peoples. Here we have a key analytical concept, one that places Jung in dialogue with both physics and philosophy, and that will serve us well in comparing Jung-ian concepts with those of Indian people.

This treatment of space, therefore, offers a way of understanding other cultures whose perspectives might be equally compatible with modern physics. Linked to some of Jung's other ideas on psychic space, however, it opens up additional speculations. If the psyche can be both universe and a fixed point, the implications of this expansive potential are staggering. In a particularly evocative musing, Jung toyed with the notion that

> infinite greatness and infinite smallness are infinitely true, and it is quite possible that we contain whole peoples in our souls, worlds where we can be as infinitely great as we are infinitely small externally—so great that the history of the redemption of a whole nation or of a whole universe might take place within us.[7]

Such a conceptualization opens the door to a number of ideas that have been discarded and rejected by the West, some of which we will touch upon later.

In spite of these intriguing linkages of psychic and physical space, Jung actually seems to have been much more interested in time. Since flexibility is also a characteristic of time, Jung could follow a similar analysis in order to account for the phenomenon of coincidence that often plays a major role in the therapeutic process. To account for some highly unlikely situations in which coincidence occurred, Jung coined one of his most popular terms: "synchronicity." According to him "synchronicity ... means the simultaneous occurrence of a certain psychic state with one or more external events which appear as meaningful parallels to the momentary subjective state."[8] Although he applied the idea to unusual events he had experienced, synchronicity can cover a multitude of events and, in its popular interpretation today, it is often reduced to simple awareness of the situation in which we find ourselves. It is perhaps most important to note when discussing synchronicity that the psyche creates and registers the connection between internal apprehensions and external events. There is the possibility that synchronous events happen more often than we believe—but we are not necessarily aware of them or do not understand their significance, and thus they simply pass by, unremarked.

The meaning of any synchronistic event is directly proportional to the capability of the individual to perceive his or her environment, and to link physical objects with the perception of a momentary mental state. Returning to a more traditional concept of time, Jung relied on chronological time as an important factor in producing the synchronous event:

> It seems as though time, far from being an abstraction, is a concrete continuum which possesses qualities or basic conditions capable of manifesting themselves simultaneously in different places by means of

an acausal parallelism, such as we find, for instance, in the simultaneous occurrence of identical thoughts, symbols, or psychic states.[9]

After arguing for the relativism of time, then, Jung turned back to the "fixed," naturalized concept of chronology. He did so, I believe, in order to argue for the apprehension of a superior timeline irretrievably mixed with our commonplace chronological time, a framework that points us toward theological concepts such as the "fullness of time." In other words, Jung wanted to suggest that—and explain how—we can have qualitative times within quantitative time. We might imagine such an experience in the frequently heard admonition to people experiencing near-death episodes that "it is not your time to die."*

Giving time "real" substance changes the nature of the discussion. If time has substance, then it must move in and of its own accord or pattern and on occasion have the capability of organizing matter to provide similarities and identities within a certain spatial configuration. Jung's experiences with the sudden appearances of a kingfisher and butterflies—frequently cited by him as evidence of synchronicity—were perhaps moments when some other kind of time, a substantial time, dominated the arrangement of our world. This model, however, requires us to return to the concept of causality—although in a much more sophisticated format. Could a superior timeline, actively involved in our lives, be understood and explained in a cause-and-effect manner? Is it psychology's task to offer a more precisely defined understanding of synchronicity that is, in effect, an overture to theology to step in and explain what are in essence meta-causes that produce the meta-effects that we experience as synchronicity?

I believe we have no choice but to follow this line of inquiry even if it does lead us to some old religious ideas and practices. Aniela Jaffé explains the Jungian position well:

> Causalism breaks everything down into discrete processes, and this is absolutely necessary if we are to gain reliable knowledge of the world.

---

* In imagining this simultaneous interweaving of sacred/superior and chronological/historical times, Jung and Deloria touch upon a similar argument made by Walter Benjamin and, through Benjamin, Theodor Adorno. See, for example, Benjamin, "Theses on a Philosophy of History," *Illuminations* (New York: Schocken Books, 1969).

But the principle of synchronicity, taking into account the psychoid archetype and a cosmic order to which both the psyche of the perceiver and that which is recognized in the perception are subject, allows us to see, behind the discrete processes, a universal interrelationship of events. A preexistent unity of being takes shape, and the seemingly incommensurate worlds of physis and psyche can be understood as aspects of this unity.[10]

This use of causality suggests that we are ordinarily handicapped in perceiving the real patterns of the world because of the discreteness and immediacy of external phenomena. The events in which we see synchronicity may have their own causality or they may represent the occasional touching of a deeper level of existence that underlies all of us. Jung's effort to provide a framework for experiences that cannot be explained by science, except to reduce them to changes in electrical energy or chemistry in the brain, deserve the highest attention. Perhaps this is why synchronicity is popular as a tool for people to think with, since it so readily leads us to consider not simply other time and space possibilities, but also the possibility that we will be able to return, through psychology, to the theological.

Nor should we be surprised to find that synchronicity brought Jung to his closest approach to modern physics. "Synchronicity," he wrote,

is no more baffling or mysterious than the discontinuities of physics. It is only the ingrained belief in the sovereign power of causality that creates intellectual difficulties and makes it appear unthinkable that acausal events exist or could ever occur. But if they do, then we must regard them as creative acts, as the continuous creation of a pattern that exists from all eternity, repeats itself sporadically, and is not derivable from any known antecedents.[11]

Acausal events, then, can be conceived as creative acts and can occur within an otherwise causally perceived world. But even this analysis is not satisfactory unless we can gather sufficient evidence that connecting the acausal events and looking for patterns will produce a common theme in them. If such gathering does in fact produce patterns—and I suspect that such events took on meaning for Jung as a result of his discoveries in therapy—then his psychology offers us a useful tool in understanding ourselves and our worlds.

We need a philosophical way to distinguish between two similar perceptions and the coincidental correspondence of emotional and physical events. Only by attaching to a physical event a transcendent meaning from an unknown source can we see synchronistic events. But are we simply trading interpretative frameworks, describing an event as "synchronic" when we formerly called it "coincidence" (or perhaps "miraculous")? Or is the psyche creating the world of meaning for us, reserving a role for the conscious mind so it can absorb the physical context of apparent causality and be able to distinguish unusual events?

We must still locate the substance of the creative act represented by the acausal. Where is this unknown source? What is it? In dealing with these issues, Jung lays the groundwork for later analyses of the status of the psyche. The synchronistic event minimally creates a superior form of knowledge, if but for an instant. According to Jung,

> The "absolute knowledge" which is characteristic of synchronistic phenomena, a knowledge not mediated by the sense organs, supports the hypothesis of a self-subsistent meaning, or even expresses its existence. Such a form of existence can only be transcendental, since, as the knowledge of future or spatially distant events shows, it is contained in a psychically relative space and time, that is to say in an irrepresentable space-time continuum. [12]

The source of the creative act, in other words, is not to be thought of in terms of meaning (Jung shifts his discussion here), but rather of knowledge—an absolute and transcendent knowledge emerging from the un-representable that underpins the synchronistic event.

This shift from creation or meaning to knowledge is significant because the knowledge that is received refers to events in the space-time continuum. It can be said to be its own initial meaning; but it also raises the question of fore-knowledge at this greater or more significant level of existence. Jung sidesteps the need of accepting "predestination" or "pre-established harmony" that religious thinkers and philosophers have used to resolve this question, although whether it is really necessary to bring the question up in this context is even debatable. "In contrast to the idea of a pre-established harmony," Jung wrote,

> ... the synchronistic factor merely stipulates the existence of an intellectually necessary principle which could be added as a fourth to the

recognized triad of space, time, and causality. These factors are necessary but not absolute—most psychic contents are non-spatial; time and
causality are psychically relative—and in the same way the synchronistic
factor proves to be only conditionally valid. [13]

It would seem to me that the synchronistic event is not conditional at all, and
that Leibniz and other philosophers who suggest a pre-established harmony
may be telling us something important on this point.

Synchronicity, we might imagine, is an idea that gives to the psychic
world the same dimension that chronological time gives to modern physics.
Where physicists transcend chronological time in order to describe motion
at sub-atomic and galactic levels of size, synchronicity offers the possibilities for a new frame of meaning in an otherwise meaningless phenomenal
world. As Jung observed:

> Just as the introduction of time as the fourth dimension in modern
> physics postulates an irrepresentable space-time continuum, so the idea
> of synchronicity with its inherent quality of meaning produces a picture
> of the world so irrepresentable as to be completely baffling. The advan-
> tage, however, of adding this concept is that it makes possible a view
> which includes the psychoid factor in our description and knowledge
> of nature—that is, an *a priori* meaning or "equivalence." [14]

An accumulation of synchronic events, therefore, would reveal a pattern of progression similar to the claims of theologians of God's plan working itself out in physical space. But, as we will see, such a pattern does not
necessarily require something like God's plan. It can be as easily seen in other
cultures and traditions as well.

In another context, Jung once noted that time,

> or the moment understood as a peculiar form of energy, coincides with
> our psychological condition. The moment is unique, so that whatever
> has its origin at a certain moment has the energy and qualities of that
> particular moment. [15]

Time, in this sense, is thus not simply substantial but it is also another way
of describing energy. "When one says time is merely an aspect of energy,"
Jung told his dream analysis seminar,

one makes it more tangible, because everyone can observe it and measure it. Time and energy are correlated concepts. If there is no energy
nothing moves and there is no longer any time. They are identical, a
certain movement of time is a certain movement of energy. When we
observe energy we really observe time, because it is through energy that
we measure time.[16]

Energy, in effect creates time. Does the experience of a different sense of
time create energy? Or does the experience of a certain movement of energy
create time?

After following Jung through the jungle of synchronicity, we discover
that we have returned to our original position with only the hope that we
can include the "psychoid factor"—the psyche with definite materialistic
overtones—in our understanding of nature. In this exploration, however,
we do not receive the knowledge of archetypes, the understanding of the
basis of instinct, or even the vocational path that forecasts the development
of personality during individuation. We do not even understand how all
individuals seem to have a personal fate or destiny and how the collection of
people with whom they have a close relationship is essential in discovering
that fate. In short, if synchronicity does enable us to include the psyche as
part of the physical world or to relate the psyche to the space-time continuum of modern physics, this relation is partly one of convenience, since we
already know that we are a part of the physical world. It is the participation
in the over-arching sense of time that worries us. Are we a permanent fixture
of the universe or a passing phenomenon? To this question, synchronicity
opens up possibilities that take us in the general direction of theology.

At least within the psyche, Jung appears to have taken space and time
as absolute concepts and therefore as ultimate elements of the cosmos, and
then made them a relative value as part of his engagement with the question
of causality. Relativization also enabled him to accord the psyche a degree of
flexibility sufficient to include it within the space-time continuum for the
purpose of valid scientific investigation. The results of such an investigation
would, presumably, be scientifically valid even though they would not be
obtained by making causal connections between the psyche and its energy
manifestations. In the end, we really know nothing about space or time in
any reliable sense, and still less about the linkage of the psyche to the rest of
the universe. These things exist primarily in theoretical terms, and largely
outside of Jung's arsenal of more familiar clinical concepts. It is worth pur-

suing these such questions through other openings, however, and so we turn to an examination of Jung's treatment of the traditional mind/matter dichotomy that has plagued Western thinking since Descartes.

In approaching this problem from the standpoint of the psychic processes, we begin with an examination of the empirical evidence available.

"There are indications that psychic processes stand in some sort of energy relation to the physiological substrate," Jung said.

> In so far as they are objective events, they can hardly be interpreted as anything but energy processes, or to put it another way: in spite of the non-measurability of psychic processes, the perceptible changes effected by the psyche cannot possibly be understood except as a phenomenon of energy. [17]

As we have seen, Jung turned at this critical juncture to the model of physics. Having explored the possibilities of time and space, he identified the psyche with energy, a notion suggested earlier, and which now requires further treatment. Sophisticated psychic events, Jung suggested, must be shaped by active archetypal guidance. He saw no difficulty in making this identification. "The analogy with physics is not a digression," Jung argued, "since the symbolical schema itself represents the descent into matter and requires the identity of the outside with the inside." Recall his dialectical argument:

> Psyche cannot be totally different from matter, for how otherwise could it move matter? And matter cannot be alien to psyche, for how else could matter produce psyche? Psyche and matter exist in one and the same world, and each partakes of the other, otherwise any reciprocal action would be impossible. If research could only advance far enough, therefore, we should arrive at an ultimate agreement between physical and psychological concepts. [18]

The analogy here seems to be one of method: physicists go into the depths of the atom to the point where they become part of the experiment themselves: the great revolution in physics came about when physicists learned to incorporate their presence in the experiment into their interpretations. The wave-particle difficulty, for example, was resolved, at least epistemologically, when physicists suggested that if they wished to describe the wave motion of particles they had to surrender the possibility of describing the action of individual particles in the wave in the same experiment. Jung felt that probing into the psyche to reach certain fundamental archetypal levels was comparable to subatomic exploration of matter. The analyst and the physicist were approaching a conjunction, therefore, although they traveled on different paths using different ends of the matter/energy polarity.

In physics, the subatomic particles begin to take on a less substantial aspect until they can only be described in a set of relationships that seem to have spiritual or mental characteristics. It is not surprising then that Jung should discover that the reverse holds within the analytic process: "The qualitatively rather than quantitatively definable units with which the unconscious works, namely the archetypes, therefore, have a nature that cannot with certainty be designated as psychic."[19] That is to say, when we approach archetypal themes in the unconscious, at a certain level they begin to appear unmovable and as possessing a substantial nature. We have already seen, in Jung's engagement with the primitive, that, as he argued,

> [t]he deeper "layers" of the psyche lose their individual uniqueness as they retreat farther and farther into darkness. "Lower down," that is to say as they approach the autonomous functional systems, they become increasingly collective until they are universalized and extinguished in the body's materiality, i.e., in chemical substances. The body's carbon is simply carbon. Hence "at bottom" the psyche is simply "world."[20]

Such an idea would at first glance appear simply a sophisticated form of scientific materialism or even a complex form of reductionism: all our mental activities are, ultimately, *chemical* processes, psychology being a restricted form of chemistry that is itself a special case of physics. But Jung rejected this chain of reasoning: "The psyche as such cannot be explained in terms of physiological chemistry," he argued,

> if only because, together with "life" itself, it is the only "natural factor" capable of converting statistical organizations which are subject to natural law into "higher" or "unnatural" states, in opposition to the rule of entropy that runs throughout the inorganic realm.[21]

In other words, at a certain point within the psyche we discover a qualitative organizing principle that counteracts the increase of randomness and channels energy into specific forms. Speaking to the mind/matter split, we might argue that this principle would hold true for both mental and physical organization. Here Jung makes a major contribution to our thinking because, although some physicists have reached similar conclusions, Jung has approached the problem of mind/body from the mental side.

Jung's understanding of the psyche is similar to the descriptions of the physical world given to us by modern physics. Consider, for example, David Bohm's idea of an "Implicate Order," in which mind and matter are two different projections or manifestations of an underlying order. They are two related expressions of a single deeper reality that can be measured or experienced.

According to Fred Alan Wolf,

> The concept of universal energy in our language might be called the "universal quantum wave function" or "matter wave" or "probability wave" of quantum physics. This "wave" pervades everything, and like the universal energy, it resists objective discovery.[22]

We can easily imagine this definition being devised by Jung to describe the psyche. Indeed, it is a pity that quantum thinking was not popularized when he was younger so that Jung could have delved more deeply into a sympathetic physics to help explain his idea of the psyche.

Fred Alan Wolf's definition is important for another reason, however; it is prefaced by the observation that "our position is close to the one discovered by basic tribal peoples."[23] In other words, some people in physics can now see that tribal peoples, taking a purely empirical approach to the world and their experiences in it, reached the conclusion that the ultimate entity in the world was the mysterious energy they could perceive and occasionally apprehend. Yet if the unconscious and its psychic energy, knowledge of which is wholly derived from psychological therapy, can be equated with the energy we describe in quantum physics, derived wholly from subatomic experiments, then we have a new format in which we can ask metaphysically oriented questions. The methods by which tribal peoples discerned this energy would be parallel in some way to the techniques used by Jung to describe his understanding of the psyche and its contents.

Jung took the step that many physicists avoided, suggesting a new model for considering the mind/matter problem. "Psychic events are facts, are realities," he said,

... and we observe the stream of images within, you observe an aspect of the world, of the world within. Because the psyche, if you understand it as a phenomenon occurring in living bodies, is a quality of matter, just as our body consists of matter. We discover that this matter has another aspect, namely a psychic aspect. It is simply the world seen from within. It is just as though you were seeing into another aspect of matter.[24]

Here we have an equivalency: mind seen from the outside is matter; matter seen from the inside is mind. When we understand that energy is personal, then we have a personal, intelligent matter that inhabits and constitutes the physical universe and a substantial personal intelligence that composes the world of mind and emotions.

And we have a triangulation of insights, with Jung and "mind" at one point, physics and "matter" at another, and our comparative dialogue pointing to the third angle among American Indian people. This condition—of a personal, intelligent, and constitutive energy—was of course well known among tribal/primitive peoples, including American Indians, who said that everything, including the rocks and grasses, was alive, and moreover had personality *and* intelligence. Since these societies were outside the Western tradition, however, and since the West was obligated to interpret other traditions as expressions of lower cultural evolutionary accomplishment, their understanding was called "animism" and regarded as superstition. Had they tediously arrived at the same conclusion after years in a Western scientific laboratory, presumably their ideas might have been acceptable. That they reached this understanding by centuries of observation of the personal behavior of nature can still seem unacceptable. In this sense, it is worth noting the *non*-theological aspects of this knowledge. Many tribal/primitive peoples refused to refer to the source of this energy with the familiar concept of "deity" but preferred to call it, in their own languages, words that translate—poorly, we might add—into the "great mysterious" or the "great holy."

The mind/matter problem is partially resolved by Jung in what may be a new approach to the old metaphysical problems. He recommends a shift from basing metaphysics on measurements and approaching it instead from an experiential perspective. "If I shift my concept of reality on to the plane of the psyche—where alone it is valid—this puts an end to the conflict between mind and matter, spirit and nature, as contradictory explanatory principles," Jung explained. "Each becomes a mere designation for the particular source of the psychic contents that crowd into my field of conscious-ness."[25] Contradictions and ambiguities will undoubtedly exist whenever we deal with the empirical evidence of psychic process, but if we trace those processes back, our sources would be the probable structure of the psyche. We would thus find unity at the deepest level of existence. We would have a new certainty that we have not had before.

When energies of that deep level express themselves in human actions, since we are—as both individuals and societies—confronting different situ-ations, we call the various manifestations by different names and identify nuances of behavior and understanding as separate experiences. Advocating intelligence as a basic constituent of all life forms would have brought Jung into confrontations with Western theologians since they admit other life forms as part of creation but refuse to credit them with any of the psychologi-cal functions that can be easily observed. Jung took his explanation right to the brink of a confrontation when he noted,

> psychic processes seem to be balances of energy flowing between spirit
> and instinct, though the question of whether a process is to be described
> as spiritual or as instinctual remains shrouded in darkness.[26]

Presumably this darkness was, to some extent, epistemological, and Jung thereby avoids the possible accusation that the substance of theology can be reduced to scientific description. In his engagement with the pos-sibilities of a deep underlying structure that offered a meta-causal under-pinning for seemingly acausal events, and in his speculations concerning a "superior," non-chronological form of time, Jung touched on the same epistemological darkness, opening up not simply the question of mind and matter, but also of spirit and instinct.

The Jungian universe is compatible with modern physics and that is because Jung sought to make it so. But it is also compatible with the worlds in which many tribal/primitive peoples live and have lived. Space and time are flexible and not absolute. Space can be collapsed so that the psyche can be either the universe or a single point. Any point in space can be the center. Time is also flexible. There are at least two time dimensions intertwined and moving in the same direction that we can experience. One we can observe, and one we find through mystical and unusual experiences. Mind and matter seem to be two sides of the same coin. So do spirit and instinct. All four ideas can appear in different combinations depending on how we understand our experiences. Jungian psychology offers a comprehensive and expansive context in which to examine ourselves and the world around us. We can conduct this examination if we focus most of our attention upon Jung's speculative insights rather than upon some of his more orthodox and doctrinaire comments. Such speculative insights, however, exist largely unmoored from any specific or concrete examples. The Sioux cosmological tradition, to be discussed in the next chapter, is certainly not meant to serve as an "example" to explain Jung's theoretical speculations. But in offering a grounded account of the Sioux universe, I hope to offer an occasion for dialogue between cosmologies that do in fact share many of these same basic frameworks, emergent in the sciences, speculated upon by Jung, and lived by Sioux people.

CHAPTER FIVE

THE SIOUX UNIVERSE

Discovering and examining the Sioux universe and placing it in comparative dialogue with the modernist universe we have sketched for Carl Jung will be a formidable task. The basic vocabularies match up only with difficulty, particularly if we take as our reference point the knowledge possessed by Sioux people of earlier times. The historical Sioux, for instance, did not conceive of the world as being logically connected in cause and effect relationships; the questions pursued by Western scholars are not those that concerned them. They saw the world as harmoniously interrelated, so that knowing how things were related to each other enabled them to develop predictive talents—comparable to those of Western science but based upon entirely different foundations. Despite these differences, however, we can explore many of the ways they confronted and interpreted their experiences, examining the knowledge they have passed down as their own philosophical traditions, still meaningful and resonant today. If the preceding chapter dealt primarily with the abstract and theoretical, this chapter will emphasize the concrete and particularistic. Recounting specifics, we can place Sioux cosmology into conversation with Jung, as both a contrasting foil and an illustration of some of his speculative concepts.

Perhaps the best way to enter the Sioux universe is to return briefly to Jung's characterization of the tribal/primitive since, had he been acquainted with the Sioux, Jung would certainly have classified them as "primitive." In a letter to Heinrich Boltz, Jung gave a useful description of the differences between civilized Western people and the so-called primitives:

> *The naive primitive doesn't believe, he knows,* because the inner experience rightly means as much to him as the outer. He adjusts his life—of necessity—to outer and inner *facts* which he does not—as we do—feel to be discontinuous. He lives in *one* world, whereas we live in only one half and merely believe in the other or not at all … [1]

Here, Jung has aptly described the ways Sioux people experienced the world. The so-called primitive consciousness accepts data from all sources. Hence, there is no good reason for "primitives" to distinguish between the information they have perceived from basic sensory experience and the data they receive from dreams and visions that occur within secular chronological time.

Jung's choice to frame the difference in this way did not simply come as a casual aside in a letter. In "The Psychological Foundations of Belief in Spirits," one of his major essays on the constitution of the psyche (and written much earlier than his letter to Boltz), Jung commented:

> Primitive man ... really lives in two worlds. Physical reality is at the same time a spiritual reality. The physical world is undeniable, and for him the world of spirits has an equally real existence, not just because he thinks so, but because of his naïve* awareness of things spiritual.[2]

Jung's characterization—which seems appropriate to Sioux understandings—does not fail to open up the questions raised in the previous chapter concerning time, space, spirit, instinct, and the possibilities for a superior structuring energy. With this in mind, we begin an inquiry into the nature of the Sioux universe, recognizing that, as part of a dialogue with Jung, Sioux cosmology represents considerably more data—and much different data—since the physical and spiritual are explicitly intertwined.**

---

*   Jung's use of the word "naïve" in this context probably is an allusion to the "innocent" quality of "the primitive," i.e., not contaminated by Western thought and reason, as opposed to an immature naiveté.

**   Readers may wonder why Vine Deloria chose the Sioux in particular and not another indigenous tradition. At the most basic level, it is important to note that he was of the Sioux tradition and able to speak to it in ways that claimed responsibility appropriately, as opposed to a comparison to the Pueblo, for instance, or some other tribe. It is also the case, however, that he seems to have found a greater number of affinities between Jung and this particular tradition, making it not only the most familiar but perhaps the most useful as well. The question, however, raises the sticky issue of generalization. On the one hand, Jung was willing to generalize a "primitive" mind and to attribute it both to people of the past and tribal and indigenous people of his present. When he wishes to draw a firm line between the West and its others, Deloria is willing to follow this line of argument (thus his shorthand conflation of "tribal/primitive"). At the same time, Deloria understood all too well the sometimes radical differences among American Indian cosmological traditions. Missing, in some important ways, from this discussion, are the insights Deloria previously developed in *God is Red* (1973) which suggest the importance of particular land bases to spiritual practice. We suspect that, with a more sustained editorial dialogue, Deloria would have engaged this important

Space, for the Sioux, manifests itself in many different ways. There is, of course, the physical space of distance, from one location to another, and usually measured in the time it takes to travel across it rather than a unit measurement involving physical length. And there is, as we have seen, the strange psychological recognition that we "take up space" with our bodies and presence. According to Esther Harding, Jung believed that

> the concept of the psyche as being a body of some kind corresponds to a universal feeling, present in every human being, that in the psychological dimension he occupies a certain space and has a definite position. In addition, he feels himself to be possessed of a certain energy inherent in his psychic contents.[3]

While this feeling is not necessarily precise in an intellectual sense, so that it provides a guarantee of individuality or personality, Jung properly connects the sense of having a position, of being in a particular space, with the energic contents of the psyche. At this deep level of emotional recognition of space, then, all humans have the same kind of perceptual experience.

Behind or underlying this basic notion of space, however, are additional experiences of space, including the "other" places Sioux people visit in dreams and the acknowledgment of the extra-material dimensions of space that they recognized in ceremonies. In using the Sacred Pipe, for example, Sioux religious practitioners always invoke the powers attributed to each of the directions. They point their pipes to the four directions and then up toward the sky and down toward the earth, addressing each these directions and the power that is characteristic of each. As we have discussed previously in terms of Jung, the psyche can be powerfully conceived as either (or both) the universe or a point within its field. In ceremonial activities, the powers (usefully conceptualized as energies) of the cosmos are invited to participate. People believe that it is impossible to use a pipe properly without this preliminary recognition. The bowl of the pipe becomes the universe when this gesture is made. The space of the universe is acknowledged, its infinite nature admitted, and its powers gathered at a single precise point in order to participate in the ceremony.

---

conceptualization of space. Readers are directed to *God is Red*, as well as to the essays in *Spirit and Reason*, in order to think through these issues in their own further dialogue with Deloria's ideas.

In many Sioux practices, we can see similar experiences in which the entire universe is present in its fullest dimensions—and yet simultaneously concentrated into a single point. The Sweat Lodge, used before and after other ceremonies, is built in the shape of a circle. The willow sticks that form its framework must be placed in the ground at a certain angle so that their curve, if carried around completely, would make a sphere, with half earth and half sky enclosed. The spacious universe is thus enclosed in the form of the lodge, for the purposes of receiving cleansing and power. At the same time, the central hole, in which heated rocks are placed, is (like the bowl of the pipe) also the universe focused on a particular point. Care is taken when putting the stones in the hole to make certain they first represent the four directions before other stones are placed on top of them. Here again, a specific place becomes the universal space at which energies are concentrated. That the proper form is critical to this practice can be seen in early ethnographic materials on the Sioux. According to ethnographer James Walker, as early as the close of the last century the Oglala Sioux Medicine men were concerned about the practice of traditional rituals because the younger generation was not making the sweat lodge in the specific manner in which it had always been made. They recognized the relationship between spiritual energy and the form in which it chooses to manifest itself.[4]

With both the Sacred Pipe and the Sweat Lodge, space becomes a physical/spiritual reality—it is experienced. The large dance circle and the central pole used in the Sun Dance—the primary annual ceremonial—also represent the universe. So too does the placing of ceremonial objects during the Vision Quest, in which an individual "cries for a vision," alone, in a private place. In such dreams and visions, space becomes flexible—following Jung, one might well use the term "relative."

Consider the vision of the Sioux man, Siyaka. He followed a crow to a village and was invited into a tent, but once inside, found that he had a long and difficult journey to reach the seat of honor opposite the door. Told to raise his hand, he "saw dragon-flies, butterflies, and all kinds of small insects, while above them flew all kinds of birds."[5] Speaking of another vision, Brave Buffalo testified to a similar experience of expansive space. He was inside a lodge (tipi or tent) and "the elks in the lodge watched me with interest and encouraged me to go on, saying they had something they wished to tell me."[6] These experiences—in which vision seekers entered the confined space of a lodge, only to find an entire world inside—are common in Sioux spiritual culture, revealing a kind of spatial relativity.

It would be difficult to argue that these experiences of space are unique, even to Sioux culture, since dreams of Jungian places have produced distortions of space similar to those of Siyaka, Brave Buffalo, and others. We can say, however, that the Sioux experiences were part of a continuing relationship with spiritual powers practiced by those communities for hundreds, perhaps thousands, of years. And that relationship took concrete form in certain spaces, which accumulated over this period of time. In the early twentieth century, for example, the ethnographer Frances Densmore went to a spot on the Standing Rock reservation with some old men who had participated in the last Sun Dance held on that reservation in 1882: "In a short time they found the exact spot where the ceremony was held. The scars were still on the prairie as they were on their own bodies." They looked for the location of the sacred pole and "there it was—a spot of hard, bare ground 18 inches in diameter." And Densmore wondered: "More than 29 years had passed since the ceremony. It is strange that the wind had not sown seeds on those spots of earth."[7] People have told me that they have gone to Canada to the site of Sitting Bull's last Canadian Sun Dance and there also, the ground still has bare spots where the various altars and poles were placed. An important hallmark of the Indian experience with space, then, may be its material imprint on the earth marking the occasion.

Yet another dimension of space can be seen in the Yuwipi ceremony, in which the medicine man works in complete darkness and the spirits come to assist him in healing and prophecies. In the Yuwipi, the medicine man is bound in a quilt or robe, his fingers laced tight behind his back, and in darkness he awaits the coming of the spirits. In the account of Lame Deer, we can see yet another expression of the relativity of space:

> While the Yuwipi lies on the floor in his star blanket, his spirit could be hundreds of miles away in the far hills, conversing with the ancient ones. He has ceased to be. It is up to us to bring him back. We must concentrate on this, help him through *wace icicya*—through praying within ourselves.[8]

Anthropologist William Powers offers further explanation of the experience:

> It is as if some of these [Yuwipi] songs, although learned through the personal experience of the Vision Quest, continue to be taught to fledgling

medicine men by the same spirits. It is believed that they reoccur because they are taught to initiates by medicine men who are now living somewhere between earth and the clouds in the West.[9]

These ceremonies and practices involve space that is boundless, relative, and flexible, and that is engaged with underlying energy and power. It was not enough for the Sioux to remember the presence of spirits in visions and ceremonies. They believed they could identify where in space those spirits might be. Men describing their experiences in dreams and visions talked about other worlds, equally substantial as our own; perhaps worlds where people might go after death, but real places just the same. Black Elk, speaking of his cousin Crazy Horse, offers a useful sense of the possibilities:

> Crazy Horse dreamed and went into the world where there is nothing but the spirits of all things. That is the real world that is behind this one, and everything we see here is something like a shadow from that world.[10]

Black Elk outlines a world we might describe as Platonic. More to the point, however, we can also read him as a thinker we might put in conversation with Carl Jung. Crazy Horse moved between, and lived simultaneously in both material and relative space, and he did so in terms of a personal relation with a transcendent energy and power, an apt illustration of concepts Jung had worked to formulate.

We can summarize the Sioux understanding of space as a collection of knowledge, and of experiences of events occurring at specific locations, that appear to violate the normal expectations of secular space and distance. In fact, remembering Jung's (accurate) admonition that these people lived as much in the spiritual world as the physical, we can say that sacred manifestations of space were a greater reality for them. These manifestations included expansive and relative space, simultaneous material/spiritual space, and even material/spiritual movements across space. A sacred place was defined by the memory of a unique experience that had occurred there. Often the place invoked a sense of sacredness to people visiting it for the first time and it raised their expectations that something unique *could* occur there. The durable markings of the old Sun Dance sites are the most prominent examples of sacredness maintaining itself in the presence of secular happenings, but they are hardly the only ones. For that reason the Sioux fought very hard to keep their lands, since a good deal of their religious life involved knowing and responding to the sacred sites where gifts and information originated. It would not be amiss to extend this conclusion to other tribes as well.

Many of these manifestations of space take us immediately to the question of time. Time, for the Sioux, was an equally flexible, relativistic thing that involved a multitude of experiences. People returning from vision quests, for example, often reported the "telescoping" of time, hardly believing that they had spent four days in their quest. Others reported that their dreams constituted a prolonged passage of time so that an hour measured in ordinary chronological time would have hardly been sufficient to accomplish everything they could remember. These reports, however, do not radically differ from the accounts of Western peoples who have extensive dreams and report the same experiences of time. So while the Sioux perceptions of space may differ substantially from that of Western peoples, at least these ideas of time seem reasonably close to that of many Western experiences.

There is, however, also an apprehension among the tribal/primitive peoples that another dimension of time exists over and above or within ordinary time. This time is sacred; that is, spirits who have their own chronology inhabit it and are bound by it. Yet this time dimension also contains human destinies and therefore is able to intrude upon secular time in order to accomplish some larger task. A good example of this sacred time involves the calling out to a human being by a spiritual voice from outside human chronology.

Black Elk was nine years old, for instance, when he heard a voice call him. "While I was eating," he remembered,

> a voice came and said "It is time; now they are calling you." The voice was so loud and clear that I believed it, and I thought I would just go where it wanted me to go. So I got right up and started. As I came out of the tepee, both my thighs began to hurt me and suddenly it was like waking from a dream, and there wasn't any voice.[11]

Black Elk then fell ill, his limbs became swollen, and he was led into the sky by two spirits to meet the Six Grandfathers.

To what does this peculiar phrase, "It is time," refer? What time is it? Why that particular moment in chronological time, when Black Elk was only nine years old? The vision that followed introduced him, as a young boy, to breathtaking spiritual (or psychological) experiences with the powers of the directions, a multitude of sacred horses, and the power to hear the sacred. It could have taken place almost any time during Black Elk's adolescence. Indeed, he did not actually perform a vision quest until he was eighteen years old, and his decision to perform this ceremony came in response to another calling from voices. After the winter of 1881, which was very difficult and depressing for his people, Black Elk remembered:

> When the grasses began to show their faces again, I was happy, for I could hear the thunder beings coming in the earth and I could hear them saying: "It is time to do the work of your Grandfathers."[12]

He then performed the vision quest where he experienced a further vision, the Dog Vision, a supplement to his earlier vision experience.

We have a situation in which nine years of chronological time pass between spiritual experiences and yet the entrée to these experiences occurs when spiritual voices tell Black Elk "it is time" to do this ceremony. When seen from a superior time dimension in which only qualitative events determine the flow of experience, there is continuity between the two events. In our chronological world, however, the two events are separated by nine whole years. From this qualitative continuity we might hypothesize that there might be no passage of time—as we know it—within the larger spiritual time frame. Western theologians might understand this phenomenon as immanence—the continuity of Eden and redemption and everything in between—or as the "fullness" of time—the moment when spiritual powers fulfill the promise of previous events. In the secular chronological interim, Black Elk is the normal Indian boy doing the things that teenagers do.

Another facet of time can also be seen in these experiences, and that is the prediction of the length of an individual's life. In his first vision, Black Elk found himself in a celestial tipi, seated with the Six Grandfathers. He later recalled:

> Now I knew the Sixth Grandfather was about to speak, he who was the Spirit of the Earth, and I saw that he was very old, but more as men are old. His hair was long and white, his face was all in wrinkles and his eyes were deep and dim. I stared at him, for it seemed I knew him somehow; and as I stared, he slowly changed, for he was growing backwards into youth, and when he had become a boy, I knew that he was myself with all the years that would be mine at last.[13]

This prediction of the length of the lifespan—which suggests a meeting between chronological and the higher-order time dimensions—is not unusual among many Indian people, not only the Sioux. Sometimes the information comes directly from animal helpers, as in the case of Brave Buffalo who reported, "The buffalo in my dream told me that I would live to be 102 years old."[14] Or consider the case of Plenty Coups, the famous Crow warrior. At the end of his vision quest experience, Plenty Coups is led by a "Man-person" guiding him over a landscape:

> I followed him back through the hole ... until we came out right over there (pointing) where we had first entered the hole in the ground. Then I saw the spring down by those trees, this very house just as it is, these trees which comfort us today, and a very old man sitting in the shade, alone. I felt pity for him because he was so old and feeble ... "This old man is yourself, Plenty Coups," he [the Man-person] told me. And then I could see the Man-person no more. He was gone, and so too was the old man. Instead I saw only a dark forest.[15]

Plenty Coups did live to be an exceedingly old man. It would appear that at least some human lives are determined in outline and have certain inviolable destinies.*

We can return to the Yuwipi ceremony, with its spiritual and material migrations across space, for another sense of time, that of an eternal "now." William Powers explains this possibility well:

> Not only are all aspects of the Lakota universe represented in the [Yuwipi] meeting in terms of ritual paraphernalia and altar decorations, but all generations are represented. The generational aspects of Yuwipi are made more consistent by the fact that all Yuwipi spirits, human and animal, are actually spirits of those who once lived on the earth. Hence the Oglala feel the sense of continuity between the living and non-living, and their belief that the spirit world is simply an extension of the earthly world is reinforced.[16]

---

* It is worth noting that during the late 1960s and early 1970s, when a number of civil rights activists were paying for their commitment with their lives, Vine Deloria Jr. commented to his family members that he was not worried about a violent political death, since he knew that he would not die in that manner.

Both human and animal spirits that appear in the Yuwipi, and other ceremonies, seem to have intimate knowledge of living people and know of their current situation. And Sioux people frequently suggest the one-ness of time in generational terms, from Black Elk's observation of a multi-generational procession of Sioux people to the Ghost Dance's dream of re-engagement with ancestors and landscapes out of historical time.

These various examples of the apprehension of time suggest that, despite their inevitable linkage, time may be more complex than space, and that we are subject to the timeline of another dimension that is itself unfolding to accomplish a specific goal. The Sioux understood the supervisory aspect of this other time dimension—and its probable inhabitants—and their understanding led to two distinct practices. On the one hand, they hoped to join this superior time more closely to their daily lives. On the other, they sought help from spirits to alter, to their own benefit, the sequences of action inspired by that dimension. They understood a universe being constantly created, and that it perhaps had even more time dimensions. If one could apprehend these, they would make daily and lifetime experiences more eas-ily understood and accepted.

Space and time are thus central concepts in both cosmologies, with intriguing overlaps. Sioux examples shed light on Jungian theories, while these theories in turn help us make sense of Sioux experiences. We now turn to an aspect of the Sioux universe that does not appear within the Jungian scheme of things but which, I shall suggest, might have been included—seem-ingly inanimate material objects, which do not exactly reflect human per-ceptions of time or the physical dimension of space, but a rather different category of experience. Most, but not all, Sioux people with spiritual powers enjoyed the assistance of intercessors in the form of material objects—often (but not always) small round stones that possessed special powers and per-formed tasks for them.[17] In the decade 1910-1920, such stones were the major remaining active entities of the old spiritual traditions and both Aaron McGaffey (A. McG.) Beede and Frances Densmore gave them serious attention. Beede linked their potency to the Sioux belief in Spirit:

> The Western Sioux believed that each being, a rock for instance, is an actual community of persons with ample locomotion among them-selves, and such locomotion not regarded as circumscribed or restricted, save as the make (*oicage*) of the whole gives to each species his own sphere.

And, they reasoned, this limitation is merely in body (*tancan*), the mind, intelligence and spirit of each is privileged to range through and blend with totality of gaining a right attitude toward Woniya (Spirit).[18]

Densmore recounts the explanation given by Chased-by-Bears concerning the shape and symbolism of the stones.

> The outline of the stone is round, having no end and no beginning; like the power of the stone it is endless. The stone is perfect of its kind and is the work of nature; no artificial means being used in shaping it. Outwardly it is not beautiful, but its structure is solid, like a solid house in which one may safely dwell. It is not composed of many substances, but is of one substance, which is genuine and not a limitation of anything else.[19]

So while all stones are regarded as self-contained entities, only those small round stones could be said to possess the power, or inclination to have a relationship with people. These stones were the physical representation of the powers of the universe.

The stones were found on the top of buttes, often after thunderstorms, and were regarded by many people as products of lightning strikes, gifts to humans by the thunders. It was not permissible to dig them out of the ground because there was a feeling that it would be stealing. Stones found sitting on top of the ground, however, were fair game for anyone who found them. The stone did not automatically begin to function as an assistant for the person who found it. Usually a stone would appear in a dream or vision and articulate both its desire for friendship with a human and announce its powers and abilities. Beede reported on the Sioux beliefs about the stones without objecting that the people were superstitious:

> The fact of a rock, or any object, being a community of locomotive persons, was based, or concomitant with, the belief that not a few of their people actually had the ability to see into and through a rock discerning its make-up, similarly as we look into a community or grove of trees. I have known many Indians believing they possessed this ability—not regarding it as anything remarkable—and there was no occasion for doubting their sincerity.[20]

Densmore gives a striking example of how medicine men would use the stones to see clearly in and through the quotidian world:

> A white man dropped his rifle into the river. The man regretted his loss, but made no effort to recover the rifle. After the man had gone, Goose [a Sioux medicine man] decided to try to find it by the aid of the sacred stones. Accordingly he took the stones with him, and rowed on the river until the stones told him to dive. Doing so, he found the rifle on the bed of the river, a strange circumstance being that when he was in the water it appeared clear instead of cloudy as usual. Goose afterwards had an opportunity to restore the rifle to its owner, who rewarded him liberally.[21]

This event was well known by people at Standing Rock but was not regarded as unusual.

Sacred stones more often performed three distinct types of tasks: providing healing information, locating things at a distance, and bringing objects or animals to the medicine man. Thus if a person had lost a horse, or some object of value, a man with stones might locate them for him. Obviously the major use of stones in this respect prior to reservation days was in locating game or in detecting the approach of enemies. Densmore gives many examples of the accomplishments of the stones in her ethnography, *Teton Sioux Music,* and I will not dwell on them at length. Bringing physical objects to the medicine man, however, was often spectacular and it is worth seeing the outer limits of the mediations into space and time the stones seem to have made possible.

My favorite example, reported by Densmore regarding the medicine man Goose, stretches the limits of belief but was nevertheless a real event witnessed by the people, white and Indian, of the vicinity:

> One day a fur trader ridiculed the medicine-man in his hearing. This white man said that all the medicine-men did was by sleight of hand, and that he would have to see an instance of their power before he would believe it. Goose entered into conversation with the trader on the subject, who offered him ten articles, including cloth and blankets, if he would call a buffalo to the spot where they were standing. Goose sent both the sacred stones to summon a buffalo. The trader brought his field glasses and looked across the prairie, saying in derision, "Where is the buffalo you were to summon?" Suddenly the trader saw a moving

object, far away. It came nearer until they could see it without the aid of
the glasses. It was a buffalo, and it came so near that they shot it from
the spot where they stood.[22]

The buffalo had long been gone from that part of the country, the last
hunt having taken place in 1883. Densmore's volume *Teton Sioux Music*
was published in 1918, and this incident was fresh in the minds of the local
people. Certainly, the buffalo might have been a survivor of that last hunt,
but could it have survived thirty years in western South Dakota without
being spotted? So where did the buffalo come from?

Another spectacular demonstration of the power of the stones was
reported by Densmore, and involved two medicine men, Siyaka and White
Shield. It seems that Siyaka had lost two horses and went to White Shield to
ask him to find them using his stones.

> White Shield asked, "What sign shall the stone bring to show whether
> your horses are by a creek or on the prairie?" Siyaka replied: "If they
> are by a creek, let the stone bring a little turtle and a piece of clamshell,
> and if they are on the prairie let the stone bring a meadow lark." White
> Shield then sent the stone on its quest. While the stone was absent the
> people prepared a square of finely pulverized earth. It was evening when
> the stone returned. The tepee was dark, as the fire had been smothered,
> but there was dry grass ready to put on it when White Shield ordered the
> light. At last the stone appeared on the place prepared for it, and beside
> it was a little turtle with a small piece of clamshell in one of its claws.[23]

White Shield then told Siyaka where his horses were and said that a neighbor
would return them to him if he didn't feel like making the trip. And Siyaka
got his horses back that way.[24]

Recounting this anecdotal evidence concerning sacred stones is important because the stones represent in the most tangible form the spiritual
energy of dreams and visions manifesting themselves in the physical world,
transcending chronological time and physical space, in a manner unknown
to the Jungian universe. Curiously, however, Jung himself had an intuitive
fascination with stone, one usefully placed alongside Sioux practices, and
perhaps read in universal terms. In 1923 Jung began to build a stone tower
at Bollingen as a means of confronting his mother's death. In his biography
of Jung, Frank McLynn writes:

Jung's Bollingen tower has always attracted extreme interest, since it seems a multi-layered focus for various Jungian motifs and almost an "objective correlative" of the Jungian self.[25]

McLynn further comments:

Bollingen answered Jung's recipe for a place where he could be completely alone and exist solely for himself. The tower-like annex functioned as a "withdrawal room," like the arcane area in an Indian house to which the master could withdraw. Jung regarded his retreat as a place of spiritual concentration, where he could paint, carve in stone or meditate; he loved painting onto the walls messages received straight from his unconscious. Jung also regarded the tower and its many later annexes as a symbol of psychic wholeness.[26]

At almost the same moment in time, then, we have Sioux Indians consulting and cooperating with stones to make predictions, to perform healings, and to call birds and animals to themselves, while a continent away a Swiss psychologist, desperate to find peace within himself, takes up the task of building a stone tower with his own hands, intellectually unaware, perhaps, of the significance of stone in the larger scheme of things. Although raised in the Western tradition in which animals and stones do not talk, Jung unconsciously brought himself into an orbit that passed close at hand to that of the Sioux universe. He almost understood, as the Sioux did, that the stone is the best physical representative of the great mysterious energy.

Following Jung, we might try to visualize the earliest scenario in which the Plains Indians grasped the essential insight that underlying the phenomenal world was a universal physical/mental reality. Certainly the regularity of the seasons and the demonstration of powerful energy in the processes of the natural world—earthquakes, thunderstorms, floods, tornados, and the like—convinced them that many energies were present in the world. Through generations of close observation and remembered knowledge, the Sioux eventually came to understand sixteen different concepts describing distinctive demonstrations of energy that they experienced. The most familiar idea was that of *Wakan Tanka*, which implied a sense of family relatedness and intimacy, a caring intelligence, a great mysterious. The physical energy that gave locomotion to physical things, they called *skan* or *Taku skan skan*. This concept is usually translated as "something that moves"—akin to the energy fields of quantum physics. In a comparative vein, we might observe that *skan* seems close to some of the Jungian ideas that suggest the unity of mind and matter, spirit and instinct, in a certain kind of intelligent existence.

Some early Western social scientists, when framing the complexity of so-called primitive apprehensions of energy, reduced complex and open ideas like *skan* or *Wakan Tanka* to the status of a single theory—that of "mana," itself a fairly open generalization. While Jung was generally sensitive to the idea of mana in his writings, he did not connect this particular idea of energy with the resolution of the mind/ matter problem. "The mana theory maintains that there is something like a widely distributed power in the external world that produces all those extraordinary effects," Jung noted.

> Everything that exists acts, otherwise it would not *be*. It can *be* only by virtue of its inherent energy. Being is a field of force. The primitive idea of mana, as you can see, has in it the beginnings of a crude theory of energy.[27]

We might equally well describe Western scholars' theory of mana itself as a very crude rendering of more sophisticated, spiritual truths that govern all the possible relationships of power.

And yet, this idea of mana returns us once again to the perennial question of time and determination. Jung saw a clear connection, observing in his dream seminar that "mana at first seems only to have to do with energy, but later it takes on time qualities."[28] Ritual actions involving a concentration of energy—the pipe ceremony, the vision quest, the Yuwipi, and the use of stones—are simultaneously concerned with the production of a transcendent notion and experience of time so that energy has the capacity of combining with form to produce a sacred occasion or event. Likewise, the concern with the shape of places where ceremonial activities take place—sweat lodges and Sun Dance grounds, for instance—suggests that the Sioux understood the importance of space in figuring this time-energy relation. We have returned to the ideas of matter and mind, and how they relate to energy. We can see that space and time are indissoluble parts of the energy concept—and vice versa, energy is a function or constituent of space and time and mind. Because these relationships exist, even though we make definite statements about them, they become requirements and boundaries of psychic events. What the Sioux tradition adds to the views of Carl Jung and of some modern physicists is a material form of triangulation, a collection of physical evidence that specific events can occur or have occurred in which all of these time, space, mind, matter, and energy constituents play a realistic, materially important role in human experience. It is necessary only that we honor the reports of the Sioux by taking them at face value, and thus allow ourselves to make the crucial theoretical connections—even if, in a Newtonian context, such events might not make perfect sense. With these groundings in mind—a basic understanding of the historical context, the productive and the dangerous uses of "the primitive," and a complex sense of overlaps and possibilities in the two cosmologies (Western and Sioux)—we can now proceed to a series of more detailed comparisons and dialogues.

CHAPTER SIX

JUNG AND THE ANIMALS

Perhaps the most extravagant pretense of Western civilization is its tenaciously held belief that only humans matter in the scheme of things. The origin of this unwarranted arrogance is unknown, but psychologically speaking it is Western culture's greatest inflation. In this tradition, humans are created last after all other creatures and are given the privilege of naming, thereby gaining ascendancy over all other beings. This is a subtle but key point in understanding the root psychology and philosophy of Western culture. With this claim to naming, something important has already happened to Western man in relation to the rest of creation.

Strangely, when first we meet humans in Western literature and myth, they are not living wild but are already domesticated. In Genesis, man and woman are carefully sequestered in a garden where they have no contact or communication with the other forms of life—save with a late-arriving serpent who leads them, and their progeny, into temptation—an act that of course results in expulsion from Eden. Humans are thus created to live an institutional life, and in that life they are charged with naming the birds and animals, thereby gaining control over them. There is no mention of other creatures living in the Garden, and with the eating of the forbidden fruit, Western history, in a real sense, commences.

Man's disobedience is so profound that, except for the Garden, the whole of creation suffers a cataclysmic moral fall, and eventually only God himself can redeem humanity. Adam and Eve are cast out of the Garden into a natural environment where they must earn their living (although tending a garden seems like steady employment that would also provide a living). Having been created in and initially confined to the Garden, humans come to view the natural world as a hostile environment—it now seems new and disorderly, as a natural environment can be. Humans hope to eventually return or be returned to their former status in the Garden, living properly with the creator. Although they appear to suffer a common fate with man, other animals and beings are not envisioned as helpers but as slaves or competitors. There is therefore a fundamental separation or dreadful alienation between man and other creatures from the very beginning. For Western people, the fall represents alienation from the earth itself.

C.G. Jung grew up as a Western European, uncritically accepting the idea that animals were lower forms of life than humans. Being a thoroughly urban man, Jung had little firsthand knowledge of animals and plants, and tended to make his most intimate acquaintances with these creatures when and as they appeared symbolically in his patients' dreams. His statements regarding animals that humans might encounter in our daily lives often merely identify their place in an evolutionary cosmos, without taking account of their natural, ecological existence. As we have seen, this study requires us to assemble many of Jung's disparate thoughts into an organized structure. Our treatment of animals will prove no different, and we will consider Jung's conceptions through three distinct formats. First, we will consider the animal as a cosmic creation, what we might call the "organic" animal. Second, the animal is understood as an intelligent being fulfilling predestined instinctual archetypal patterns of behavior. Finally, we will consider the animal as a symbolic participant in Jung's patients' dreams.

Despite his cultural heritage, Jung was surprisingly flexible and open when discussing other forms of life and our commonly shared biological heritage. "Nowadays," he wrote,

> ... we have to start with the hypothesis that, so far as predisposition is concerned, there is no essential difference between man and all other creatures. Like every animal, he possesses a preformed psyche which breeds true to his species and which, on closer examination, reveals distinct features traceable to family antecedents. We have not the slightest reason to suppose that there are certain human activities or functions that could be exempted from this rule. [1]

The "preformed psyche" seems to imply a universe of Platonic forms. Since Jung was seeking here to demonstrate the viability of the archetype, there is no reason to suppose that he carried his inquiry beyond the idea that each species had a particular psychological makeup unique to itself. Presumably during many millennia of evolutionary development, animals accumulated physical and psychological characteristics unique to each species that separated them from one another.

The topic becomes complicated when we try to conceive how this "pre-formed psyche" might function in an evolutionary setting. In a letter to Robert Eisler in 1946, Jung speculated that the

> lowest layers of our psyche still have an animal character. Hence it is highly probable that animals have similar or *even the same archetypes.* That they do have archetypes is certain in so far as the animal-plant sym-bioses clearly demonstrate that there must be an inherited image in the animal that drives it to specific instinctive actions.[2] [emphasis added]

The Jungian system, therefore, relies on the similarity of the psychic contents across species lines linking everything together in basic organic relationships.

Anticipating theory that would be articulated and formalized nearly a half century later with the establishment of "evolutionary psychology" as its own discipline, Jung understood the present psyche of living creatures as an evolutionary product. Consequently, there exists a psychic as well as an organic unity we share with other forms of life. In his "Commentary on 'The Secret of the Golden Flower,'" he suggests that "the various lines of psychic development start from one common stock whose roots reach back into the most distant past."[3] And if this was true, he argued, then "theoretically it should be possible to 'peel' the collective unconscious, layer by layer, until we came to the psychology of the worm, and even of the amoeba."[4] Because of the evolutionary origin of the psyche, we enjoy the remote possibility of contacting the lowest and earliest levels of the expression of life itself. It could even be an intangible thought that preceded any physical development, if we take quantum theory seriously.

Jung conceived of a gradual development of consciousness during the course of evolutionary time that reflected the physical structure in which other forms of life existed. "Plants are entirely rooted in the *earth,*" he observed,

> helpless victims or absolutely at one with the basic law of nature. Ani-mals have the faculty of moving away and seeking their own place; they are literally less attached to the laws of the earth. And the life of man is detached to a very high degree; we have produced an artificial world for ourselves that is very far from the laws of nature and has an entirely different rhythm.[5]

It follows that psyches must be distinguishable by physical form since the body alone provides the means of enjoying a variety of experiences.

Organic unity, however, must hold in spite of the great difference in capacity that characterizes trees, animals, humans and other life forms. Jung pointed out that

> trees cannot exist without animals, or animals without plants, and perhaps animals cannot be without man, or man without animals and plants and so on. And the whole thing being one tissue, it is no wonder that all its parts function together, just as the cells in our bodies function together because they are part of the same living continuum.[6]

Given this belief, it is surprising that Jung was not led to emphasize an intimate contact with the natural world. His psychology forms a perfect background and justification for expressing environmental concerns. Indeed, one can read these words favorably in light of another twentieth-century science, that of ecosystem biology. Perhaps what kept Jung from more fully realizing the necessity of a positive relationship with the earth and its creatures for human mental health was an overriding cultural assumption that the world was created for humanity alone.

If we accept the commonality of archetypal presences in the animals and ourselves, to what degree does that commonality issue in defined physical relationships between ourselves and other creatures? Here, Jung recognized that, in the deeper layers of the cosmic psychic structure, similarities could be discovered to account for the conscious behavior of all beings. "Emotional manifestations are based on similar patterns, and are recognizably the same all over the earth," he observed. "We understand them even in animals, and the animals themselves understand each other in this respect, even if they belong to different species."[7] In Jung's view, not only do we share basic archetypes with animals, we also observe a large set of similar emotional and instinctual responses to the physical world. In an evolutionary process, survival techniques would undoubtedly be important and might even be shared, as would more mature emotional responses to the surrounding environment. To the degree that we can see a similarity in their actions with our own responses to similar situations, animals may be "peoples" like us. In his conceptualization of physical and psychological worlds, Jung seemed to envision a "peoplehood" that would be rooted in the initial structure of the universe in which everything was ultimately related.

Trees and plants, it seems, follow basic *psychic* laws but they are inhibited because of their lack of mobility. Animals achieve a slightly higher status and according to Jung always respond to a "higher law." "The animal is a well behaved citizen in nature," Jung maintained, "it is pious, it follows the oath with great regularity, it is doing nothing extravagant."[8] Not only is the animal pious, "it is the only thing except plants that really fulfills its destiny or the superior will—the will of God, if you want to put it into religious language."[9] Expressed in these theological terms, such ideas might be unacceptable to many current scientific thinkers. Jung seems to suggest a creationist understanding of the psychic nature of all forms of life except humans:

> Only domesticated animals misbehave; a wild animal never misbehaves, it follows its own natural law; there is no such thing as a good tiger that eats only apples and carrots! A wild animal is a pious, law-abiding being who fulfills the will of God in a most perfect way.[8]

Here Jung appears to embrace a set of assumptions that have no correspondence with the rest of his psychology. Can the "will of God" apply to us also? Can we formulate "laws" that give us some knowledge of the way the organic world functions? Or was Jung speaking metaphorically when he used such words as "pious," "citizen," and "law-abiding?"

Jung never explained the somewhat careless phrase "will of God," at least in this context. Jolande Jacobi, however, offers a partial explanation:

> The migrations of animals, the rhythms and rituals in man's daily life are correlates. Adherence to imprinted modes of behaviour and experience is a safeguard, deviation from which must be paid for with anxiety and uncertainty. The animal will give up these "safe-guards" only when constrained by outward force; man, through the relative freedom of his consciousness, has the possibility of departing from them voluntarily.[11]

Subsequently, the piety of the animal consists in remaining faithful to instincts responding to changes in the environment congruent with its type. Humans have the ability to violate their psychic type, but in doing so we estrange ourselves from nature—and from our natural selves. Are our natural selves then not something over and above what the evolutionary process tells us?

Whether we know the "will of God" or not with respect to our own species, if we have similar emotions to animals, can we not be similar in our intelligence? Could some animals even be superior? Jung appears to say "yes" and then quickly "no." There are, he suggests,

> very similar "intelligent" acts of compensation in nature, especially in the instinctual activities of animals. For us, at least, they do not have the character of conscious decisions, but appear to be just like human activities that are exclusively controlled by the unconscious. The great difference between them is that the instinctual behaviour of animals is predictable and repetitive, whereas the compensatory acts of the unconscious are individual and creative. [12]

Here Jung's perceptions contrast with ethological observations. In a familiar landscape, an animal may appear to naturally respond with predictable instincts in an absence of cognition, as we would describe them. Place an animal in a new and unfamiliar landscape, however, and one quickly observes behavior that testifies to the presence of complex thinking processes. This is not surprising. When an unexpected situation occurs, human behavioral responses are similarly driven by both the instinctual and the cognitive, suggesting more similarity than difference.

This apparent lapse in his otherwise perceptive assessments of animal behaviour reveals Jung's limited experience with animals in their natural state. He therefore offers only speculations based on his own doctrines. The real issue, it seems to me, is the degree to which animals can be said to have a consciousness. They share a common psychic heritage with us and at our deeper levels they share archetypal patterns. Jung suggests that "Animals have little consciousness, but they have many impulses and reactions that denote the existence of a psyche." [13] If they have a psyche, and we derive from similar organic circumstances, would it not be possible that they have a consciousness comparable to ours except expressed in different ways? Animals may also, at least theoretically for Jung, have a "self"—the entity that gives meaning to organic life. Viewing all life from a universal perspective Jung felt that

> the individual self is a portion or segment or representative of something present in all living creatures, an exponent of the specific mode of psychological behaviour, which varies from species to species and is

inborn in each of its members. The inborn mode of *acting* has long been known as *instinct* and for the inborn mode of psychic apprehension I have proposed the term *archetype*.[14]

These categories of instinct and archetype, however, do not detract from animals, nor demonstrate that they have no consciousness, but enhance a claim for the possibility and open the door for a more serious investigation of the actual capabilities of animals.

Can animals reason? Western people applaud reason as a distinguishing characteristic that separates man from the animals. "The idea that man alone possesses the primacy of reason is antiquated twaddle," Jung wrote to pastor W. Arz.

> I have even found that men are far more irrational than animals. Since we know from experience that the psyche can be grasped to only a very limited degree, it would be best to regard it as a tiny conscious world influenced by all sorts of unknown factors lurking in the great darkness that surrounds us.[15]

If the psyche is but a tiny entity in great darkness, Jung's idea that animals have a limited consciousness does not preclude them from being as intelligent as we are.

Can animals construct systems of thought or perhaps even their own mythologies? Or, being perfect citizens, wouldn't animals simply follow the "will of God"? Would the expression of their instincts be consonant with the "will of God"? Here again Jung is uncertain.

> If the animal psyche were capable of such an accomplishment [creating a mythology], we would be able to recognize the mythology which the weaverbird is expressing when it builds its nest, and the yucca moth when it deposits its eggs in the yucca flower. That is, we would know what kind of fantasy images trigger off their instinctive actions.[16]

But why would we necessarily be able to learn how weaverbirds and yucca moths thought? Or what they fantasized? Would these entities begin to appear in our dreams?

Can animals demonstrate a thought process superior or equal to that of humans? If they can—and again, how would we know and define such a hierarchy?—would we then need to rethink the category of "instinct," which is usually seen as a primary mental exercise of animals? If animals are simply expressing a "different" form of intellect, then how are we to categorize and define "instinct"—in the case of animals and humans alike? I wonder if what we have here is a condition similar to the Jungian distinction made between plants and animals, in which almost everything may be determined by the degree of physical freedom that an organism possesses. At one point, Jung came close to engaging such a position:

> Modern investigation of animal instinct, for instance in insects, has brought together a rich fund of empirical material which shows that if man sometimes acted as certain insects do he would possess a higher intelligence than at present. It cannot, of course, be proved that insects possess conscious knowledge, but common sense cannot doubt that their unconscious patterns of behaviour are psychic functions. [17]

One could argue, then, that insects may well have an ability to entertain abstract thoughts, with the results not radically different than our own when we face problems requiring generalized thinking.

In truth, it is unfair to judge Jung's statements on understanding animals from our contemporary viewpoint because he only had the scientific findings of his day available for reference. Since then many of the theories upon which Jung derived his concepts about natural history have been substantially superseded. We have infinitely expanded our knowledge of the organic world in the last half-century in that respect. A glance at current newspaper stories on animal behavior will show that the idea of animal intelligence is now becoming widely respectable in scientific circles. In an article entitled "Animal Intellect Gaining Respect," John Yaukey reports:

> While the conventional wisdom on animal intelligence has swung back and forth over the past 150 years, scientists believe it's now on a permanent march towards a great appreciation of how animals naturally think rather than how much like humans they can be taught to think. [18]

Had this data been available to Jung, his psychology might have been radically different. The barrier to achieving this kind of recognition decades ago was the tendency of Western scientists to project their personal beliefs into their interpretation of their subject matter. The criteria for determining whether other life forms can think and reason was largely based on whether *they think as we do.* Where animals could be trained to do simple tasks, we have assumed that this achievement was the summit of their accomplishments. Yaukey suggests that

> studies of everything from chimps and elephants to whales and porpoises indicate they are capable of untrained thought well beyond mere instinct and can often communicate in high levels of detail. It's not so much that animals are performing more elaborate tricks; rather they're showing signs of reasoning rather than conditioning, such as playing tricks and hiding tools. [19]

Some animals, on the other hand, seem to be able to master the acquisition of knowledge in the format used by humans. Dr. Irene Pepperberg reported on the feats of Alex the parrot:

> ... he could identify 50 different objects and recognize quantities up to six; ... he could distinguish seven colors, five shapes and understand "larger," "smaller," "same," and "different," and he is learning the concepts of "over" and "under."*[20]

Would Jung be horrified that animals can think like us while we can't think like them? Would he have concluded that we are not as smart as they are? Don't we avoid this question by relying mostly upon the category "instinct" when discussing animal intelligence?

Surprisingly, although Jung failed to decide on whether animals had intelligence, he found that they possessed something equally important. "Viewed from the psychological standpoint," Jung wrote to J. B. Rhine,

> ... extra-sensory perception appears as a manifestation of the *collective unconscious.* This particular psyche behaves as if it were *one* and not as if it were split up into many individuals. It is *non-personal* (I call it the "objective psyche"). It is the same everywhere and at all times. (If it were not so, comparative psychology would be impossible.) As it is not

---

*   Before he died in September 2007, Alex, an African Gray Parrot, had learned a vocabulary of over a hundred words and was able to communicate boredom, affection, and mischief.

limited to the person, it is also not limited to the body. It manifests itself therefore not only in human beings but also at the same time in animals and even in physical circumstances.[21]

I do not believe that we are talking about the extraordinary hearing or sight animals often possess. Rather, Jung means those singular times when dogs howl at their master's death although that death occurs miles away at obscure places.[22] Books are filled with similar examples that suggest that extrasensory perception is a gift shared by the more developed birds and animals. According to a number of studies, animals even have languages. Constantine Slobodchikoff of the University of Northern Arizona, for example, detected a complex system of warning of the approach of specific predators in a study of prairie dogs. According to him they can distinguish between kinds of predators and communicate precisely the degree of danger they pose.[23]

In examining how Jung saw real-life animals, we face the same problem we encountered when determining what he thought the primitive was: there are doctrinaire statements acceptable to the scientific readers of the day, and then there are "throw-away" comments suggesting his intuition that the doctrine was wrong, and that we should pay attention to those aspects of animal psychic life that are equal to or better than our own. If we knit together Jung's diverse interpretations of the animals that we encounter in our daily lives—that is to say, non-dream symbol animals—we find no essential difference between them and ourselves. They have a psyche; they have a self. They have intelligence, they can reason, they share with us at the deeper levels of the psyche certain basic archetypes. Many seem to have languages, and some of them even have extrasensory perception equal or superior to that of humans.

The animal also plays a critical role in Jung's effort to define the structure of the psyche and to interpret dreams. In this respect, we discard the goal of understanding animals in and of themselves and see how Jung introduced the animal as symbolic of certain elements that he believed constituted the psyche:

The unconscious consists, among other things, of remnants of the undifferentiated archaic psyche, including its animal stages. The reactions and products of the animal psyche have uniformity and a constancy of which we seem able to discover only sporadic traces in man.[24]

Here, of course, we do not deal directly with animals but with the requirement of evolutionary doctrine to regard humans as evolved animals constituting a new species. When we begin to investigate the psyche we find, or are supposed to find, fragments of the former animal stage of our development. But as we have seen, there are no fragments or remnants. The developmental stages that preceded us remain complete in themselves since every step in evolution requires that an organism is able to survive in its environment and successfully compete.

Inconsistency seems characteristic of Jung's treatment of animal symbols. Perhaps he was more concerned with keeping his psychology intact in spite of the contradictory evidence. Alternatively, he might have encountered a part of the psyche where energies and images were so puzzling that he was unable to adequately describe what he was encountering and turned to familiar, if forced, interpretations. We can see deep ambivalence in some of his reflections on dream symbols, for example. "Theriomorphic symbols are very common in dreams and other manifestations of the unconscious," he said.

> They express the psychic level of the content in question: that is to say such contents are at a stage of unconsciousness that is as far from human consciousness as the psyche of an animal. Warm-blooded or cold-blooded vertebrates of all kinds, or even invertebrates, thus indicate the degree of unconsciousness.[25]

Unfortunately, we do not know exactly how these symbols of other creatures appeared in dreams. Were they active participants in the dream narrative? Monsters that the person had to overcome? Or were they merely background images that helped to provide a context within which the persons found themselves?

Animal symbols, Jung suggested, appear as indicative of the level of the psyche where problems occur, and thus as symbols acting as orientating mileposts for the therapist. But Jung also finds theriomorphic symbols representing the Self.

> The commonest of these images in modern dreams are, in my experience, the elephant, horse, bull, bear, white and black birds, fishes, and snakes. Occasionally one comes across tortoises, snails, spiders and beetles. The principal plant symbols are the flower and the tree. Of the inorganic products, the commonest are the mountain and the lake.[26]

In this respect it seems as if Jung almost arbitrarily takes any animal, bird, fish, or natural feature that occupies an important place in his patients' dreams and interprets it as symbolism of the Self. This observation is not made frivolously, because it may be that the particular dream animal or plant represented a particular quality or kind of energy that the patient lacked. When the therapist has such wide discretion in interpretation of symbols, though, the process looks suspicious and perhaps lacking in the kind of close, thoughtful attention to its meaning necessary to interpretation:

> All the lions, bulls, dogs, and snakes that populate our dreams represent an undifferentiated and as yet untamed libido, which at the same time forms a part of the human personality and can therefore fittingly be described as the *anthropoid psyche*. Like energy, the libido never manifests itself as such, but only in the form of a "force," that is to say, in the form of something in a definite energic state, be it moving bodies, chemical or electrical tension, etc.[27]

Granted that the psyche presents novel questions that have not previously been discovered or resolved, it nonetheless seems that having animals represent both the structure and content and the active concern of the dream presents an unsolvable, and perhaps contradictory, problem of interpretation. Indeed Jung himself asserts that

> dark and unfathomable as the earth is, its theriomorphic symbols do not have only a reductive meaning, but one that is prospective and spiritual. They are paradoxical, pointing upwards and downwards at the same time.[28]

Such an application of symbols covers the function of time, and suggests that different functions of a symbol occur at successive stages of therapy and require interpretation relative to a given context.

In his *Seminar on Dream Analysis*, Jung makes a most surprising and discordant admission that seems to contradict his other explications and use of animals as symbols of psychic processes. Recall his comment, discussed in an earlier chapter:

> I analyzed dreams of Somali Negroes as if they were people of Zurich, with the exception of certain differences of languages and images.

Where the primitives dream of crocodiles, pythons, buffaloes, and rhinoceroses, we dream of being run over by trains and automobiles. Both have the same voice, really; our modern cries sound like a primeval forest. What we express by the banker the Somali expresses by the python. The surface language is different yet the underlying facts are just the same.[29]

This transfer of dream images is a far cry from the carefully scripted appearance of animals in dreams that we see elsewhere in his work and that we have discussed above. We saw that the animal appears in dreams because it represents an earlier stage of evolution, represents the Self, or represents libido. The animal therefore represents "layers" of the psyche that have accumulated over the eons of evolutionary time. Jung suggested, at its outer limits, that one might be able to return to the amoeba's psyche. If trains, automobiles, and bankers can now supplant these ancient symbols and forces, why wouldn't Jung's patients have produced a maximum of these images and a minimum number of animal images?

Jung was quite emphatic about this substitution:

Dragons are in our day great machines, cars, big guns, these are archetypes now, simply new terms for old things. These new things are just as valid as the old ones; as the new things are merely words for images, so the old things were words for images. The mythological idea of the dragon is probably derived from the idea of huge saurians; it is really quite possible that the dragon myths are the last vestiges of ancestral memories of the saurians—the terrifying thing of which man in the dim past was afraid.[30]

The identification of modern machines with creatures of the remote past is staggering in its implications, and if it leaves unanswered the question of why such images could be so easily supplanted by machines, it nonetheless points to the possibility of evolutionary memory in the unconscious.

Does Jung mean that we have a memory of the days when saurians ruled the earth? He has partial support from David Jones, a professor of Anthropology at the University of Central Florida, who suggested in *An Instinct for Dragons,* that

the dragon image, fermented in the primal soup of man's first nightmares, is a composite of the carnivores who fed on human ancestors when they were tree-dwelling monkeys: the pythons, the big cats, and the raptors.[31]

Of course, these creatures look very little like dragons. Dinosaurs, however, were living creatures and presumably had psyches of some complexity, since their physical structures were innovative in many ways. Either remnants or the whole of their psychic constitution might then occupy a "layer" of psychic material, precluding us from simply making a transfer of images to suit our convenience. We may see them in our dreams when remote layers of the unconscious appear, or perhaps even in the sense that we have witnessed them as real living threats to human existence.[32]

In addition to animals representing the Self and libido, they also represent themes that persist as patterns of behavior and sometimes, but not always, achieving the status of an archetype. According to Jung:

> Over the whole of this psychic realm there reign certain motifs, certain typical figures which we can follow far back in history, and even into prehistory, and they may therefore legitimately be described as "archetypes." They seem to be built into the very structure of man's consciousness, for in no other way can I explain why it is that they occur universally and in identical forms, whether the redeemer-figure be a fish, a hare, a lamb, a snake, or a human being.[33]

Jung's turn once again to the figure of the redeemer, of course, reveals yet again a European cultural bias, for the link to animals in general is a weak one. A much better motif is available elsewhere. In one of the dream scenarios discussed in his Visions Seminars, Jung discussed the actions of an animal that played a prominent role in the narrative.

> This is the motif of the helpful animal intervening when everything is impossible and people expect a catastrophe—help out of a tight corner. What do these animals mean? They are merely representatives of lower instinctual forces in man and helpful in the same way.[34]

When read in terms of their symbolic appearance in dreams and visions, it would seem that Jung's ultimate position on animals and other forms of life is that they are simply lower level energies reduced to aspects of man's "lower" instinctual nature. Animals must be recognized, of course, as important symbols of psychic processes, and they must appear as lower order manifestation in the unconscious. Indeed, without animals, Jung's entire schema is forfeit, since it relies upon animals as exemplars of the unconsciousness and early stages of development that are foundational to his thinking. In this sense, animals are good to think with—they offer comparisons and baselines—but Jung does not imagine that animals could, *in and of themselves*, be helpful to humans.

If Jung effectively severs the connection between his psychology and the physical world around us by reducing animals to mere symbols of psychic energies or the Self, he also opens up new possibilities, admitting that animals and humans share a common psychic structure that reflects an evolutionary past and raising questions about the nature of animal psyche, consciousness, capability, and peoplehood. It is my belief that if Jung had opened himself to the natural world for a prolonged period of time, his thinking on this subject might have been even more productive. What is lacking in modern industrial people, including Jung, is the talent and sensitivity to pay respect to animals. This absence leads us to wonder: if the world were different—if, say, we were talking about the acts and understandings of "primitives"—what kinds of connections might exist between humans and animals?

CHAPTER SEVEN

ANIMALS AND
THE SIOUX

It will come as no surprise to learn that the Sioux relationship with other creatures differed considerably from that of Western Europeans and Americans. As described in the last chapter, the Book of Genesis gives man dominion over the other forms of life when he is allowed to name them. Adam is created last and is therefore considered the apex of creation. In the West, this implied superiority has produced a context in which killing other creatures is done for sport, in which animals are tortured in laboratories, in which they are "factory farmed" for hamburger and bacon, and in which they are put to use in myriad other ways, all in service to human beings.

In contrast to Western myth and practice, Sioux stories of their cosmology do not grant humans any special status. All beings are regarded as equals in the presence of the Great Mysterious. In the Sioux belief, man is also created last, but not as the ultimate achievement. According to William Powers:

> For whites, humans were the last to inhabit the earth, and are therefore a crowning glory of all that preceded them. For the Lakota, humans were the last, and that makes them newest, youngest, and most ignorant. [1]

The Sioux thus looked to other forms of life to take their cues on how to live in this world.

Careful observation of the behavior of other creatures by the Sioux revealed that each kind of animal—and here I am referring to birds, land animals and water animals—had its own unique way of adjusting to the world. Yet they also had many things in common with humans, and these things encouraged people to seek to understand them. Like humans, the other creatures had limitations beyond which they could not go. Although these limits were largely dependent on the physical shape of the bird or animal, keen attention showed that they were quite like humans in having strong and weak individuals among their groups, in demonstrating joy and sadness, and in confronting unusual situations and finding ways to solve their problems. Like humans, each individual creature had the ability to vary its behavior while continuing to follow the basic pattern of its life. Attributing this condition to the Great Mysterious, the medicine man Lame Deer remarked,

> He only sketches out the path of life roughly for all the creatures on earth, shows them where to go, where to arrive at, but leaves them to find their own way to get there. He wants them to act independently according to their nature, to the urge in each of them.[2]

Certainly here is a belief that Jung would have savored.

The Sioux saw in animals personality traits that they saw in themselves: bravery in the face of danger, mothers' concern to protect their young, ways of gathering food, the desire to seek shelter and build homes, and love of play and recreation. They came away believing that these creatures had the same capabilities as we do. This belief grew over many years of experience with animals, during which they came to know the full scope of bird and animal powers. Eventually the people came to realize that birds and animals had more knowledge than we do, and thereafter sought animal aid in the chores and hazards of everyday life. Establishing relationships was always described as "making friends" with a bird or animal. Both men and women would do vision quests by spending several days in solitude, under the direction of a medicine man, asking the Great Power to take pity on them and grant them additional knowledge and powers. As a rule, these powers were vested in the creatures that might agree to be friends and share with humans. During this time of fasting and petitioning, a bird, land or water animal or even insect might come, converse with a person or guide them on a journey to another world, and, in the end, agree to become their friend. The animal was always regarded as a representative of the Great Mystery who had answered their petition.

Among the tasks and favors that the animals performed are included the knowledge of healing herbs that human could use to cure illnesses, locating sources of food, warning humans of future events, and giving them powers to deflect or avoid dangers. It was essential, therefore, that individuals have as many animal friends as possible, since each animal had its own unique powers to share with them. Great honors had to be shown to these animals, and songs were composed to express human thanks for favors bestowed.

The birds and animals also gave the people songs that could be used to call the animal for assistance. Some restrictions were placed on humans when entering into a relationship with another creature. Animals and birds were always to be treated with respect and often could not be hunted without first gaining their permission.

Living in this manner, in a world which believed that everything not only had life but also a fully developed emotional life, is foreign to most Western peoples. Most Westerners would probably scoff at the idea of receiving assistance from another creature. It is perhaps best, then, to discuss the kinds of animal behaviors observed by the Sioux which led them to conclude that animals were at least our equals and in many respects our superiors.

First and foremost in the Sioux mind was the idea that other creatures were "peoples" like us. Again, while this notion is largely viewed in the West as fantastic and anthropomorphic, we must nonetheless confront a historical fact. The Sioux lived wholly in the natural world their entire lives. They had infinitely more opportunity to observe animals than do modern people—and that includes scientists. Thus their accounts of animal behavior should be given credence. We have no basis for believing that animals in a natural state do *not* demonstrate the aspects of personality and thought that we see in ourselves. Indeed, science is "discovering" what the Sioux knew all along: animals and humans share much in common. The Sioux watched animals closely so that people could predict their behavior. In this way, they were natural historians *par excellence*.

It is important to understand how the Sioux came to conclude that animals and birds were worthy of our friendship. Let us examine some unusual but typical reports by various Sioux people of demonstrations by animals that convinced the Sioux that these creatures had the same personality traits and potential as humans. We will also see that there is indeed overlap with some of the possibilities raised by Jung's writings as we have applied them to animals. On the one hand, if I read Jung's argument correctly that the animal is pious because it plays to type, then Jungian animals could be expected to behave in easily predictable ways. On the other hand, the ideas of "peoplehood" and consciousness suggest the possibility of less predictable characteristics usually associated only with humans: abstract thought, willpower, vanity (showing the presence of an ego or Self), play, and the need for companionship.

The Sioux had too many unusual experiences with animals not to place them in this latter category. The early twentieth-century Sioux author

Charles Eastman recounts an experience of his uncle's which would suggest that animals are far more intelligent than Jung might have suspected. East-man's uncle had been hunting, killed two deer, and hung the meat in a tree to keep it away from wolves. He told this story:

> Having cooked and eaten some of the venison, I rolled myself in my blanket and lay down by the fire ... I had scarcely settled myself when I heard what seemed to be ten or twelve coyotes set up such a howling that I was quite sure of a visit from them ... I watched until a coyote appeared upon a flat rock fifty yards away. He sniffed the air in every direction; then, sitting partly upon his haunches, swung round in a circle with his hind legs sawing the air, and howled and barked in many different keys. It was a great feat! I could not help wondering whether I should be able to imitate him. What had seemed to be the voices of many coyotes was in reality only one animal.[3]

Surely we have a unique and complex thought process displayed in this coyote's actions. What kind of instinctual/archetypal behavior could this incident possibly illustrate? Here the coyote is alone; he is hungry and knows where food is, and he knows immediately that the human is alone. He acknowledges that the human has the upper hand and has made it difficult for him to go after the meat.

The coyote must make a rapid selection from a variety of possible responses and choose a course of action that will enable him to get the meat. His solution is so unique that in our understanding only a very clever human could have conceived it. He pretends to be a pack of coyotes. His bluff fails and he goes away, but he has demonstrated a strategic thought process second to none. If we analyze the situation precisely, the coyote has estimated the possible response of the human when confronted by the possibility that he will be overrun by a pack of coyotes, lose his meat, and possibly be killed himself. The coyote gambles that he can frighten the man away. There is a recognizable coyote "type" of behavior in hunting that the uncle could expect and so the possible presence of a pack of animals should have solved the problem. In stepping outside type, the coyote has changed the situation in his favor. When individual animals add their own distinctive personal touch to a situation, they demonstrate a thought process comparable to our own. As the Indians observed them, animals had the same spectrum of personality as humans and often displayed variant behavior that sometimes fooled the humans completely. Therefore a smart animal was often equal to any kind of human cunning, and had to be approached as if it were another human being.

Some may discount these kinds of stories as the superstitions of a primitive mind or a story made up to teach children the value of cleverness. But it is only the assumption of superiority that allows Western readers to doubt such an account. The chances to observe this kind of behavior are few and far between. One would have to be living in the woods and prairies, hunting almost continuously, to have a chance to witness a coyote working through such a problem. The story certainly has little "scientific" value since it describes an incident that a new and "objective" observer cannot repeat. Not even a Sioux could repeat such an experience at will. Yet the knowledge of Sioux people—and of Westerners too—who live day in and day out in nature are filled with such experiences and stories.

Let us now examine an instance where an animal demonstrates willpower. Luther Standing Bear recounted an experience he had with the black-tailed deer. The traditional knowledge of the Sioux suggests that this animal could not be killed unless it was willing to die. It had the power to deflect arrows and bullets and turn the hunter's task into one of puzzling frustration. Several other tribes have this same belief, and some tribes feel that the animal has prophetic powers. These beliefs come from hundreds of years of hunting it.

"Many times I heard this story," Standing Bear said.

Then one day I had an amazing experience with this animal that puzzled me as it had other hunters. A friend and myself were hunting on horseback. The wind being right, we came close upon a black-tailed deer before it saw us. I quickly dismounted to shoot while my companion held the reins of my horse. The deer did not run, but stood looking at me, wagging its tail steadily back and forth. With every assurance of getting my game I fired. To my astonishment the deer stood still and looked intently at me. I was a good marksman, the animal was only a short distance from me, and fully exposed, yet my shot had gone astray. Seven times I shot at this animal, missing every time, the deer never moving. The seventh bullet was my last and I could shoot no more. My ammunition was gone, and there the deer and I stood looking at each other. So close were we that I could see its lips twitching. It pawed the earth once or twice with its front hoof, then clashed away. My friend accused me of being nervous, but I am not a nervous person. When I reached home, I got some more ammunition and tried out my gun. It was in perfect working order.[4]

Now what can we, or should we, make of this story? It was Standing Bear's spur-of-the-moment intention to test the teachings of his elders and disprove their belief in the animal's power to protect itself. That test failed. We could say that his experience with the deer was a psychological projection from the unconscious that seized Standing Bear and made it impossible for him to hit the deer. But we were not with him and his companion. Hypothesizing Standing Bear's psychological state is merely an attempt to explain the incident *away*, not to try to explain it.

It is neither satisfactory nor logical to discard the incident because it does not fall into the familiar cause-and-effect explanation that we would ordinarily use to interpret our data. We might be better served by concluding, as the Sioux did, that this animal has power to avoid being killed unless it consents. Invoking that power had to have been an exercise of will by the deer, since the instinctive thing for an animal to do would be to freeze, giving the hunter one easy shot before his intentions were known, or to flee him hoping to escape the range of his weapon. Instead of these natural options, the deer moves closer to Standing Bear, in effect daring him to shoot. Standing Bear also commented that "the prairie dog and the prairie chicken both have the power to keep a hunter from hitting them,"[5] suggesting that several animals had developed a powerful willpower that enabled them to deal with humans.

Goose, a Sioux medicine man, reported a similar incident to Frances Densmore, recorded in her *Teton Sioux Music*:

One morning I arose before daybreak to go on a hunting trip. As I went around a butte I saw an antelope, which came toward me and stood still a short distance away from me. The antelope looked at me and then began to graze. I took my rifle and fired several shots with no effect. I fired sixteen cartridges and wondered what could be the matter. I put in four more cartridges and fired again, but with no effect whatever. Then the animal stopped grazing and began to move slowly away. Then I heard a voice speaking three times, then a fourth time, and the voice said it was going to sing something and I must listen.

Goose received an herb and a sacred stone and the song. After telling Densmore the story, he remarked, "I do not consider that I dreamed this as one dreams in sleep, it appeared to me when I was early on the chase."[6] Although this experience was a prelude to a religious revelation, with the spirits communicating to Goose through the behavior of the antelope, there is also the practical side of the story involving the functioning of the gun.

In examining other psychological characteristics of animals within the Sioux understanding of the world, we find further evidence of the similarity between humans and other forms of life. The bear, for example, was regarded as a vain creature prone to adorn himself in finery like some middle class humans. The bear, according to Standing Bear,

> likes to beautify himself by painting his face with earth mixed with water. He finds a clear pool, in which he can plainly see himself, then takes some earth in his paw and mixes it with water until he has a paste. This he spreads on the left side of his face, never on the right side. Then he looks at himself in his mirror of water. If not satisfied with his first attempt at beautifying, he repeats his work until he has the side of his face fixed up, as he should have it.[7]

This kind of behavior surely helped convince the Sioux that animals were people like themselves. They may even have gotten the idea of painting their faces from the bear.

We also find examples of games, levity and play among the animals.

> We admired the beaver, for he is very industrious. Just the same he likes to play. They like to splash water over each other with their tails. Then they build slides of earth and mud, and carry water up to them with their tails until the slope is smooth and shiny. When the game is going big, even the old ones join the young ones, and everybody has a good time.[8]

And for recreation and vanity, Standing Bear pointed out that buffalo

> loved the simple and odorless sunflower just as did the Lakota. These great beasts wandered through the sunflower fields, wallowing their heads among them. Sometimes they uprooted the plants and wound them about their necks, letting sprays dangle from their left horns.[9]

It would be difficult for people living with these animals and observing them daily, not to conclude that they had the same mental and emotional constitution as we do—animals were a "people" in almost every sense. On the other hand, it is not surprising that a Swiss psychologist having no first-hand knowledge of animals in a natural state and having lived a life very much apart from nature relative to the Sioux, might insist that animals were inferior to humans as a matter of course and incapable of displaying this kind of behavior.

Sioux stories provide us with even more examples of the close relationship between animals and people. It is well known that in a catastrophe such as an earthquake, other creatures panic and seek the companionship of humans. And on rare ordinary occasions, even wild animals will seek to be with us. This trait might better explain domestication of animals than our current scenarios. Two Shields, a Sioux elder from Standing Rock, related a tradition of the first time the people had a relationship with the wolf:

> Many years ago a war party was in their camp when they heard what they believed to be the song of a young man approaching them. They could hear the words of the song and supposed the singer was one of their party, but as he came nearer they saw that he was an old wolf, so old that he had no teeth, and there was no brush on his tail. He could scarcely move, and he lay down beside their fire. They cut up the best buffalo meat and fed him. Afterward they learned his song, which was the beginning of all wolf songs (war songs).[10]

So even wild animals sometimes seek human companionship and, notably, humans show something other than domination toward animals; here they show empathy to their animal neighbors.

Charles Eastman gives an example of how animal virtues were identified and evaluated when he describes how his grandmother posed questions for the small boys in the family to answer. I include it here because it illustrates how precisely the Sioux observed and knew animals and birds, and how they sought to find virtues that humans shared with other creatures. Eastman repeats the whole conversation, which is too long to reproduce intact here, but I have abstracted the essence of the discussion. The grandmother asked two boys: "What bird shows most judgment in caring for its young?" Chatanna, Eastman's cousin, and Eastman gave their answers:

Chatanna: The eagle is the wisest of all birds. Its nest is made in the safest possible place, upon a high and inaccessible cliff. It provides its young with an abundance of fresh meat. They have the freshest of air. They are brought up under the spell of the grandest scenes, and inspired with lofty feelings and bravery. They see that all other beings live beneath them and that they are the children of the King of Birds. A young eagle shows the spirit of the warrior while still in the nest.

Eastman: My grandmother, who was it [who] said that a mother who has a gentle and sweet voice will have children of a good disposition? I think the oriole is that kind of parent. It provides both sunshine and shadow for its young. Its nest is suspended from the prettiest bough of the most graceful tree, where it is rocked by the gentle winds; and the one we found yesterday was beautifully lined with soft things, both deep and warm, so that the little featherless birdies cannot suffer from the cold and wet. [11]

The grandmother decided in favor of Eastman because Chatanna had mistakenly identified the teaching of a warlike spirit with actual care of the young birds. In the extended conversation each boy recited many other bits of evidence to support his position. Of importance here is the precision that the boys achieved in identifying the personal characteristics of each bird. The oldest traditions say that humans learned politeness and courtesy from the animals. Jung, on the other hand, might simply find in the boy's lesson a projection of human values on the birds, and that would be an adequate response. Generations of elders had already observed the behavior of birds, however, and had decided that emulating them was the proper way for humans to act.

It is interesting to recount some of the things that the Sioux learned from these observations that proved useful in the functions of everyday life. Standing Bear observed, for instance:

The calls of the sand or prairie cranes were announcers of the always important weather changes; a croaking frog proclaimed a tiny marsh or a hidden spring. … Even the black, horned ground-beetle commonly called tumblebug, once common on the plains, the scout stopped and attentively watched, providing the scout [was] looking for buffalo. The two horns on the top of the insect's head were movable in all directions, but were invariably pointed and held toward the buffalo herd, probably attracted in that direction by stamping hoofs too distant for even sensitive human ears to detect.[12]

And more:

When the swallows, which were called *icapsinpsincela* on account of their swift and bold darting here and there, came in flocks flying audaciously about, we knew a shower was coming our way. While it rained we saw no swallows, but as soon as it had gone, again would come the swallows more hilarious than ever.[13]

Some observations were remembered even though there was no good explanation for the given observed behavior of the animals. Living on the high plains, the Sioux needed to know where grass and water might be found in sufficient quantities so they could make their camp in the most suitable location. Over a long period of time they discovered that two animals were always connected with water, the turtle and the beaver.

Sometimes we discovered that a beaver colony had moved to another creek, but we never saw a beaver on land, nor did we ever catch a colony of these animals on the march moving their town site.[14]

Since the Sioux occupied areas where beaver thrived for thousands of years, this observation is important because it hints at special knowledge by the beaver of the land and its possibilities. Neither a beaver nor a turtle colony could move haphazardly because out of the water they would be virtually helpless to escape a predator. They must have done considerable planning to make the right nocturnal moves. Again we can imply a sophisticated animal intelligence and an appreciation of such by the Sioux.

The same can be said, with even more emphasis, about the turtle.

The Sioux name for the turtle is "water-carrier," because when a turtle left a pond or stream, that body of water became dry as if they took the water with them. Great numbers of these water-loving animals moved over the land in changing their places of living, yet like the beaver we never saw them on the march.[15]

This observation, if true (and we certainly have no good reason to doubt Standing Bear), does pose a problem. How *did* the turtles move from place to place? Why were the people unable to detect their migrations? What kind of planning must the turtles have made when moving from one water source to another so that their temporary vulnerability to predators did not result in their extermination? If medicine men had the powers of the beaver and turtle and knew the answers to these questions, they kept their understanding a secret.

According to the Sioux, some animals helped humans with the healing of physical illnesses by teaching them healing songs or identifying useful plants for a particular ailment. Prior to the relationship between humans and the other creatures, perhaps even before man made his appearance on earth, animals helped each other. William K. Powers noted:

> Certain animals and birds are believed to be companions. For example, the Yuwipi man George Plenty Wolf was instructed in his visions that the swallow was the companion of the black-tailed deer, the magpie of the buffalo, the crow of the whitetail deer, and the meadowlark of the elk. In this case, the bird nations are regarded as the *akicita*, "soldiers," of the advance guard of the animal nations they accompany. [16]

Once a person knew these animal relationships, if a bird or animal was seen, people would look for his companions. If, however, a bird or animal appeared alone, that might be a sign that something was askew. It could also mean that the companion was acting on behalf of both animals. In ceremonies, birds and animals could substitute for each other and in visions they could transform themselves into each other when the occasion warranted. If we analyze the long vision sequences, we often find several changes from bird to animal to human and back again. People cherished these changes because they gave the vision questing individual an insight into the larger cosmic world of the seen and unseen.

Living completely within the natural landscape and faced with the necessity of feeding themselves and warding off enemies, the Sioux had to be alert and always seeking allies to ensure their survival. If animals could provide the information they needed, then it was important to have a good relationship with the animal. It must have taken thousands of years to begin to accumulate the proper knowledge so that serious approaches could be made to the animals. The secret, of course, was to regard dreams as having an equal status to that of the waking observations and to act on the basis that dreams were an important source of reliable information. A good bit of the animal relationship, then, originated in dreams in which the human was expected to obey the messages they received. The men and women who had received special consideration from the birds and animals were called "dreamers," which meant that they could call upon these animals for assistance.

The healing powers received from animals might properly be discussed as religious beliefs ungrounded in ethological knowledge except that healing powers in cooperation with animals were so common in Sioux practice as to be understood on their own terms. The importance of dreams is a premise common to many schools of Western psychology, and this is perhaps most true in Jungian psychology. For Jung, the "real" and the "dream" animals are almost always kept separate from each other. As we have seen, however, there are elements in a Jungian approach to animals that are similar to Sioux beliefs. Recall that, in his Visions Seminars, Jung introduces the "motif of the helpful animal intervening when everything is impossible and people expect a catastrophe—help out of a tight corner."[17] Helpful animals do appear at times in patients' dreams, sometimes at a crucial point in therapy, and they can act as a motivating force in resolving problems. Indeed, Jung suggests that "instinct appears in myths and in dreams as the motif of the helpful animal, the guardian spirits, the good angel, the helper in need, the saint, saviour, etc."[18] But within the Jungian framework, which generally precluded a material linkage between dream events and events in the physical world, animals were generally restricted in their definition as "lower instinctive forces."

To grasp the substantial difference between worldviews on this question, imagine a debate between a Western psychologist and a medicine man over the question whether or not the animals had special powers. The psychologist might well insist that the Sioux belief was simple primitive superstition; Jung himself would do better, but would, in the end, probably suggest that these animals were only projections of the psyche of the Indian observers. In response, the medicine man might demand that the psychologist provide observational proof that, say, beavers and turtles moved overland either singly or as a group in some uncomplicated fashion to find their new sources of water. More intense observation might eventually provide evidence that these creatures actually did migrate from water to water, but this question would have to be resolved by empirical evidence, not doctrinal arguments.

The intimacy between human and animal in Sioux life is illustrated in other ways. The Sioux felt that the animals actually *chose* the people they wanted as human companions. Luther Standing Bear, for example, observed:

> While in the spirit condition the dreamer was in contact with the spirits of all things of the world, though in the case of the Bear Dreamer only the bears spoke to him and gave him bear powers. The bears told him to recognize all things of nature and to observe and learn from them. *The animals would thereafter observe and learn from the dreamer, and he should do likewise.*[19] [emphasis added]

The animals—as active subjects—thus gain knowledge of the human as he accommodates himself to their overture.

The bear was the most prominent of the animal healers because he knew a great deal about the roots and berries that could be used for food and for medicinal purposes. "We have in the Sioux tribe what we call 'Bear Dreamers'," Standing Bear recalled. "They are the medicine men who, during their fast, have had a vision in which the bear has come to them and revealed a useful herb or article with which to cure the sick." It should be noted that this herb is not symbolic. It is a real herb that can be located in the vicinity, and does not represent psychological growth or expansion of consciousness as it might for Jungians.

> Whenever the bear dreamer is called to attend to a sick member of the tribe, he uses whatever the bear brought to him in a vision. For instance, if the bear told the medicine man that a certain herb would be good to give to the sick person, the medicine man would get some of this herb and use it in his ritual over the patient.[20]

Here the animal plays the critical role in diagnosing and healing in cases of human infirmity by making himself available to the medicine man during a scheduled ceremony rather than appearing symbolically in a nighttime dream state.

How, exactly, did these relationships with animals come about? According to Standing Bear,

> If a man could prove to some bird or animal that he was a worthy friend, it would share with him precious secrets and there would be formed

bonds of loyalty never to be broken; the man would protect the rights and life of the animal, and the animal would share with man his power, skill, and wisdom.[21]

Certainly these deliberate bonds of friendship could be forged by careful behavior of the human, but perhaps as often, information would be revealed in a nighttime dream. If the information came in a dream, the person having the dream would be obligated thereafter to demonstrate the special powers he had received and maintain the relationship with the bird or animal.

It is important to note that the other creature most often initiated the friendship, and to grasp that these relationships were reciprocal. It would, therefore, be difficult to fit them into a Jungian context in which there is not a mutual exchange of knowledge but merely symbolic relationships and the assumption of human superiority and animal inferiority. Jung would describe the event of a dream or real animal approach as a result of deep archetypal behavior and as a projection on the part of the human being. But since these relationships exist over long periods of time, it is difficult to imagine how a psychic projection could maintain its potency beyond the immediate psychological crisis of the individual.

An example of this animal initiative, from Standing Bear again, is instructive:

> Long ago the wolf came to the medicine man and told him how to use the tobacco plant. The wolf digs into the earth and is wise about the things that grow up from the soil, so he told the medicine man that if tobacco plant was burned in the tipi, it would keep away disease and purify the air. The women threw leaves over the coals. As the smoke arose, they covered their heads with their blankets and bent over the coals so they could breathe in the smoke.[22]

Of importance here, and what I believe takes this kind of experience outside a strictly psychological interpretation, is the practical use of the plant by people following the acquisition of the information. It was not simply having dreams in which animals appeared and talked with people; it was the fact that what they told people had immediate practical medicinal value.

The Duck Dreamer examples given by Standing Bear indicate that transmitting data from animal to human was not restricted to medicinal herbs.

The duck, who brought many good plants and roots to the tribe, told the Duck Dreamer medicine man about it and named it *psa*. In the early spring and summer we welcomed this plant, which was pulled up by the roots, and the white part eaten like celery.[23]

In this instance a nourishing food, apparently having no medicinal healing value, was brought to the tribe. Standing Bear said he was

once in a tipi where the medicine-man was giving a patient treatment. The medicine-man happened to be a Duck Dreamer, so, of course, the duck was helping him to find a cure for the sick man. The medicine-man asked me to bring him some water, so I brought him a vessel holding two quarts or more. He drank every drop and then quacked in perfect imitation of a duck. In a moment or so he called for more water and that he drank, too.[24]

Here, water became a healing entity even though it was not used directly on the patient and the prodigious consumption of the water gave evidence of the power of the duck.

The relationship between people and birds and animals could well be based on their common archetypal heritage. However, the nurturing of the friendship through direct communication between the two relatives was the responsibility of the human being. The Sioux received new information about the physical world from other creatures in dreams and visions and also through direct vocal communication. As experienced by Standing Bear,

the prairie chicken, the meadowlark, and the crow are birds that make sounds that can be interpreted into Sioux words. We Sioux knew, of course, that birds and animals had a way of talking to one another just as we did. We knew, too, that the animals and birds came and talked to our medicine men. Our legends tell of a time when bird and animal life communicated with man.[25]

It is well known among Dakota people that in the 1880s, when some of the Sioux people left the reservation to seek work elsewhere, they returned, complaining that the birds in the far west did not speak Lakota.

One rather mysterious explanation by Paul Radin of why humans and animals can communicate speaks of a very remote time in planetary history:

According to Winnebago thinkers no beings had any permanent form originally. They were all a kind of *tertium quid,* neutral beings that could at will transform themselves into human beings or spirit-animals. At one particular period in the history of the world they decided to use all their unlimited power of transformation to change themselves definitely either into animals or human beings. Since then, animals have remained animals and human beings, human beings, except for those few human beings who still possess the power of transforming themselves, for short periods of time, into animals.[26]

I cite this explanation because some people in the Sioux tribe seriously believe it, and many other tribes have similar stories. If the world is merely an idea, as we see argued often in quantum physics and the near-death experience literature, then the Winnebago memory may recall a time when the physical world was being created and the spirits were finding their own way in the developing cosmos.

Of course, many of us shudder when we think of some of our companions who do talk with inanimate objects or invisible friends. Yet even here, I think that psychologists' scholarly prejudices have often overcome their common sense and analytical skills. The point is not whether people talk to animals and plants, but *the validity of the messages that are given and received.* In other words, people picking up gibberish should be given therapy. When a person is told, however, that a certain plant, used in a particular way, is excellent for curing boils, stopping bleeding, or reducing fevers—and the cure works—that is another matter altogether. By making empirical verification a standard test of the information, it should not be difficult to separate fantasy from a real unique experience.[27]

Jung believed that animals, or at least the relationships that he could find between them and civilized educated people, were projections from deep in the psyche that suggested primeval psyche-forming times during which personalities were being created. In his case they might well have been such. Perhaps more than most Westerners, Jung had truly begun to glimpse and understand the deep connections between humans and animals with which the Sioux were so familiar. Unfortunately, Jung assumed a kind of expertise in tribal/primitive cultures, like that of the Sioux, which were grounded in the landscape and intimately familiar with bird and animal behavior over thousands of years, and then proposed that those intimate knowledges represented little more than raw energy in the psyche. Clearly they represent something more. Today, there are dozens of books comparing animal behavior with that of humans. Now that many species are tragically gone or facing extinction, the Western mind is gradually coming around to an appreciation of other forms of life, recognizing that these creatures may well teach us something significant about time, space, psyche, and a cosmology based upon relations with other beings in the universe.

CHAPTER EIGHT

THE INDIVIDUAL
AND KINSHIP

The mysteries of the universe—Sioux, Jungian, or otherwise—are experienced and understood through the daily practices of social life. In previous chapters we have looked in some detail at the non-human world, and we will consider the practice of spirituality in subsequent chapters. Here, I want to embark upon an important path of social inquiry by looking at the family, which is the earliest and perhaps most important formative influence on individuals. Carl Jung seemed to see the family as part of an ongoing organic process, one containing temporal dimensions that other psychologies did not take fully into account. "A human life is nothing in itself," he said.

> It is part of a family tree. We are continuously living the ancestral life, reaching back for centuries, we are satisfying the appetites of unknown ancestors, nursing instincts which we think are our own, but which are quite incompatible with our character; we are not living our own lives; we are paying the debts of our forefathers.[1]

If the psychology of the parents affected the infant, it was largely because the parents themselves were subject to influences that had been accumulating for many generations. When it came to the individual, Jung considered the person as but a brief episode in a much larger family spanning generations and perhaps centuries:

> We ought rather to say that it is not so much the parents as their ancestors—the grandparents and great-grandparents—who are the true progenitors, and that these explain the individuality of the children far more than the immediate, and, so to speak, accidental parents.[2]

The raw material of the infant psyche, then, was only secondarily derived from the parents:

The true psychic individuality of the child is something new in respect of the parents and cannot be derived from their psyche. It is a combination of collective factors which are only potentially present in the parental psyche and are sometimes wholly invisible. Not only the child's body, but his soul, too, proceeds from his ancestry, in so far as it is individually distinct from the collective psyche of mankind.[3]

The psychological conflict of early childhood must therefore reflect an adjustment to the immediate environment of the psychic factors inherited from previous generations. The attitudes received from the parents are patterns of behavior that have been made conscious by the parents and create friction because they are similar to what the child has inherited from long ago.

Rather than a negative value, Jung sometimes saw this limitation as a positive thing: "It is possible that one sets out to live the ancestral life right in the beginning, as most people do who develop in a reasonable and positive way; they grow out of several ancestral lives into all-around individuals."[4] If the ancestors play such a critical role, and all the elements they contribute are inherent in the personal unconscious when the person is born, then the individual in fact provides only a new perspective for a point of view already embraced by previous generations. "Normal" people are then those individuals who allow the inherited ancestral propensities to develop and who are not handicapped by early traumas created by the living family.

We may simply absorb everything around us and in that sense are pre-determined by the family. Rural people, for example, can live for generations in a small social environment and repeat almost exactly the patterns of living practiced by their ancestors. Indeed, it is necessary to do so in order to survive. In fact, rural people having a limited geographical environment might well regard as different, impractical and foolish those individuals who reject the life of their ancestors. While there may be a degree of pre-determination in Jung's assessment that Western people would not welcome, few thinkers have suggested a more realistic basis upon which human personality might be built. Are we little blank minds that develop simply by taking in data and interpreting it in self-centered ways to create our mentality and personality? Or do we in large measure absorb the influences around us when we make choices of the data that we will consider valuable to us?

We have expectations that our children will resemble us physically and follow our beliefs and values rather closely. One cannot look at a child without seeking some assurance that he or she looks like the parents, Uncle Mike or Aunt Blanche or even great grandpa Max. Given this propensity to seek physical similarities, we should be prepared to affirm the possibility of psychic inheritance also. And we do in fact find ourselves looking for character traits across generations. As children's personality traits develop, we can often see close similarities with the personalities of various relatives in their actions and beliefs. We are recognizing the existence of psychic heredity even if we cannot prove it in terms that are rigorously scientific.

Fulfilling the expectations of ancestral influences is not as easy as it first appears. Looking at the individual, Jung saw that the personality was made up of many inherited constituents that did not always fit together. Taking into account all the possible ancestors from which individual traits could be drawn, we would expect considerable *conflict* inherent in the new personality. There must be "dominant" inherited characteristics that create their own hierarchy within the newborn individual. There must also be a sorting and choosing of the psychological inheritance. Jung warned that these constituents

> may be irregular, perhaps, on account of some inner friction, but through the development of life, in the course of years, these constituents ought to function in such a way that there will be in the end a complete synthesis, the integration of human personality.[5]

This synthetic ideal limits the possible paths on which individuals could proceed in life. It removes the arbitrary aspect of personality development and provides for the orderly growth of the conscious part of the psyche. Jung is correct here. We often identify personal characteristics of individuals with past members of their families whom we have known personally. We see similar psychological traits continually manifested in families generation after generation so that once data about the ancestors is known, our knowledge of people can take on a predictive nature.

Jung was encouraged in this belief of psychic heredity by his own experiences. In his autobiography, *Memories, Dreams, Reflections*, he recounted the many instances in which he believed he was not living his own life but rather fulfilling unfinished tasks that his ancestors had undertaken:

> It has always seemed to me that I had to answer questions which fate had posed to my forefathers, and which had not been answered, or as if I had to complete, or perhaps continue, things which previous ages had left unfinished.[6]

And he reflected: "I feel very strongly that I am under the influence of things or questions which were left incomplete and unanswered by my parents and grandparents and more distant ancestors."[7]

If the family fits so easily into a cosmic pattern and enables us to conceive of the process for smoothly developing the mature individual, wherein does the psychological problem of our species lie? Why do we so often see trauma, when we might see instead adjustment and harmonious development? One answer might be the tremendous rate of change that civilized societies have imposed upon themselves. When conditions change quickly for living persons, the mass of inherited ancestral constituents requires time to absorb and adjust to the new situation. We find ourselves not simply being conservative; we develop phobias and complexes as we try to adjust consciously to the new situation.

When the discussion moves from Jung's personal feelings about his ancestral family to the often-theoretical nuclear family of psychological doctrine, the cosmic warmth he shows towards his progenitors begins to fade. "Man needs a wider community than the family," Jung advised in discussing psychology and education, adding that the family had complications that would stunt moral and spiritual growth.

> If he is burdened with too much family, if, in later life, his tie to the parents is too strong, he will simply transfer the parental tie to the family he himself has raised ... thus creating for his own progeny the same suffocating psychic atmosphere from which he suffered in his youth.[8]

Jung thus poses critical questions: How do we determine when we have too much family, or when the ties are too strong to break, or even whether the wider community is an adequate substitute for the family?

We must, according to Jung, avoid the stifling atmosphere that may be thrust upon the next generation by the parents, or inherited from their ancestors by the children and foisted upon the unsuspecting brood. Jung suggests that

> all the libido that was tied up in family bonds must be withdrawn from the narrower circle into the larger one, because the psychic health of the adult individual, who in childhood was a mere particle revolving in a rotary system, demands that he should himself become the centre of a new system.[9]

Presumably individuals, forming new families, would be able to distribute energy between the ancestral family and the new families they are creating. The "larger circle"—a gesture to the social relations outside the family—would seem to be critical in assisting this redistribution.

The necessity to redistribute libido or psychic energy poses a major problem for the family. Adjusting the demands of the individuals constituting the family, and allowing for the growth of the individual and of the various family relationships, would seem to be the goal of the normal family in its psychological development. In the West, the effort to extend the distribution of psychic energy beyond the family has resulted in the creation of a number of formal social institutions. Most familiar to us is the school, where children can learn to adjust to a larger world of people and establish new loyalties and friendships that in some respects are competitive with family relationships. In the West, we have addressed this issue of competition by attaching adults to many of the institutions that transcend the family and act as its substitute. We then vest a significant portion of our psychic energy in the institutions and their non-family adults, with a decreasing amount of energy invested in the family. One might argue that it is these particular forms of distribution of psychic energy that drive people in civilized society to the point of abandoning or mistreating families, and that may help to produce psychologically unstable individuals. Institutions, over a long period of time, cannot handle psychic energy in a positive manner.

What to do? Not surprisingly, Jung returns to "the primitive" as most able to deal with the transfer or the investment of psychic energy. "Psychic development cannot be accomplished by intention and will alone," he wrote in "The Structure and Dynamics of the Psyche," suggesting that we require intelligible symbols and an expressive process to transfer psychic energy:

> If man lived altogether instinctively and automatically, the transformation [of psychic energy] could come about in accordance with purely biological laws. We can still see something of the sort in the psychic life of primitives, which is entirely concretistic and entirely symbolical at once. ... In civilized man the rationalism of consciousness, otherwise so useful to him, proves to be a most formidable obstacle to the frictionless transformation of energy. [10]

For Western man, then, even as reason defines the institutions that channel the psychic energy of the family, it also severs the intimate connection between symbols and their concrete expression, equally critical to psychic development.

If ancestral fragments influence the family and the personalities of the children are formed more by grandparents, and if the collective unconscious has an ancestor relationship to the conscious personality, then the family might best be seen to be organized around the concept of several generations instead of a two-generation nuclear family. Let us see how the family is arranged when this insight occupies the center instead of the periphery of our concerns. Sioux society offers an excellent example of this multi-generational family concept, for a Sioux child was born into a complex system comprised of personal parents, a kinship family, the extended community, a cultural collective, and the living presence of ancestors, all psychically present in powerful ways.

By all accounts, Sioux people believed that life began when the mother recognized conception. Childcare actually began with this recognition, so that there was no sharp transition from married couple to family. Between conception, birth, and the moment when the child had attained two years of age, special activities had to be undertaken to ensure that the child received a proper beginning in life. If there was life in the mother, then it had to be respected and included in the daily activities of the mother. Early twentieth-century Dakota writer Charles Eastman described the practice of the traditional Sioux mother upon learning that she was with child:

> From the moment of her recognition of the fact of conception to the end of the second year of life, which was the ordinary period of lactation, it was supposed by us that the mother's spiritual influence counted for most. Her attitude and secret meditations must be such as to instill into the receptive soul of the unborn child the love of the "Great Mystery" and a sense of brotherhood with all creation. Silence and isolation are the rule of life for the expectant mother. She wanders prayerful in the stillness of great woods, or on the bosom of the untrodden prairie, and to her poetic mind the immanent birth of her child prefigures the advent of a master-man—a hero, or the mother of heroes—a thought conceived in the virgin breast of primeval nature, and dreamed out in a hush that is only broken by the signing of the pine tree or the thrilling orchestra of a distant waterfall.[11]

This description of the behavior of the expectant mother during pregnancy is, of course, overly romanticized by Eastman and represents the ideal traditional way of his people, translated for a turn-of-the-century audience fascinated by Indian primitivism. But the custom was generally practiced and was the goal toward which good women strived. In more abstract terms there was a belief among the Sioux that mothers could, by serious meditation, begin forming the personality of the child before it was born. By thinking, prior to the birth of the child, of the qualities and talents that the new child would need to become a contributing member of Sioux society, the mother sought to lay the groundwork for a healthy personality.

Had Jung known of its existence, he might well have endorsed this Sioux practice of preparing the baby for birth into the family. Indeed, he arrived at a similar idea in *The Development of Personality*:

> Just as the child in embryo is practically nothing, but a part of the mother's body, and wholly dependent on her, so in early infancy the psyche is to a large extent part of the maternal psyche, and will soon become part of the paternal psyche as well. [12]

If he had recognized the influence of the mother after the child was born, would he not have admitted the possibility that the mother's psyche was critical in initiating the child's personality prior to birth? Since there is strong and intimate communication between the mother and the embryonic child, the development of a positive personality begins prior to any face-to-face contact.

These Sioux practices affected the manner in which the mother responded to the living child once born, and the goal in this instance was to prepare a loving welcome for it. The environment of the unborn child was not restricted to the family. Meditating and daydreaming about the child in a natural setting, absorbing the sounds and smells of the natural world meant that, in a peculiar way, the natural world was also understood as a relative, as part of the family, and as something to which the family naturally belonged.

A mother-to-be might indeed call upon various helpful and familiar birds and animals to see that she was carrying a child and that, at some future date, she hoped these animals would take pity on her child and assist him or her. If the bird or animal was previously known to assist living family members in some way, more emphasis was placed on attracting that particular creature to help maintain the existing continuity that family had with the non-human forms of life. This practice was continued for two years after the birth of the child so that there was continuity between what the expectant mother desired and the first years of development of the baby.

Unfortunately these practices have all but disappeared today, since the Sioux have been forced to adopt the customs of non-Indian society. Only among very traditional families today might one find behavior that resembles this manner of placing pregnancy within the scope of tribal society so that it was not merely an individual affair. When we compare Jungian psychology with the old ways of the people, we seek to understand principles of psychology that each might affirm. Many of these principles transcend issues of family and individual to take on larger social import. Indian women, for example, yearned for a more peaceful life since the burden of sorrow always fell hardest on them. After the sacred pipe had established a means of making peace with one's enemies, according to Luther Standing Bear,

> women had begun the necessary foundational work for the elimination of war by raising sons who could participate only in pursuits of peace. War was excluded from the existence of a certain portion of the male population and in this move the Indian mother pointed the way and the only road to the realization of peace between all men. The acceptance of a kinship with other orders of life was the first step toward humanization and the second step was the dedication of sons to peace, the spiritual value of which is incalculable.[13]

The Sioux approach to the problem of the early orientation of the child to the world sought to take seriously their notion of what a family was. The first name given to a child after birth, for example, was often that of an ancestor whom the parents and grandparents wished the child to emulate. As the child grew up and people observed how its personality was developing, and on the basis of their knowledge of previous family members, a child's name might be changed to correspond to the newly identified emerging personality. When a child did not demonstrate familiar personality traits of the family, it might be named after a living person in the tribe who the family respected. This new name, given in honor of a friend, would serve to encourage the child to observe its namesake and bring honor to the name. As the child grew, it might receive several different names to commemorate his or her achievements. Over a lifetime a person would receive several names to indicate changes in psychological development or, as an adult, to note special deeds they had accomplished or talents they displayed.

In the kinship system of the Sioux, the family was not a small nuclear construct but extended outwards to include every person who was a relative by blood and by marriage law, thus linking families together in a complex set of relationships. A short discussion of these relationships is instructive because it offers a sense of the roles and responsibilities that membership in a family required, far in excess of the expectations that we have in today's world. No one was omitted from the family circle, and as people matured and married, an individual could find him- or herself with roles and responsibilities in several families. Everyone dreaded the possibility that they would one day find themselves without relatives, so every effort was made to follow the kinship duties towards others.

Briefly, an individual's possible family relationships of blood and marriage were: grandfather, grandmother, father, mother, brother, sister, aunt, uncle, cousin, nephew, niece, twin. Recognizing the existence of each of these relationships, the Sioux carefully defined how each relative should act toward every other relative. And they further subdivided the sets of responsibilities by gender to cover all possible situations in which the child might find itself. In early childhood training, everyone—the entire social group—worked together to acquaint the child with these roles.

Black Elk spoke of the time when this system was created. Its purpose was not simply to find ways of anticipating and resolving family problems or to make peripheral relatives feel wanted. Kinship, he made clear, was designed to reflect the cosmos and the larger unity of the people. "The old would guide the young," he explained,

> the young would give their strength to the old; and all together would give one strength to the nation, that it might be strong and live. The nation was itself a being with a grandfather, a grandmother, a father, and a mother. The Great Mysterious One is the grandfather, the Earth is the grandmother, the Sky is the father, and the mother is where the growing things come out of the ground and nurse with all that live.[14]

This system organizes the universe around the family structure and the family structure becomes consonant with the perceived universe and provides comfort and security for everyone in it.

The Sioux allocate different kinds of behavior to each relative so that they can understand their role in the family—there were different responsibilities for people on the father's side of the family from those of the mother's relatives, for example—and further differentiate responsibilities for the male and female actors within these roles. Finally, recognizing that people occupy a different social status as they age, the Sioux again distinguish roles and responsibilities according to age, thus giving distinct values to younger and older members of the tribe. The kinship network is so complex that only a few traditional Sioux today can recite properly and comprehensively the responsibilities each relative has toward all the others. Yet children quickly learned these customs by watching the behavior of older people toward each other. They also learned that as they grew older they had to adopt new ways of approaching and dealing with other family members. Ceremonies often marked the transition from one role to another.

The system functioned in specific ways. The discipline and teaching of the children were duties allocated to the brothers and sisters of the parents, generally the father's brothers having responsibility for the sons, the mother's sisters taking care of the daughters. By shifting the role of teacher/disciplinarian to aunts and uncles, the parents were freed to give love to the child in the best parental ways. Children were never puzzled about their relationships with their parents. Instead they were encouraged to act in such a manner that the parents would always be proud of them. It would be unthinkable for a parent to chastise a child; that would be the role of uncles and aunts.

The aunts and uncles teach the child about the family and everything appropriate for their gender. They also encourage the child to do things that will make the family proud of them. The child thus justifies itself and returns the love they receive by behaving properly. Standing Bear said,

> For an older person in the Lakota tribe to strike or punish a young person was an unthinkable brutality. Such an ugly thing as force with anger back of it was unknown to me, for it was never exhibited in my presence.[15]

Instead of punishment, as a rule, the possibility of bringing social shame on the family was sufficient to keep the children in line. Children behaved themselves because it was the proper thing to do as a family member, not because of their fear of punishment.

Children were taught that they had special duties toward each other. Often the older children functioned in the place of aunts and uncles when the adults were not present. But the custom extended beyond the family to the tribe as a whole. Standing Bear recalled,

There was a custom among the Lakota often followed by young men whereby an older boy voluntarily adopted as a special charge some younger boy. The older one appointed himself as guardian and helpmate to the young, the obligation to last throughout life; and through war or peace, in times good or ill, the brotherhood was to exist. If the two went with the same war-party, the older boy gave up his life if necessary to save that of the younger.[15]

To avoid constant bickering among siblings, brothers and sisters usually did not speak to each other directly. Standing Bear noted:

> The ties of sentiment between brother and sister were strong. Neverthe-less, no Lakota boy ever spoke directly to his sisters or girl cousins. This rule of conduct a Lakota boy dare not violate, for to do so was showing the utmost disrespect for them.[17]

Girls were expected to have a good reputation so as not to embarrass their brothers, while boys were encouraged to perform heroic feats so their sisters could honor them. Deep ties were developed even though direct social contact was minimal.

The recognition of gender difference required certain kinds of behavior in proper families, and the females who benefited from it socially and emotionally rigorously enforced these customs. "It was different with a man's own relatives," noted the Lakota holy man Lame Deer, with

> his sisters or female cousins. You don't look them straight in the eye, kid around or touch them. And a girl has to be very reserved with her brothers and male cousins. But between a man and his mother-in-law, a woman and her father-in-law—why, it is just as if there was a brick wall between them. They avoid each other completely. That is because your in-laws are looked upon as real parents.[18]

With three sets of real parents supervising family relationships there was a greatly reduced chance that any serious conflict would be generated within the family circle that could not be handled immediately.

Grandparents generally expressed a parental concern for the children distinct from that of the parents. One generation removed from the responsibility of feeding, clothing, and housing the children, they frequently indulged themselves by giving the children gifts and assuming the task of supervising the religious and philosophical teaching of their grandchildren. They would almost always step into a situation when the family suffered the loss of a father or a mother and raise the children themselves. On other occasions they would intervene in the treatment of the children by the aunts and uncles when they believed that the relatives were being too harsh or too lax. They told stories and kept track of the ancestral and kinship ties. People knew that elders had had many experiences in life and therefore that their counsel and advice was more informed than that of anyone else. Elders also knew tribal history and how their family was related to the other families in the band and tribe. They were the representatives and judges of family morality and were responsible for insuring peaceful relations among their relatives and between their relatives and other members of the tribe. Their role perfectly reflected Jung's insights regarding the influence of grandparents. In simple ways, they were indeed shapers of the child's personality—far more than the parents.

In-laws had special rules to inhibit or encourage their participation in the family. Wives were forbidden to communicate directly with their fathers-in-law and, as we noted, husbands avoided contact with their mothers-in-law (a custom that would probably be welcomed in Western society today). These customs eliminated the friction that would ordinarily occur in families when anxious in-laws, wishing to help younger people adjust to marriage, begin to intrude on the new family unit established by their children.

The mother's brothers were expected to be gentle and protective of their nephews while the father's sisters sought to favor their nieces. Thus a balance was struck between the uncles and aunts so that if the father's brothers treated a child harshly, it was the responsibility of the mother's brothers to comfort the child and smooth over the difficulty. Every relationship with disciplinary or teaching duties also had a corresponding role that protected and advocated on behalf of the child, so that its relationship with adults was clearly defined. Brothers-in-law and sisters-in-law were encouraged to tease each other in specifically designed patterns so that should tensions arise between adult siblings who represented the two families, they could be deflected into a ritual situation where no one could take offense. Since teasing was a duty and expected by the targets of the teasing, bad feelings were minimized. This ritualized teasing brought adults closer together and enabled people to spar with language before any serious discussions of the family could take place. Teasing continues today and serves as an extremely valuable social cement in many Indian communities.

Families did not always have a large membership. The Sioux tried to space their children, so two or three children would have been the typical size family. In any one generation, there might be several kinship roles that would not be filled. Older people, recognizing the scarcity of relatives, might adopt one or more children and thereby come to fill one of the missing kinship roles. Adoption was a more serious matter traditionally, and the people becoming new relatives took their task very seriously. There was also a ceremony in which two people took each other as special friends with the equivalent kinship responsibilities of a blood relative. Lame Deer described this relationship:

> The young men who vowed to be a *kola* to each other would almost become one single person. They shared everything—life and death, pain and joy, the last mouthful of food, even their women. They had to be ready at all times to give their lives for each other. In the same way an older man could adopt a younger one by becoming his *hunka.* By this ceremony, the younger man became the son of the older, even if only a few years separated them in age. Men sealed these special friendships with a ceremony. [19]

The grandmother was usually the most influential member of the Indian family. Since Sioux society was basically matrilineal, the oldest female in the family became the grandmother who supervised everything—unless the biological grandmother was of a strong personality and could imprint her leadership on the family. Her role was to determine and articulate what was proper behavior for members of the family. Thus while custom might dictate a certain course of behavior, the grandmother would determine whether, in spite of custom, the proper solution to the problem was a variance from custom on that occasion.

Some traditional families were very rigorous about maintaining these very detailed kinship connections and responsibilities. They would treat second, third, and sometimes fourth generations as if they were first generation cousins, uncles and aunts, thus severely limiting the eligible marriage pool and extending the family far beyond its natural boundaries to include ancestral ties also. Often families would treat second cousins as if they were brothers and sisters of the original children of the marriage, making the family a much tighter group and providing additional people to carry on the kinship responsibilities. The advantage in extending the basic family—and even the basic kinship group—lay in securing allies and loyalties within the larger tribe, beyond the limiting boundary of the smaller band to which they belonged. Thus when hunting bands gathered in the summertime, people already had relatives in the other bands that they could visit and this reduced the sense of strangeness that might otherwise have occurred.

Within such an extended family, a person *always* calls another person by the kinship name, never by the personal name that is used when referring to the person in the larger tribal context. This practice served to bolster proper behavior among family members and reminded individuals of their responsibilities to others. Of course when these words are translated into English, they make it appear that the individual has no distinctive name or personality because he is always calling his father "father," his mother "mother," and his cousins "cousin." When spoken in the Lakota or Dakota language, however, these words function as terms of endearment, moral admonitions, and reminders of what the two people have in common. Most of the Sioux families today have kept this part of the kinship system intact, and individuals consequently have these extended kinds of relatives on almost every one of the fifteen Sioux reservations. The extended family functioned like the clan system of other tribes in that distantly related people were obligated to perform traditional family functions whenever two separate bands happened to meet. And while a member of the family was visiting another band, he or she received the same courtesies that would be extended to him in the intimate family circle back home.

This ingenious and effective social system originated from entirely different premises than the family and society of Western civilization. It took seriously the social context in which families originated, prospered, and dissolved. The Sioux would not have understood the Western idea that the family is composed of isolated individuals connected primarily by biology. Sioux kinship recognizes that, as individuals, we live as a composite of the ways we relate to a wide range of people in our personal relationships. Sioux society was built upon the allocation of duties and responsibilities rather than the recognition of "rights." If it worked with maximum efficiency, everyone, over the course of a lifetime, was a beneficiary of the system. It particularly helped the young and the old people who were unable to contribute much to the welfare of the tribe, and they were vigorously protected by the able-bodied adult members of the family on all occasions. As the generations matured, they received, and expected to receive, the benefits they had extended to people when they were younger. Mature adults cheerfully gave food, clothing and shelter to the infants entering the family and to the elders who could no longer contribute.

In contrast, Western society and the Western style family are often built upon the premise that each family member has "rights" in relation to every other member. These "rights" arose, perhaps, in the relation between the psychic energy of kinship libido and the development of social relations based upon property, and thus upon property rights. "Rights" suggests, at an abstract level, the practice of law, which replaces the rather different strictures found in the kinship concept of "taboo." It may be that this distinction is usefully linked to the rise of monotheism, and is perhaps best illustrated by the rivalry described in the Bible between Joseph and his brothers, and between Isaac and Jacob. The child in Western society is born into a situation in which competition is the likely outcome of all his experiences in the family, and then later in society as a whole. The Indian child experiences within an extended family a variety of relationships that encourage not only competition, but that more actively emphasize cooperation and concern. Living inside this system provides considerable security for the individual and enables him or her to meet every challenge as a member of something greater than himself or herself. That the federal government intuitively wished to break this system as soon as the tribes were on the reservations is testimony to its effectiveness.

The Sioux took pains to remember the psychological traits of the people in each generation, so here too the comparison provides an apt illustration and elaboration on Jung's speculations about psychic heredity. When I was young, before World War Two, the stores in Martin, South Dakota, where I lived, had benches outside that were sheltered from the sun. There the old Indian men would sit and visit when they came to town. In addition to recent gossip and recounting stories about the old days, much of the discussion was devoted to genealogies. People kept track of everything. When discussions turned toward recent local events, the old men would issue predictions on how various people were going to behave. They had identified traits of family members past with the emerging behaviors of people living in the present, and they would make remarkably accurate prognostications on how personal situations would develop: "So-and-so acts just like his great uncle; he pouts to get attention. So-and-so will weather this storm; she has her grandmother's determination." There were always fascinating conversations and commentaries going on that gave everyone an insight into the local Indian community. Of course, whenever we repeated what we had heard we were warned that it was not in good taste to do so. I remain amazed yet today at the knowledge possessed by these old men about families in the tribe.

When a child, I noticed other things about the ancestral presence that always struck me as strange. If a child came from a good family, he or she was not introduced as himself or herself but as the son, daughter, grandson or granddaughter of an older member of the family who had enhanced the family name. The Sioux thus reflected Jung's intuition about psychic heredity, but put this knowledge to practical use. Nowhere was this knowledge of family and ancestry more useful than in arranging and approving marriages. Knowing nothing of modern genetics, the Sioux nonetheless did not want to pollute the family bloodstreams by close intermarriages. Although scholars have written on how easily marriages were arranged among Indians, as if proffering a few ponies would close the deal, for good families the process was agonizing. When two people were attracted to each other, family elders would begin to trace marriages and relatives back many generations to see if the family lines had drawn together in any previous generation.

One of the most frequently-invoked ideas from Sioux culture—that one must think of the people's welfare in terms of seven generations—has its roots in the multi-generational, complex kinship system we have been using to deepen Carl Jung's insights. Certainly in genetic terms, the care taken by elders in supervising intermarriage to non-family members over six marriages and perhaps two hundred years would radically change the physical and psychological nature of the present generation of the family. The Sioux recognized these kinds of changes, of course, but they had something else in mind. They had a saying that each generation must think of "the seven generations" when they considered important actions or were faced with an impending crisis. The great Sioux leader Red Cloud, in negotiating for the taking of the Black Hills, told the federal treaty commissioners that he wanted his people clothed, housed and fed for seven generations. What did he mean?

Although dying in battle was considered a virtue—since no one wanted to be old and helpless—it was also the case that old age was considered a blessing among the Sioux. If a person lived the proper life, he or she could expect to know, while a child, his or her great grandparents and, while an elder, to know his or her great-grandchildren. Any individual, then, could imagine three generations back and three generations forward, for a total of seven. A person must therefore act so that their great grandparents would not be ashamed of what they were doing in the present and so that their great grandchildren could point with pride at what their ancestors had done.

Red Cloud wanted to ensure that his people would be well treated, so that his great grandchildren, looking back at tribal history, could see in the far distant past the thoughtfulness of the people of his generation. Even more, he wanted to put his great grandsons, who would be responsible for the tribe's prosperity, in the same position vis-à-vis the United States that he himself then occupied. This provision would ensure that the Oglalas would maintain their political status over this period of time. With this kind of foresight, the generations were tied together as if they were all present in the flesh.

With the deep and intricate example of the Sioux before us, we can return to Carl Jung's effort to deal with the family in historical and ancestral terms. "If our impressions are too distinct," he reflected,

> we are held to the hour and minute of the present and have no way of knowing how our ancestral psyches listen to and understand the present—in other words, how our unconscious is responding to it. Thus we remain ignorant of whether our ancestral components find an elementary gratification in our lives or whether they are repelled. Inner peace and contentment depend in large measure upon whether or not the historical family which is inherent in the individual can be harmonized with the ephemeral conditions of the present.[20]

Here Jung touches on one of the fundamental aspects of ancestral heritage in the social situation. Personal development involves the reconciliation of the ancestral with the present, and social systems—including family, kinship, and institutions—play a key role in such harmonization.

The recognition that, in addition to one's individual desires, one represents *a family* can, as we have seen, provide a powerful self-regulating ethic for social life. Personal embarrassment, for the Sioux, was not as traumatic as the realization that one had brought discredit on the ancestral line. Many people, both vertically in ancestral time and horizontally in kinship space, are psychically injured if a family member acts wrongfully. A person's individual trauma can be reconciled by condolence ceremonies and the use of mediators or intercessors to bring alienated families together again in friendship. But it is difficult to erase the dirt on the family name. An injury done becomes part of the community memory. Older family members take special care to monitor family members during times of crisis so that they do not take actions that will bring shame upon the family.

All of these things are implicit in Jung's conceptual musings on the ancestral and collective nature of the psyche. Indeed, we can look back and think it a pity that Jung did not spend more time with the Pueblos in New Mexico or make his way to the Sioux reservations to see how people acted toward each other. Having massive amounts of social science data at his command, he somehow failed to understand adequately the *function* of kinship in terms of distributing the intense psychic energy that invests a family. Other Western scholars who have studied kinship patterns have generally done well in explaining the mechanics of kinship, and their charts often give a good explanation of how it works. But they too have generally neglected to credit tribal/primitive peoples with the understanding that such a network is necessary if society is going to minimize conflict within its basic unit.

It is important to note, however, that later Jungians have taken up these questions, moving into the void left by Jung's inability to speak to the extended family situation and reaching conclusions that show a definite inclination towards what we might call a "Sioux way" of understanding the larger family network. Murray Stein's fine book of essays, *Jungian Analysis*, contains several reflections worth mentioning in this respect. Thayer Greene, in an article entitled "Group Therapy and Analysis," writes:

> The model that most adequately corresponds to the dynamic of group process is the family. Every person entering the group is in some sense reopening the repressed and unconscious memories of early family experience. In one form or another, the family has been for everyone the primary and primal group.[21]

If the group, because it resembles the family, is used as a therapeutic tool, would not the full development of the possibilities of the family also have relevance in establishing proper psychological growth processes?

Edward C. Whitmont argues that

> the ego complex, as Jung called it, is the "actualization" of a transpersonal Self in a personal shell of conditioned ideas and images of what one has been trained by family and culture to assume one is like or should be like, in terms of standards, values, and aspirations. Hence what we have called our ego turns out to be "determined" by an "experience" that is but the expression of the way the Self has been "actualized" by parental and cultural conditioning.[22]

This definition expresses precisely what the Sioux aimed to accomplish with their use of the kinship system. And Whitmont comments that

> individuation need no longer be seen then in the light of a need to renounce the ego for the Self, but rather as the development and differentiation of a new ego position, of a Self-oriented, truly individual ego, in which outer and inner directions are balanced. Nor need individuation be considered limited to the second half of life, nor defined exclusively in terms of introversion. [23]

More compatible with "the Sioux way" is Whitmont's redefinition of individuation so that it "means not only a conscious relationship to the archetypal world, but also a conscious relationship to interpersonal reality and social collectivity." [24]

The kinship system prepared the Indian child for entrance into adult life and acceptance of the particular responsibility that is his fate in a far more comprehensive fashion than any of the institutions we find in Western society, and it does so in a way that accounts fully for the collective ancestral legacy. Luther Standing Bear reported that by the time he was twelve years old, he had gone on a war party, killed a buffalo, and joined the Fox society. In terms of the maturing process and the necessity for individuation, the Sioux extended family customs were highly efficient. The Sioux youngster of adolescence preparing to experience the vision quest—to which we shall turn next—had been well prepared to seek his vocation and the realization of his Self.

We cannot pretend that every Sioux Indian child today has this support system during his or her childhood. "Civilization" has been immensely destructive toward the functioning of such kinship systems, and it is probably a rarity today if an Indian child has such a family network into which he or she is born. Only the very traditional Sioux families still make a deliberate effort to maintain this kinship network. But the importance of the kinship system to this dialogue and comparison is that it provides a complete map of the possible relationships that a person will have during his or her formative years, and it does so in a way that makes concrete sense of Jung's formulations. It reveals the connections between the ancestral, the psyche, the individual, and the social, and it establishes the context in which we can more fully consider the nature of the experiences to be found in the dreams and visions of any given individual.

CHAPTER NINE

THE VOICE AND THE VISION

"True personality," according to Carl Jung, "is always a vocation and puts its trust in it as in God, despite its being, as the ordinary man would say, only a personal feeling. But vocation acts like a law of God from which there is no escape." The word "vocation," as it is used here, has a strong sense of a kind of sacred calling. Jung goes on to point out, however, that "the original meaning of 'to have a vocation' is 'to be addressed by a voice.'"[1] As we have seen in the case of Black Elk and others, the visions that took Sioux people into superior time and space relations, and that defined their life courses, were initiated by the calling of a voice. Here we have yet another common concept, "the voice," upon which to build a comparative dialogue between the Sioux tradition and the psychology of Carl Jung, and this chapter will take up that point of intersection.

For both Jung and the Sioux people, "the voice" stands as that mysterious call we hear that urges us toward greater spiritual depth. The Sioux regard hearing a voice as a critical event that initiates the process of seeking assistance from the spirits. For the Sioux, that meant the questing for visions, which we will take up shortly. Jung finds it to be critical to the process of individuation since it separates out the person for greater growth and development—thus the linkage between voice and personal vocation, which Jung described as "an irrational factor that destines a man to emancipate himself from the herd and from its well-worn paths."[2]

The clearest examples of the linkage between vocation and voice, Jung suggested,

> are to be found in the avowals of the Old Testament prophets. That it is not just a quaint old-fashioned way of speaking is proved by the confessions of historical personalities such as Goethe and Napoleon, to mention only two familiar examples, who made no secret of their feeling of vocation.[3]

Indeed, many people have stated that at certain climatic moments they recognized their destiny and then acted upon it. The voice not only commands the attention of the individual but also determines his or her life as one that stands out from the crowd. In effect, it moves people in a predetermined way. This idea is in close accord with the Sioux understanding that a person who hears a voice responds through ceremonial means. He or she then receives special powers and is set aside from the rest of the tribe because of the ability to perform certain functions—although always in cooperation with the spirits—which could not otherwise be performed solely by human beings. Vocation, in other words, is the prize that everyone seeks.

The Sioux tradition may differ from that of Western peoples, however, in that modern industrial man has largely exchanged the unconscious of nature for the unconscious of his collectivity. It is not clear that the traditional Sioux had done so. "As a rule," Jung noted,

the miseducated civilized human being is quite incapable of perceiving the voice, which is something not guaranteed by the current shibboleths. Primitive people have a far greater capacity in this respect; at least the medicine-men are able, as part of their professional equipment, to talk with spirits, trees, and animals, these being the forms in which they encounter the objective psyche or psychic non-ego.[4]

The relative capacity for this kind of encounter may well place the primitive/ tribal person in a far better position for understanding his or her life than the "civilized" man. But a traditional Sioux person would go farther, maintaining that the objective psyche or the psychic non-ego appear as real entities, easily distinguishable from their own human subjectivity.

Unless I am reading Jung terribly askew, the call to have a vocation brings forward the responsibility to individuate, or in laymen's terms, to reach full psychological and emotional maturity. "Individuation is the fulfillment of the law of life, so to be individuated is to be quite naturally united with the laws of the universe," in Jung's understanding. And he continues:

the fulfillment is on the conscious level if it is a matter of the human individual; such consciousness accords naturally with the totality of nature; that is what is expressed in the idea of Tao. So, insofar as one can speak of complete individuation at all, I should say it would be a conscious experience of the totality of nature.[5]

Jung clearly saw individuation in an almost cosmic context. And yet, it is difficult to know exactly what he may have meant. We cannot quite tell whether Jung is speaking of a recognition of the scope or essence of Nature, an experience or vision of *cosmic* wholeness, or a sense of eternal value which floods the soul and releases it from illusions. The fact that Jung insists on the *conscious* realization of this experience suggests that he may be placing individuation within a scientific context, rendering the term both problematic and intriguing. Certainly, everyone can intellectually affirm a relationship with *cosmic* wholeness, and we can often experience it aesthetically. But can we go further, to become active participants in this wholeness, our consciousness in accord with that of the totality of nature?

My question arises because of Jung's estimation of what is possible for individuals to achieve within today's world. "What does lie within our reach," Jung says,

> is the change in individuals who have, or create for themselves, an opportunity to influence others of like mind. I do not mean by persuading or preaching—I am thinking, rather, of the well-known fact that anyone who has insight into his own actions, and has thus found access to the unconscious, involuntarily exercises an influence on his environment. The deepening and broadening of his consciousness produce the kind of effect which the primitives call "mana." It is the unintentional influence on the unconscious of others, a sort of unconscious prestige, and its effect lasts only so long as it is not disturbed by conscious intention.[6]

The result of individuation, then, would be the development of a unique personality to the point that it becomes empirically visible, an obvious personal and social fact to anyone capable of observing it. Here, we might recall Jung's various uses of the "positive primitive," noting in particular that this kind of powerful personality is prevalent in older tribal peoples.

If the Jungian voice calls us to individuation, that of the Sioux calls us to ceremony, most frequently the vision quest, which stands as a useful example of a consciousness in accord with nature, which in turn produces the kind of unconscious power of the individuated person. Let us examine, then, the experience of a Sioux medicine man who answered the voice, made it a concrete physical reality through ceremony, and was then later able to reflect on what he had experienced. Readers familiar with accounts of Sioux visions as reported in such books as *Black Elk Speaks, Singing for a Spirit,*

Lame Deer, Seeker of Visions and *Fools Crow* will instantly see the commonalities of these visions. Below is the edited vision quest account of Siyaka, as recorded by Frances Densmore in *Teton Sioux Music*:

When I was a young man I wanted a dream through which I could know what to depend upon for help. Having this desire, I went to a medicine-man and told him about it. He instructed me what to do, and I followed his instructions in everything. He told me to get four well-tanned robes, with one for my own use, also a decorated pipe and offerings of tobacco, and to appear before him on a certain day prepared to seek my vision. I prepared the articles as he directed and went to him on that day. He painted my face white, and before leaving him we went together into the sweat lodge and while we were there he told me of his own dream and gave me an idea of what a dream was like. I had already selected a hill on which to await my dream, and after leaving him I went to this hilltop to follow his instructions. I was not required to fast before seeking the vision but of course took no food with me when I went to the hilltop. In the middle of this hilltop I dug a hollow about two feet deep and large enough so that I could crouch against its side when weary with standing. At each of the four points of the compass I placed one of the robes and some of the tobacco. These offerings were to show that I desired messages from the directions of the four winds and was waiting anxiously to hear the voice of some bird or animal speaking to me in a dream.

Having placed these offerings in position, and according to the advice of the medicine-man, I stood facing the west and watched the sun disappear. As soon as the sun was out of sight I closed my eyes and turned my face to the east, standing thus for a while, then facing the north and the south. So I stood, wrapped in a buffalo robe. I was not exactly singing, but more nearly lamenting, like a child asking for something.

As I still faced the west, after the sun had set and when it was almost dark, I heard a sound like a flying of a bird around my head, and I heard a voice saying, "Young man, you are recognized by *Wakan Tanka*." This was all the voice said.

All night I stood with my eyes closed. Just before daybreak I saw a bright light coming toward me from the east. It was a man. His head was held up, and he held a tomahawk in his hand. He said: "Follow me," and in an instant he changed into a crow. In my dream I followed the crow to a village. He entered the largest tent. When he entered the tent

he changed into a man again. Opposite the entrance there sat a young
man, painted red, who welcomed me. When I was thus received I felt
highly honored, for as this was the largest tent I knew it must be the
tent of the chief. The young man said he was pleased to see me there.
He said, further, that all the animals and birds were his friends, and that
he wished me to follow the way he had used to secure their friendship.
He told me to lift my head. I did this and saw dragonflies, butterflies,
and all kinds of small insects, while above them flew all kinds of birds.
As soon as I cast down my eyes again and looked at the young man and
at the man who had brought me thither, I saw that the young man had
become transformed into an owl, and that my escort had changed again
into a crow.

The owl said, "Always look toward the west when you make a petition, and you will have a long life." After this the owl commanded me
to look at him. As soon as I did this he changed into an elk and at his
feet were the elk medicine and a hoop. As soon as I saw him changing, I
began to wonder what marvel would be next. Then I heard a song. I tried
to learn the song, and before I realized what I was doing I was singing
the song.

The hilltop where I had my dream was quite a distance from the
camp. My friends knew I had gone there, and in the early morning they
sent a man with my horse. I came home, and the first thing I did was to
take a sweat bath. In the lodge with the medicine-man I told him my
dream.[7]

Let us examine this material and see the elements involved. First, Siyaka's experience is wholly physical, both when he is fasting and later when the
birds and animals accompany him. The experience is also rational; there are
no fantasy creatures, monsters, or puzzling symbols here. The setting is not
unlike what we experience every day. The vision quest is an effort to relate
to the higher spiritual powers by eliminating distractions and cleansing the
body of food and water in order to minimize the effect they have on the
mind. The quest begins and ends in ordinary time and space, and consumes
anywhere from one to four days of regular chronological time. Within the
sacred world of the vision, however, time and space are experienced in a
different manner. Both appear to change, from secular to sacred, at the
moment when Siyaka is taken to the village and the larger tent. They return
to their original secular status when he finishes his quest.

Other creatures speak to him, telling him specific things he had not known before, and they become his friends and helpers thereafter. He receives a song that can be sung to summon his bird and animal friends whenever he needs assistance. In changing their shapes, the animals reveal the intimacy of their own relationships—the crow becomes an elk, indicating that these two have a relationship different than their connection with humans and other creatures. Finally, Siyaka is told how to use the powers given him.

The symbolism and the narrative could easily have been experienced by a non-Indian, even by one of Jung's patients, so the vision could be subjected to a Jungian analysis. The important thing to keep in mind, however, is that after the experience Siyaka could perform feats that violate the routine activities of secular time and space. Regardless of the interpretations an analyst might give to this vision, the pertinent fact is that Siyaka received special powers that he exercised on behalf of the people, and which were qualitatively different powers than those of anyone else.* Many Jungians would correctly point out that the individuation process, particularly when realized in analysis, can indeed leave individuals with "special powers" of vision, intuition, and sometimes healing. Jung himself stands as an excellent case in point. Still, to the best of my knowledge, while individuating Jungian patients grow considerably in maturity and understanding, they do not receive these particular kinds of powers from entities outside themselves.

Jung observes that,

> Individuation can only mean a process of psychological development that fulfills the individual qualities given; in other words, it is a process by which a man becomes the definite, unique being he in fact is.[8]

"At all events," Jung concluded in another passage, "only those individuals can attain to a higher degree of consciousness who are destined to it and called to it from the beginning, i.e., who have a capacity and urge for higher

---

*   Readers are again directed to Vine Deloria's penultimate book, *The World We Used to Live In*, which contains numerous accounts of the feats of medicine men. Deloria's argument in that book, important to understanding his argument here, is that the accounts of Indian spiritual powers have been easily separated out from one another, and then bracketed as folklore, anomalies, superstition, and fiction. Deloria took these accounts seriously and, in collecting them together, sought to show the reality of the power wielded by men like Siyaka and Black Elk.

differentiation."[9] If some aspects of the Sioux experience remain distinct, the experience of Siyaka and others nonetheless illustrates the possibilities for individuation. He heard the call of "the voice," and opened himself to the powers of the universe. He received a basic knowledge of his destiny during the experience, and might well be described as having a higher consciousness, one able to bring additional powers to his ceremonies, and one who understands when it is and is not appropriate to do so.

Individuation posed in traditional Jungian terms involves a great degree of social conflict and disapproval in Western society. Jung observed that:

> A person who by reason of special capacities is entitled to individuate must accept the contempt of society until such time as he has accomplished his equivalent. Only a few are capable of individuating, because individuation rules out any renunciation of collective conformity until an equivalent has been accomplished whose objective value is acknowledged. Human relationship establishes itself automatically on the basis of an acknowledged equivalent, because the libido of society goes directly towards it.[10]

Here Jung admits the tendency of Western civilization to reject or punish people who move to deeper levels of awareness. In the Sioux tradition, these people, while sometimes feared, are more typically honored and cherished.

Jolande Jacobi is helpful in understanding the religious significance of individuation. "From the religious point of view," Jacobi writes, individuation

> creates a living relation between man and the suprapersonal and gives him his proper place in the order of the universe. Through the encounter with the contents of the unconscious realm of the psyche and their integration with consciousness, it lays the foundation of an independent, personal philosophy of life which, depending on the individual, may also ally itself with a particular creed.[11]

Individuation—at least in Jacobi's understanding—thus seems to be a process of connecting the person to higher powers, but without the certain prospect of any special future participation in cosmic activities. It is not difficult to claim a suprapersonal relationship, particularly if it speaks mainly to the self; it is another matter to demonstrate it in physical terms. It seems almost as if individuation re-establishes a connection to the greater cosmos by overcoming a psychological deficit, but then fails to move on toward a greater goal. This somewhat limited understanding was likely *not* that of Carl Jung. Still, there seem to be important distinctions to be drawn between the Jungian and Sioux understanding; these differences are as important to our dialogue as are the revealing overlaps and similarities.

The similarity in how people are called seems so great that the two things, the voice and the vision quest, might be cultural variations of a single important psychological/religious theme. But individuation for Western man seems to be, as Jacobi reports, "a deepening by a process adapted specifically to the nature of Western man, as is also attempted in other spheres of culture by corresponding rites and religious forms."[12] Individuation may be a process that exists in all cultures, although expressed more often as religious experiences in many non-Western traditions, and understood inadequately in the West. The question of individuation, as we have seen, is reasonably resolved in the Sioux cultural context. Kinship responsibilities focus the individual's attention on others and create a society in which the most respected and admired behavior is to give, not to take. That an individual developing his personality would face the contempt of his society is quite out of the question. Marie-Louise von Franz observes that "in primitive communities there are not many personal problems; a personal problem is really everybody's problem,"[13] and this is indeed true because community harmony must not be disturbed without good reason. The converse also holds true. One person's success is everyone's success because people act for the benefit of the community whenever possible. At a minimum, then, the social context in which individuation takes place or the vision quest is completed is entirely different. The Western experience is more inclined to be hostile to the individual; the Plains Indian context more inclined to be supportive, and focused on the good of the community.

Almost unanimously the Sioux medicine men and most of the secular adults who achieve particular vocations—warriors, hunters, scouts, arrow makers—reported that they heard voices prior to the time when they performed their vision quest, heeded the signs and instructions, and acquired special skills and knowledge. As a rule, people generally tried to avoid having this difficult experience because it set them aside from ordinary folk and placed heavy burdens on them. They had to use their powers to help others, and that became their destiny. Throughout their lives they were constantly aware that they lived in two worlds—the secular world and the world of those times when the suprapersonal powers required them to use their powers. The vision was not anything that people sought; it was thrust upon them by higher powers.

Presumably, upon hearing a voice, a Western person, if at all sensitive to the nature of the experience, begins to deal with the elements of his or her conscious personality, moving quickly into a situation where he or she can bring from the unconscious those configurational patterns of growth that must be understood if the personality is to continue to develop. "It is one of the main tasks of an analytically assisted individuation process to stimulate the symbol-producing capacity of the psyche and its natural tendency to self-regulation and assignment of meaning," according to Jacobi, in other words, to promote its "transcendent function."[14] Here we again see a major difference between Jungian psychology and the practices of tribal peoples. For the Western thinker, everything vested with meaning must be symbolic and intangible; for the Sioux it must be capable of repetition and have physical expression.

The medicine man that supervises the vision quest offers a pragmatic critique of the experience during a sweat lodge conducted after the lamenter comes down from the hill where he has been fasting. Very good medicine men have a mysterious connection with the questor in that they have a means of sharing the vision while it is occurring, and can gauge the veracity and character of the lamenter by what he shares afterwards. Here the question of symbolism looms. Crow, elk, stones, or fish are not understood by medicine men as symbols of some psychic complex or energy pattern. Rather they are a part of the everyday natural world and the lamenter can expect to encounter them as living beings. The unusual in nature, a bird talking and then turning into a small animal, for example, is a wondrous experience but is not understood as existing outside the possible experiences of everyone. Medicine bundles are usually made up so as to contain the physical representations of the creatures in the vision. The near physical presence of bird and animal helpers is required so that the helpers are manifested as a concrete physical presence and will always be a part of the person's life. There is, therefore, no "supernatural" as there is the Western culture; the natural is simply larger and more comprehensive.

Voices can be heard in everyday life, of course, without the preamble of a vision quest. Many ordinary people have heard voices that warned them of danger or cautioned them to refrain from doing something. Voices can sometimes simply convey information. They can vary considerably, while always remaining an audible experience. Black Elk was once hunting when a blizzard came up and he found himself lost and stranded:

> The wind went down that night and it was still and very cold. While I was lying there in a bison robe, a coyote began to howl not far off, and suddenly I knew it was saying something. It was not making words, but it said something plainer than words, and this was it: "Two-legged one, on the big ridge west of you there are bison, but first you shall see two more two-leggeds over there."[15]

The next day everything happened as the coyote had predicted. Black Elk found an old man and a boy huddled in a snowdrift, starving and freezing. Beyond them in a draw, trapped by snowdrifts were some buffalo. How does this experience fit into a Jungian context? Specific practical information was transmitted audibly although it was not in one language.

Here we find one of the gaps between Jung and the Sioux, for I cannot see how Western psychology can adequately explain this kind of experience using standard frameworks. If the other two-leggeds and the bison had appeared as Black Elk heard this message, we would have said that it was a case of *synchronicity,* but with a cold snowy night intervening between the time Black Elk heard the voice of the coyote and the discovery the next day of two people also stranded in a blizzard, the message also has a prophetic dimension, in addition to being a communication from the higher powers and animal helpers. How could Black Elk have received this specific yet seemingly trivial information from the unconscious?

A Western psychologist may object that the experiences of Indians doing the vision quest are fantasies brought on by lack of food or projections from the unconscious into the objective nature within which the vision questor is located. But fasting generally brings on an amazing surge of energy instead of faintness and fantasy. Voices heard during the vision provide specific practical instructions or data that can be verified easily. A fantasy would likely have no immediate application to the circumstances and no relationship to ordinary life at all. All testimony from people, both Indian and non-Indian, who have had a vision quest experience suggests, in fact unquestionably contends, that actual physical visitations are made by spirits, birds, animals and other forms of life. Assuming that the lamenter has had a successful experience and received special gifts, a number of things now become possible. They can exercise powers of healing, prophecy, or protection in ordinary secular life. People suffering from fatigue and embroiled in fantasy from lack of nourishment do not emerge from the experience with new talents and capabilities.

Individuals are sometimes given the broad details of certain parts of their future life in a vision, but they are never given the specifics. Crazy Horse was told that his war medicine would make him invulnerable to his enemies but that he would be killed as a result of the betrayal or the conniving of his own people. Roman Nose, the great Cheyenne warrior, was given special medicine that made him invulnerable to bullets in battle. Each man achieved prominence in his tribe and eventually did the things that were predicted of them. Crazy Horse was virtually invulnerable in battle against other tribes and the cavalry but he was killed as a result of the machinations of some of the reservation Indians and the government at Fort Robinson, Nebraska, as predicted in his vision.

Roman Nose was the foremost warrior of the Cheyenne, a man who invoked fear in every fighting man who opposed him. During the fight at Beecher's Island he was visiting a nearby Sioux camp where he was feasted. Younger Cheyenne warriors came to him and asked him to lead the next charge against the troopers. Roman Nose discovered that he had eaten food that had been stirred and served with an iron spoon or ladle that, according to his vision, made him vulnerable to the white man's bullets. Without time to perform the necessary purification ceremonies, he knew that if he led the charge it would mean his life. His responsibility to his people left him no choice and so he mounted his horse and rode to his death and into the lasting memory of his people.

Successful medicine men almost always obtain their powers through the vision quest. Additional powers could be given in later dreams and visions but the initial experience largely determined the future configuration of events. Songs played an important part in every encounter with the higher powers. Some songs called the spirits to the medicine man, others were used for healing illnesses, and still others were songs of thanksgivings for blessings received. Some scholars have suggested that Indian healers use singing, rattles and drums as a technique of exciting the patient, building the emotions to frenzy, with the hope of invoking the spirits. One needs only to hear the actual songs sung by medicine men to see that they stir up only the deepest solitary thoughts and not the emotions. Songs and other ritual actions bring the helping animals and birds to the location where in a cooperative effort they can work together with the medicine man to conduct the healing.

The preponderance of evidence from Indians and non-Indians alike is that, while the healing is taking place, some of the helping animals are seen in the vicinity of the healing ceremony and over or around the person who is being healed. A white woman once had a bad back, for example, and attended a Sioux ceremony where she was to be healed. The medicine man told her to go home and on a certain day and time to go out into her back yard. She followed his instructions and as she was standing in her yard an eagle flew overhead almost so high that she could barely make it out. As he passed over, her back straightened out completely. Perhaps such incidents can be explained as coincidence or as a special kind of synchronicity but it may also be a certain indication that animal spirits are working actively in the situation.

One can only approximate Jung's response to the similarities found in the voice, individuation, and the vision quest—and to the significant distinctions between these two sets of practices. In considering such distinctions, between the psychic and the material, Jung once wrote that,

> the fact that all immediate experience is psychic and that immediate reality can only be psychic explains why it is that primitive man puts spirits and magical influences on the same plane as physical events. He has not yet torn his original experience into antithetical parts.[16]

Jung suggested that

> the more limited a man's field of consciousness is, the more numerous the psychic contents (imagoes) which meet him as quasi-external apparitions, either in the form of spirits, or as magical potencies projected upon living people (magicians, witches, etc.).[17]

If it is the case that human experience must be contained—analytically—within a discrete system of thought, I suppose that these responses are adequate. They illustrate the scientific way of describing phenomena. Testimony from tribal peoples, however, offers a different world, one in which Spirits are not mental images projected outwards but have real power in the physical world as entities in themselves.

As was the case of the "primitive," Jung's more formal definitions do not always accord with some of his less formal admissions. I suspect that if he had been able to spend some significant period of time living among the Sioux, Jung's responses would have been qualitatively different. In many instances, he demonstrated an openness to experiences like those of Sioux vision questors. "Those who are convinced of the reality of spirits should know that this is a subjective opinion which can be attacked on any number of grounds," he once wrote.

> Those who are not convinced should beware of naively assuming that the whole question of spirits and ghosts has been settled and that all manifestations of this kind are meaningless swindles. This is not so at all. These phenomena exist in their own right, regardless of the way they are interpreted, and it is beyond all doubt that they are genuine manifestations of the unconscious. [18]

Cutting through some of his scientific rhetoric, as we did with the positive primitive statements, we find such indications that Jung may well have understood and embraced something like Sioux interpretations of these experiences.

Jung's indecisiveness on this point has its irony. If he was willing to tar the primitive with a broad brush on the subject of spirits, there were also occasions when, confronted with the experiences of American Indians, he did not respond dogmatically. Consider one of Jung's utterances that we have examined previously, this time in the context of his willingness to consider a range of possibilities:

> It is generally supposed by the Red Indians, that in a wood at night they can talk to the ghosts; and it is assumed that in the initiations people will hear voices when they fast and remain alone for a long time. This general expectation shows that to be a very frequent phenomenon. As a matter of fact under certain strained conditions people frequently do hear or see queer things. [19]

Standing alone on a hilltop for four days would be a strain for a European. As it would be rigorous but reasonably commonplace to a Sioux, we can move beyond the culture-bound suggestion that the vision questor is under considerable stress and suggest instead that when the people do these things, they may well be communicating with the Spirits, bending space and touching some superior timeline, experiencing some kind of cosmic wholeness.

The appearance of the voice often foretells this kind of cosmic intimacy for the solitary individual. There is evidence from many cultures that the voice sets aside the individual for larger spiritual tasks. In Jungian psychology it guides the final maturation process. "All life is bound to individual carriers who realize it and is simply inconceivable without them," Jung observed. "But every carrier is charged with an individual destiny and destination, and the realization of these alone makes sense of life."[20] Following the call in the proper way enables the cosmos to be what it is. Perhaps that is why the animal is the most pious of the creatures we know. While other creatures follow their voices without friction, we humans have used this experience as a springboard to greater understanding and power. And while Jung's theoretical apparatus may not easily accommodate the voice that comes to Sioux people, it is clear that the deep similarities between visions and the process of individuation visibly manifest a number of important affinities that become clear in the comparison. Are these simply different cultural expressions of similar psychic experiences? It is quite possible. In the next chapter, let us continue with the consequences of these experiences of calling and vocation, which take concrete shape in the form of dreams, visions, prophecies, and healing gifts, manifested and performed in the physical world.

CHAPTER TEN

DREAMS AND PROPHECIES

Human beings, across historical time and across a range of cultures, have taken seriously the interpretation of dreams. In both of the systems of thought under consideration here, dreams are critical to understanding cosmology, space and time, family structure, and relations with animals and the non-human world. Indeed, since many of the most revealing relationships between Indians and the cosmos occur in dreams, it is fitting that we see, first, how Jungian psychology understands dreams and then look how the Sioux interpret and use them. Carl Jung, of course, made dream interpretation one of the cornerstones of his psychology, and in this case his writings reveal a fairly systematic body of thought. One central problem in selecting Sioux dream data is that the most frequent translation of the vision experience uses the English word "dream" to describe the psychological state in which the Sioux find themselves in the vision. The Sioux themselves generally use the same words—dream and vision—and sometimes do not distinguish one from another, making it difficult to separate out grand visions from nighttime dreams.* Indeed, dreams themselves often carry powerful content, sometimes akin to that found in visions, so this overlapping of translated terms is not altogether inappropriate.

For the Sioux, the dream/vision is a wholly different experience than everyday life, comparable in some ways to the near-death experiences described by a number of doctors. The famous Sioux medicine man Black Elk, for instance, had his tremendous vision when he mysteriously fell ill. He was taken to another place where he met the Six Grandfathers and the powers of the directions, was introduced to the various spirits, and given a bow, a cup, and a staff that enabled him to do many things. Later, his family

---

* Although Jungians would distinguish between (waking) visions and dreams, the manner in which each is treated psychodynamically in the analytic context would be the same in most cases.

testified that while Black Elk had been in the midst of the vision, he had appeared to them to be close to death. In a number of cases, bystanders have assumed the death or impending death of the person undergoing the vision experience. Of primary importance to us here, however, is Black Elk's reaction to the experience after he had returned back to normal life:

> I remember that for twelve days after that I wanted to be alone, and it seemed I did not belong to my people. They were almost like strangers. I would be out alone away from the village and the other boys, and I would look around to the four quarters, thinking of my vision and wishing I could get back there again. [1]

Black Elk's experience imprinted another sense of reality on him, suggesting that he felt that while in the vision he was in an alternative world that had as much substance and reality as his everyday world. It took him more than a week to readjust to the everyday world.

The similar nature of dreams and visions suggests that we can proceed cautiously with a discussion of dream accounts even if we cannot always determine precisely which Sioux accounts are visions and which are night-time dreams. I will, however, exclude vision accounts wherever it is possible to understand them as deriving from a vision quest, so as to better focus on the question of dreams. Before examining the Sioux experiences and their relevance for Jungian thought, we should first examine Carl Jung's theory of dreams in a systematic way.

The dream is the most important analytical tool in the Jungian school of psychology. It is, according to James A. Hall,

> to the psyche as an x-ray is to the body; it truthfully pictures the actual state of a portion of the whole organism/psyche. Just as x-ray images are not the body itself—although skillful understanding of them may give invaluable knowledge about the state of health of the actual body—so dreams are not the actual psyche, but offer rich images of its structure and dynamic movement. [2]

Unlike an x-ray, however, we cannot demand that dreams inform us of the state of affairs in our inner selves. "We do not feel as if we were producing dreams," Jung observed,

it is rather as if the dreams came to us. They are not subject to our control but obey their own laws. They are obviously autonomous psychic
complexes which form themselves out of their own material. We do not
know the source of their motives, and we therefore say that dreams come
from the unconscious.[3]

The assumption, therefore, in Jungian analysis, and probably in other
psychologies as well, is that the dream takes the initiative in showing us
the most pressing element or fragment of our psyche that demands attention. The dream, in this sense, is a psychic alarm system if we are able to
heed it.

The dream has other important qualities. It is "a fragment of involun-
tary psychic activity just conscious enough to be reproducible in the waking state."[4] That a dream can be made conscious (or at least its important
symbols and sequences can be made conscious) suggests that it resembles a
mediating guidance system rather than an intrusive element from the deeper
levels of the unconscious. In this sense it can serve, one might say, as an ego-
corrective; an attempt on the part of a conscious unconscious to redirect a
wrongly oriented ego path. Dreams might therefore be, in one sense, part
of the ongoing movement toward finding and understanding one's vocation. If we grant dreams a partially teleological function—that is, directed
toward the specific goal of vocation—rather than simply a reproductive
"x-ray" role, we can say that they are a part of the purposeful movement of
the larger sense of time that we have discussed before, and that dreams may
have a divine aspect in so far as we are able to fathom the meaning of divinity.

Jung also spoke to the divine nature of dreams when he said that the
dream

is a little hidden door in the innermost and most secret recesses of the
psyche, opening into that cosmic night which was psyche long before
there was any ego-consciousness, and which will remain psyche no matter how far our ego-consciousness may extend ... [A]ll consciousness
separates; but in dreams we put on the likeness of that more universal,
truer, more eternal man dwelling in the darkness of primordial night.
There he is still the whole, and the whole is in him, indistinguishable
from nature and bare of all egohood. Out of these all-uniting depths
arises the dream.[5]

In this sense it is both personal and, at the same time, can tap into the transpersonal realm of knowing and of human experience that is "indistinguishable from nature and bare of all egohood." Dreams are "... pure nature; they show us the unvarnished nature truth ...", and can function as a conveyor of divine inspiration and initiation when nothing else will suffice. This latter dimension of the dream, as described by Jung, is more in keeping with the Sioux orientation to the vision/dream.

This interpretation credits dreams with sufficient characteristics of our own personality that the dream may be said to operate as a superior guiding spirit in directing and conversing with our perceptual functions, while at the same time informing us of psychic realities that do not derive directly from the ego's experience in the outer world. Thus many of the thoughts, sensations, and intuitions that we might ordinarily have in a conscious state appear in a half conscious state so that they can participate along with relatively objective functions of ego perception. The ego's perceptions, it seems to me, are means of filtering the enormous amount of data that reaches us—from both inside and outside—and arranging it in a particularly useful way. The concept of "amplification" in dreamwork addresses this issue of perception and consciousness, and bridges the Sioux experience of visions and the dream as viewed from a Jungian perspective. Jung's concepts of "active imagination" and "guided imagery" may be seen to represent other dimensions of this same psychic process.

At the same time as opening up possibilities, Jung also considered dreams to have a kind of limiting or braking effect on consciousness, acting as a corrective as much as an additional source of information and information processing. "Dreams are impartial, spontaneous products of the unconscious psyche," he said,

> outside the control of the will. ... [Dreams] are therefore fitted, as nothing else is, to give us back an attitude that accords with our basic human nature when our consciousness has strayed too far from its foundations or runs into an impasse.[6]

The function of the dream in this context is consequently to correct our attitude, to reorient a wrongly directed ego more than to provide a supplement to our perceptions.

Dreams, whether in a Jungian or a Sioux context, are always personal in the sense that they affect us directly and are not merely an abstract picture of other realities to which we have no responsibility or relationship. Jung observed, however, that some dreams seem to transcend the purely personal:

> Normally, the dream material serves only to compensate the conscious attitude. There are, however, comparatively rare dreams (the "big" dreams of primitives), which contain clearly recognizable mythological motifs. Dreams of this sort are of especial importance for the development of personality. Their psychotherapeutic value was recognized even in ancient times.[7]

So where do mythological motifs originate and how do we recognize them? Jung admitted that

> We seldom meet with a completely transparent and coherent dream in an adult. Frequently the dreams of adults belong to the class of dreams which, though meaningful and logical in themselves, are unintelligible because their meaning does not in any way fit the thought-process of the waking consciousness. The great majority of dreams, however, are confused, incoherent dreams that surprise us by their absurd or impossible features.[8]

It is not easy, it turns out, to come to an understanding of Jung's idea of the mythological motif dream. Does the Jungian analyst "supply" the mythological motif him or herself? Does the dreamer?

Mythological motifs are certainly useful as central themes of dream expression, and particularly so if we can discover the actual function or even indeed the status of such dreams. Jung said that dreams could be "big" in the sense that they touched "upon the characterological structure of the personality" and had a "valid meaning over months or years." "All such dreams," he observed,

> can be considered symbolic statements, but some reach even the archetypal level of symbolization, using images that are meaningful in mythological or religious systems that may not even be known to the dreamer's waking mind.[9]

It is, therefore, the images in dreams (rather than any dream narrative) that have a similarity to mythological motifs; the motifs themselves are only inferred from the appearance of familiar symbols that have other connections with already conscious and objective themes. Presumably these images were once unconscious, and when they appear they initiate or help to sustain religious and mythological interpretations and explanations of human experience.

Dream symbolism is a major source of data supporting the idea of the archetypes (along with myths, stories, fairy tales, and other narrative forms, and in addition to patterns of behavior). Jung's constant position on archetypal themes was that they applied always to everyone everywhere; they were the structural components of the universe when it was viewed from the perspective of mind rather than matter. But there is no reason to suppose that archetypal patterns or themes have always been inherent in the universe, in universal mind, or in a universal form. They may well have a history—or histories. Indeed, depending upon the school of Western psychology that one chooses, dream images can represent almost anything, as Jung unwittingly demonstrated when comparing his results and interpretations with those of Freud and Adler in similar circumstances.

"Big dreams," for Jung, carried the symbolic weight of mythological themes and perhaps archetypes; for the Sioux, they were decidedly practical, and had implications not only for the individual life, but for the community as a whole. Indeed, when he deals with the subject of myth, Jung seems to move, not simply toward the familiar cultural symbols coded in myths, but also toward the idea of prophetic or prospective dreams. "The real difficulty begins when the dreams do not point to anything tangible," he observed,

> and this they do often enough, especially when they hold anticipations of the future. I do not mean that such dreams are necessarily prophetic, merely that they feel that way, they "reconnoitre." These dreams contain inklings of possibilities and for that reason can never be made plausible to an outsider.[10]

Among tribal peoples the content of an important dream is immensely practical, warning of danger or informing the dreamer about future events. These kinds of dreams are common enough that people do not regard them as extraordinary. "Big," in this context, may simply be a kind of dream that Jung had not previously encountered, one that needed no interpretation of symbols and that related directly and powerfully to events in the physical world. Speaking on a Munich radio show of his trip to Africa, for example,

Jung recalled what he characterized as a *big dream*, which suggests exactly this kind of function:

> The only dream that occurred while I was there—at least, the only one that was reported to me—was the dream of an old chief, in which he learnt that one of his cows had calved, and was now standing with her calf down by the river, in a particular clearing. He was too old to keep track of his many cattle that pastured in the various open places in the forest, so he naturally didn't know this cow was going to calve, let alone where. But the cow and the calf were found just where he had dreamt they would be.[11]

This dream may have been "big" for Jung, but it was perhaps a more ordinary event for the chief.

To bring this discussion to a more grounded level, let us examine several dreams of the Sioux as recorded in a variety of sources. In 1911, Frances Densmore visited the Standing Rock Reservation, which straddles North and South Dakota, to record Teton Sioux music from the elders of the Sioux tribe. Instead of merely recording their music, she studiously transcribed the explanations given by the elders regarding the origin of their songs. Many of them said that they had received songs during their vision quest as a gift of a spirit. Several others said they had received songs in nighttime dreams and were able to recount the important parts of the dream in which they had received certain powers. They were obligated to display these dreams before the people to verify receiving the power.

One of the most interesting elders Densmore met was Brave Buffalo, who had received many powers from different animals through the traditional dream format. Over the years, he was able to increase his powers as a medicine man when different animals adopted him. Jung might have classified these dreams as "big," and they certainly were important to Brave Buffalo. His first dream came when he was a young boy:

> When I was 10 years old, I dreamed a dream, and in my dream a buffalo appeared to me. I dreamed that I was in the mountains and fell asleep in the shade of a tree. Something shook my blanket. It was a buffalo, who said, "Rise and follow me." I obeyed. He took a path, and I followed. The path was above the ground. We did not touch the earth. The path led upward and was smooth like smooth black rock. It was a narrow path,

just wide enough for us to travel. ... We went upward a long distance and came to a tent made out of buffalo hide, the door of which faced us. Two buffalo came out of the tent and escorted me in. I found the tent filled with buffalo and was placed in the midst of them.

The chief buffalo told me that I had been selected to represent them in life. He said the buffalo play a larger part in life than men realize, and in order that I might understand the buffalo better day by day they gave me a plain stick (or cane) and told me that when I looked at it I should remember that I had been appointed to represent them. The cane was similar to the one which I now carry and have carried for many years.[12]

After receiving this dream and the cane, Brave Buffalo was required to demonstrate the buffalo power before his community. He clothed himself in a buffalo skin, complete with head and horns, and allowed the people in the village to shoot arrows at him. In spite of best efforts by men in the camp, no one could wound him while he was clothed in the buffalo skin. He said later that when he was much older he often performed the same feat with people shooting guns at him. Clearly we have phenomena far different than what we encounter in Western dream analysis and interpretation. We can pass the demonstrations off as some form of "superstition," but might be better served by assuming that Brave Buffalo's power actually worked. Certainly, the people in his camp would have made every effort to discredit anyone so bold as to demand this kind of test of his powers. (Since there were frequently great jealousies between medicine men, there would have been several people in the crowd eager to prove him wrong!)

Brave Buffalo had another dream when he was twenty-five years old and camping in the mountains:

The dream came to me when I was asleep in a tent. Someone came to the door of the tent. He said he had come for me, and I arose and followed him. It was a long and difficult journey, but at last he led me to a beautiful lodge. All the surroundings were beautiful. The lodge was painted yellow outside, and the door faced the southeast. On entering the lodge I saw drawings on the walls. At the right of the entrance was a drawing of a crane holding a pipe with the stem upward, and at the left was a drawing of a crow holding a pipe with the stem downward. I could see that the occupants of the lodge were living happily and luxuriously. I was escorted to the seat of honor opposite the entrance and reached it with difficulty, as the lodge was filled with brush, and I was not accustomed to making my way through thickets. [At this point the occupants of the lodge seem to have been recognized as elks:] The elks in the lodge watched me with interest and encouraged me to go on, saying they had something they wished to tell me. At last I managed to reach the seat assigned me, and when I was seated the elks rose and said they had heard that I was a great friend of the buffalo, and that they wanted me to be their friend also. They said they had tested me by requiring me to reach this difficult place, and as I had succeeded in doing so they were glad to receive me. They then said that they were going to sing a song and wished me to learn it. [13]

In the narrative recounted by Brave Buffalo, we are not dealing with visions, either induced or spontaneous, but rather with nighttime dreams comparable to those that Jung's patients must have reported. And clearly this dream scenario is different from the traditional dream narrative that a Western psychoanalyst might encounter. Why is this dream different? It comes in the same manner, as do other dreams—since Brave Buffalo had been asleep in a tent and not performing a ceremony. Jung might say it represents a classic case of the "friendly animal" motif. Yet there was no immediate crisis that the dream resolved. On awakening, Brave Buffalo had new powers transcending those he had previously received. The elks noted his friendship with the buffalo, his fidelity to that responsibility, and wished to make an alliance with him. The consequences of that alliance were visible in the material world.

Suppose we return to Brave Buffalo's youth. He was raised within the traditional kinship family. He had no obvious talents that distinguished him from any other young boy. Yet by age twenty-five, as the result of two dreams, he had tremendous powers that were demonstrated in a physical event. This kind of experience occurs in many small tribal societies but does not appear in Western society or psychology. It cannot be subsumed under any existing doctrinal rubric on dreams. Can this experience merely be a "projection" from the unconscious in the Jungian sense of the term? What has been projected? The elk, traditionally, was regarded as having prodigious sexual powers yet Brave Buffalo was not provided with sexual prowess but instead received powers not usually associated with the elk.

Brave Buffalo did have an intense desire to understand the world around him and wanted to gain special powers to help him through life. Thus he was open to what Jung might have named as archetypal experiences. Brave Buffalo related the circumstances leading to his openness to dreams, which came about at a very young age:

> When I was ten years of age I looked at the land and the rivers, the sky above, and the animals around me and could not fail to realize that they were made by some great power. I was so anxious to understand this power that I questioned the trees and the bushes. It seemed as though the flowers were staring at me, and I wanted to ask them, "Who made you?" I looked at the moss-covered stones; some of them seemed to have the features of a man, but they could not answer me. Then I had a dream, and in my dream one of these small round stones appeared to me and told me that the maker of all was *Wakan Tanka*, and that in order to honor him I must honor his works in nature. The stone said that by my search I had shown myself worthy of supernatural help. It said that if I were curing a sick person I might ask its assistance, and that all the forces of nature would help me work a cure. [14]

These dreams might have been produced by a vision quest experience, but Brave Buffalo observed that he did not perform that ceremony:

> I am not required to fast, only to smoke, showing that I am at peace with all men. Dreams come to me now in a natural way. Often during the day when I am alone on a journey, and my mind is on many things, I stop to rest awhile. I observe what is around me, and then I become drowsy and dream. [15]

Most unusual would have been a ten-year-old boy receiving a healing stone for use in curing people. If this dream can be understood as a projection from Brave Buffalo's unconscious, it shows unusual twists and turns, because his initial desire was presumably to *understand* how things came to be, not to become a participant. Nevertheless, he is drawn into an active role, that of representing the higher powers.

We might also look at an extremely old dream, written down in the 1860s by a non-Indian who admired a Sioux man named Thick-Headed Horse. This dream features some motifs that are familiar to Jungians, the foremost of which is that Thick-Headed Horse discovers and rides a large snake monster into the spirit world where he encounters a number of Sioux medicine men who had lived long ago. He has many adventures, including a war with the Pawnees, traditional enemies of the Sioux. As the dream nears its conclusion, Thick-Headed Horse learns that the snake-monster is actually an old and very powerful medicine man named Big Snake, and he receives from Big Snake the power to return home and become one of the most capable of all historic Sioux medicine men.

The snake in this dream could represent the shadow, the libido, a present physical situation of sparse hunting, or some other, generalizable idea that might lead to an archetypal or mythological interpretation. It might be compared even with the snake that appears in the Garden of Eden or Jesus as a snake. One can look comparatively across the numerous societies that have featured snake motifs and discover many apparent similarities. Within the Sioux context, however, there is a simple and more specific explanation. The snake monster is a form in which Big Snake, a medicine man who once lived, chose to manifest himself to Thick-Headed Horse. For the Sioux it is possible in ordinary life for a man to have the power to assume or adopt other forms in which to express himself. That is what Big Snake did; no symbolic or mythological dimension need be involved.

After naming a number of similarities, overlaps, and concrete (Sioux) expressions of abstract (Jungian) concepts, I want to stress here the discontinuities created by crossing cultural traditions. Apart from instinctual patterns of response, I think that symbols and motifs—although they appear to have similarities—often are distinctly different across cultures. Though Jung's archetypal themes may be considered to exist in one way or another in every culture at every period of time, it is also the case that different archetypes carry different weights at different times and within different cultures. And yet, regardless of the psychic task to be accomplished, Western psychologists have frequently chosen mythological motifs with a Greek origin and story line. They have needed little encouragement to appropriate a symbol from one culture and insist that it is present in other cultures, and it appears they have made Greek mythology the standard against which other cultures are judged.

The most abused symbol in this sense may well be Oedipus, who comes through Freudian psychology to stand in the popular mind for all manner of incestuous relationships, for the problem of breaking from the mother and achieving maturity, and for the reconciliation of the individual with his or her origins. To cite Oedipus as a universal mythological motif, and to suggest that it tells us about family relationships, strikes me as a problematic instance of this inclination to universalize the symbolic. Indeed, only by doing violence to the Oedipus story, and to other mythological narratives, can Oedipus be regarded as a universal archetype. Oedipus, you will recall, is the subject of several Greek plays in which his life is presented as predestined, hinting at the possibility of a cosmic vocation. It is well worth noting, however, the nature of that predestination. His story does *not* end with his entry into his mother's bed or his slaying of his father; it ends at Colonus, where he is a respected prophetic figure, blind to this world but able to see into other worlds. Powerful Greek cities all hoped that he would be buried within their territory.

Oedipus is thus a blessed figure at the end of his life. Extracting the incestuous and patricidal image from this longer, vocational drama may actually misread the mythological motif. Indeed, if we were to focus on the later Oedipus, the blind man who can see between two worlds, we find a similar number of parallels in other cultures. Samuel the prophet, Tiresias, Milton, and even Black Elk are blind, or nearly so, when they achieve their greatest fame as wise old men. Why not use the story to constitute the old wise blind man as an archetypal figure? I am not suggesting this kind of redeployment of the story, of course, but wish simply to make the case for the virtues of specificity in thinking about archetypes, and for the utility of engaging in such comparative dialogues. Indeed, if we were to pursue the question of the blind wise man, we might find ourselves turning back to the question of prophecy and the prospective dream. After all, the fame of the blind wise man derives from his ability to view multiple times and spaces simultaneously, and thus to predict the future.

Jung down-played the prophetic importance of prospective dreams but he could not deny the possibilities they held out:

> The occurrence of prospective dreams cannot be denied. It would be wrong to call them prophetic, because at bottom they are no more prophetic than a medical diagnosis or a weather forecast. They are merely an anticipatory combination of probabilities which may coincide with the actual behaviour of things but need not necessarily agree in every detail.[16]

Why, we might ask, did Jung reject the prospective reality of dreams in this manner? Did he want overwhelming evidence of predictive capability, so there would be no doubt of the prophetic nature of dreams? His suggested answer is dependent largely upon the unconscious:

Dreams prepare, announce, or warn about certain situations often long before they actually happen. This is not necessarily a miracle or a pre-cognition. Most crises or dangerous situations have a long incubation, only the conscious mind is not aware of it. Dreams can betray the secret. They often do, but just as often, it seems, they do not. Therefore our assumption of a benevolent hand restraining us in time is doubtful. Or, to put it more positively, it seems that a benevolent agency is at work sometimes but at other times not. [17]

Sioux tradition, as we have seen, differs radically on this point. The dream, in Sioux context, is a communication between individuals and the powers of the universe, working with and through various helpful birds and animals. The dream is almost always prospective in the sense that it commands that the individual remain faithful to the narrative of the dream and reveal parts of it to the public, often in a display of powers. The dream is always the beginning of a new kind of life, now enhanced by a closer relationship with the friendly animal. In searching through written accounts of prospective dreams, however, I have found hardly any Sioux dreams that would be similar to prospective dreams as found in the Jungian literature. The Sioux dreams are almost unanimously directed to future action rather than future situations and possibilities.

Such dreams, often forecasting dire future events, can be as common-place among non-Indians as they have been among Indians. But perhaps Sioux people understood cosmic processes with greater clarity and had access to more powerful channels of communication, and so the *déjà vu* nature of the dream did not impress them. They expected it. They were intensely interested in the prospective knowledge that could be obtained in visions and dreams, and by using their sacred stones and other techniques.

If we have drawn these distinctions between Sioux and Jungian thought, it is also worth pursuing other kinds of overlaps and dialogues. When Jung said "the dream is a *spontaneous self-portrayal, in symbolic form, of the actual situation in the unconscious*," [18] what exactly was he saying? Here, Jungian and Sioux understandings speak to one another in productive ways. The "actual situation in the unconscious" must be understood at the deepest and most profound level of the collective unconscious, at that place where space, time, mind and matter are one basic unity proceeding in a forward direction at a specific pace. At those places and times where the collective unconscious has major influence in our lives, the movement of time can "push" forward all the layers of the individual unconscious and thereby promote specific personal actions.

I mention layers of the unconscious because Jung implied that, behind the personal unconscious, there were an increasing number of layers of universal possibilities and similarities. Beyond the personal, one might find family, town or city, geographical location, nation, race, historical time period and so forth, all of which composed the individual in one sense or another. All of these layers and categories would have to be affected if the impingement of *cosmic* time, and the power of cosmic space, were to be expressed or realized physically. Hence the movement of cosmic reality forces everything else that is more specific to shift or to move forward. For people who have not yet realized themselves as personalities, the personal unconscious and its repressions move forward into consciousness in the confused manner in which they have been repressed. The fewer the repressions, the greater the *chance* of receiving clear directions. Consequently the most mature and profound individuals would be those people who have not only been capable of individuation but who have benefited from a number of experiences—the clarity of interspecies communication, for example, or the acquisition of power through the medium of the vision. These individuals would be capable of receiving information in their dreams about where the physical realization of *cosmic* process might move.

This interpretation is not the only way that we can understand dreams. But I would argue that it presents a viable and entirely consistent view of dreams that takes into account the significant distinctions between tribal/primitive peoples and "civilized" humanity. Why should we suppose that a people who have systematically devised a procedure for minimizing traumatic personal relationships, who have identified and developed a means of determining individual vocation, and who are completely at home with and accept the presence of other forms of life, should not be such natural people that the preponderance of their dream experiences would be prospective dreams? On the other hand, is it not possible that a civilized people with few family linkages, in a society that stresses individualism at all costs, and that considers only the tangible physical existence of something as "real," would have prospective dreams—but would be so mistrusting as to experience them as simply the perpetual circling of the Self around the objective existence of the ego?

Jung himself said,

Although dreams in which these mythological parallels appear are not uncommon, the emergence of the collective unconscious as I have called this myth-like layer, is an unusual event which only takes place under special conditions. It appears in the dreams dreamt at important junctures in life. [19]

Here, I think that Jung determines "important junctures" from a predominantly European point of view. It is well known that so-called primitives have ceremonies designed to bring about the transposition from one critical juncture to another, whether these are initiation rituals or condolence rites. That Western Europeans have needed some kind of archetypal structural guidance at such junctures—and during particular stages in life—should come as little surprise. They have little psychological protection from the world in the sense that they are unable to realize, ceremonially and physically, the important movements that growth entails.

I will not belabor this point since it should be reasonably clear that in the matter of dreams Indian people have a concrete understanding of what is happening, whereas the civilized subjects of Jung's psychology are subject to a more arbitrary functioning of the unconscious. It might be useful to suspend the application of archetypal symbolism when interpreting dream materials and act as if the dream provided a glance at future probabilities. Ultimately, if Jungian psychology and Sioux traditions are to speak to one another, the Jungian concept of the Self needs to be extended to consider the Sioux view of dreams, which always addresses the outer situation (whereas for Jung it can be completely intrapsychic). The primitive traditions do speak profoundly of rocks, animals, and so forth, but these things do not necessarily function as symbols that lead back to the Self. Dreams, I would suggest, following Sioux tradition, are also tangible intersections with a reality that looms in front of us. By understanding this broader canvas on which our psychic life is painted, we can make considerably better use of dreams and understand our vocational responsibilities with greater precision.

COMING TOGETHER

We began by noting the affinities that some Jungians have found among the traditions of Plains and other Native American people, and we have now explored a number of overlaps and possibilities existing between the two bodies of thought. As the compatibility between Jungian psychology and Sioux religious traditions becomes clearer, additional connections may be discovered that highlight new issues not previously considered. Some of us might even contemplate the possibility of a transcendent framework that would incorporate the best insights of each body of knowledge in a new psychology. What frameworks and approaches would best encourage the creation of such a synthesis? What points of connection and overlap would be most productive? We can conclude our comparative dialogue by exploring these issues in broad strokes.

Before beginning, it will be important to remind ourselves to guard vigilantly against the unfortunate tendency of Western scholars to reinforce pre-existing worldviews. As we have seen, scholars have often incorporated evidence and anecdotes from the experiences of primitive peoples into their own frameworks, and then cited such evidence as additional proof of the universality of their own beliefs. Consider, as a brief example, the question of Noah's Flood. For some Western people, the tales of monstrous floods found in other people's traditions are often cited as evidence proving that Noah's Flood was a historical event, thereby validating the beliefs of Christianity. Flood stories from around the globe actually have value to the extent that they suggest that there might have been a universal flood some time in the past. To name such a flood as "Noah's," however, is to wield the power held by the West over these other peoples and other traditions, reinforcing in an intellectual context what has already been accomplished through histories of colonialism and other forms of domination. This issue is not insignificant. Currently psychologists, physicists, astronomers and other scholars are visiting Indian country in search of bits of evidence they can add to bolster existing intellectual frameworks and edifices. Optimistic plans are being made by some physicists to create a language that will incorporate non-Western insights and better express ideas in physics. The assumption is that the Western explanation needs no more than minor adjustments whereas the non-Western scheme only hints at a solution.

It is also worth noting that in psychology and anthropology, and many times in comparative religion, the imprecise translation of words by Western thinkers makes it impossible to transmit the proper meanings from one cultural context to another. Adding a concept from non-Western sources does not necessarily ensure a proper interpretation of data, and often eliminates the nuances that gave content to the original idea. Indeed, many concepts are often inhospitable to literal transmission. Time, space, and other ideas take on different meanings when found in non-Western traditions. In discussing a possible psychology that builds on both Jungian thought and Sioux traditions, we must approach the task from a neutral perspective, in effect transcending the parochial nature of both bodies of knowledge, escaping the Western tendency to incorporate others rather than to dialogue with them. To do so, we must necessarily treat psychology as a philosophy—an effort that Jung himself would have eventually undertaken, I believe.

We can begin with the recognition that the fundamental reality in our physical world is a strange kind of energy that is found within everything—from stars to humans to stones to quantum energy fields. This energy is personal—or can be experienced personally. It is mysterious, and so potent and varied that it is useless to explore all the possible ways to define it. If we say anything about this power or energy, we say that the world we live in, sustained by this power, is ultimately spiritual and not physical. Here we have the opportunity to unite psychology and religion with the energy fields of quantum physics. As the English physicist and mathematician Sir James Jeans, theoretical physicist F. David Peat, and others have proposed, the world might simply be something like a giant thought.[1] Investigators of near-death experiences suggest the same thing.[2] And many Indian tribes start from similar propositions.

Carl Jung went a good distance toward theorizing the ways that psyche and matter might be connected. "The deeper 'layers' of the psyche lose their individual uniqueness as they retreat farther and farther into darkness," he said, and we can productively revisit this assertion, previously discussed in an earlier chapter:

"Lower down," that is to say as they approach the autonomous functional systems, they become increasingly collective until they are universalized and extinguished in the body's materiality, i.e., in chemical substances. The body's carbon is simply carbon. Hence "at bottom" the psyche is simply "world."[3]

Jung was not engaging in simple reductionism here, but truly believed that some effort needed to be made to resolve the mind-matter split of Western scientific thinking. "The microphysical world of the atom exhibits certain features whose affinities with the psychic have impressed themselves even on the physicists," he observed. And he concluded that "Here, it would seem, is at least a suggestion of how the psychic process could be 'reconstructed' in another medium, in that, namely, of the microphysics of matter."[4]

In other words, psychic processes could be represented in the same manner in which we observe how matter reacts in our experiments. Since our experiments are rigidly controlled ways of forcing the physical world to respond to mathematical questions, the results of our scientific investigations already suggest evidence of the psyche. "It is not only possible but fairly probable," said Jung, "that psyche and matter are two different aspects of one and the same thing."[5] In many writings, he adopted this premise, and it proved exceedingly useful in explaining unusual psychic phenomena. The identification of psychic energy with physical energy effectively moves the discussion of the physical world into another framework—and vice versa. One could now accept the occurrence of physical events that had no obvious physical relationship with what had gone before. Jung devised the term "synchronicity" to describe such unusual conditions, in which mind and matter seem independently to create an event. He then suggested that "the synchronicity phenomena point, it seems to me, in this direction, for they show that the nonpsychic can behave like the psychic and vice versa, without there being any causal connection between them."*[6]

If the psyche could act in a manner similar to "matter" as we know it, then it seems likely that space and time are not the boundaries we have been taught to believe. As we have seen, it then followed for Jung that "the psyche could be regarded as a mathematical point and at the same time as a universe

---

*   For a stunning example of this observation, see pp. 159-161 in *Living in the Borderland: The Evolutions of Consciousness and the Challenge of Healing Trauma.*

of fixed stars," in effect negating the Newtonian belief in rigid categories for these two basic ideas but not quite reaching the Kantian belief that they were means of apprehension.[7] If the psyche were to be regarded as a part of the substratum of the physical world, then that world would have to be infused with, supported by, or connected with a form of personal energy. Jung speculated on "the hypothetical possibility that the psyche touches on a form of existence outside space and time" and therefore "presents a scientific question-mark that merits serious consideration for a long time to come."[8]

These ideas sound like the speculations of the philosophical physicist rather than the findings of a practicing psychoanalyst, but they represent Jung's efforts to extend the reach of psychology to the other sciences. Clearly, he was willing to engage a search for a metaphysical common ground that would help to make sense to modern science. That science has often been an expression of a deeply materialistic practice that aggressively asserts a position largely devoid of the metaphysical. Ironically, Western science's insistence on material proof for such entities as "the soul" stands in stark contrast to the fantastically abstract technological world and culture that has created science and in which it functions.

In contrast, Jung's proposed extension of the psyche to a fundamental place in the material world—at least to the world that we have been taught to believe as material—gives us a possibility for the unification of knowledge and a metaphysics that is neither ethereal nor material, but which consists of "mind-stuff" or "thinking matter." So we begin with a recognition of the existence of "substance-thought," which appears to be the basis for the physical universe and offers the possibility of apprehending it. We have a self-aware, thoughtful universe that is also the psyche. Here, we might imagine, archetypes become something akin to the equivalent of the formulas describing the physical universe in physics, and may well be seen as comparable to the prophecies of visions, as they give us access to other spaces and superior, non-chronological time.

Jung grasped the possibilities of this unity when he speculated that at bottom the body was pure carbon and the psyche was simply "world."[9] Were Jung alive and writing today he would likely embrace the concept that the universe is composed of "mind-stuff," since it gives mind equal status with matter. Jungians today might well go beyond Jung's own thought and demonstrate the broader relevance of Jungian psychology by thoroughly examining phenomena of mind that have previously been rejected as topics for serious scientific inquiry.

We still have the problem, however, of approaching this mysterious energy on its own terms. In the West, because of the spectacular progress of hard science, we treat the energy as a wholly physical phenomenon. The physical energy that we identify and use in physics, and apply in our technology, becomes the only kind of energy we can accept or visualize.

The Sioux approached this mysterious energy differently, by recognizing it first in personalities, then in the motions of the natural world. They reasoned that it was necessary first to seek a personal relationship with the Great Mysterious, knowing that physical manifestations would follow. Western science, following Roger Bacon, worked from the opposite direction, believing that humans could force nature to reveal its secrets, which, in the end, did not allow science to consider the concept of personal relationships at all.

The Sioux simply petitioned nature for friendship. As we have seen, there is a good deal of the Sioux attitude to be found in Jungian thought. For Jung, the unconscious produced data for the conscious mind. It could not be commanded or forced to produce data or to reveal its ultimate nature. In therapy, Jungian psychology has sought to rearrange the symbols and energies of the conscious mind, making room for the unconscious to offer its message. In this sense, Jungian techniques also petition nature, and they do so in the interest of personality and maturation, rather than reductionist science.

The scientist produces complex mathematical equations to demonstrate his or her knowledge of the physical world, and while some of these formulas are exhaustingly complex in mathematical terms, quite often they can be summed up in simple equations such as $F=ma$ or $E=mc^2$. One goal of science is to produce a body of knowledge such that these formulas can be understood and used by anyone with a minimum of training. They become "laws of nature" when they gain acceptance by a large number of people. This abstract knowledge is then taught from generation to generation until it becomes commonplace. At that point, questioning it is regarded as nonsense or insanity. But such knowledge is severely limited as an explanatory scheme since it only tells us how nature responds when subjected to force and required to do extraordinary things. We still do not know what nature, left undisturbed, could tell us if we were merely patient petitioners.

Instead of formulas derived from an instrumental encounter with nature, the Sioux opened themselves to communications from nature, allowing nature to speak to them in dreams or visions. Birds, animals, and even rocks—each representing the higher spiritual powers—educated the people about the structure of reality. Descriptions of the destiny of individuals, revealed in these experiences, introduced the people to the idea that, in addition to the passage of mundane chronological time, there was another temporal realm in which a different reality was working to create the future of chronological time. Quite often the person receiving assistance from the higher powers was given songs to share. The songs and the stories of how they were given were remembered and used as models for increasingly sophisticated approaches to nature. These songs often led to other songs in the same manner that Newtonian physics provided the foundation for theories of relativity and indeterminacy in the exploration of the physical world.

If the so-called primitives had an understanding of the physical world equivalent to that of modern physics—expressed in personal rather than mathematical terms—then Jungian psychology does not need the concept of "the primitive" to explain its findings. Indeed, such a categorization gets in the way of a meaningful inquiry and exchange. We have seen the sometimes ludicrous characterizations of the primitive articulated by Jung. The belief that primitive man could not distinguish himself from his environment, for instance, prevents us from understanding the complex relations humans have had with their environments. Jung did use "primitive" in a positive fashion when referring to non-Western peoples' subjective relationships to the world, and to their eschewing the objective materialistic interpretation of natural phenomena. He did not, however, reconcile his contradictory views on the primitives. Eliminating the concept of the primitive from Jungian psychology does not injure that psychology—unless, of course, one feels it is necessary to maintain Jung's reliance on outmoded cultural evolutionary doctrines. Rather, such a cleansing enables his psychology to understand and participate more easily in the experiences and thoughts of other cultures. It avoids the obvious problem, highlighted earlier, of presenting the primitive as at once nearly inert and at the same time as the best living example of psychological maturity. And, more important, it prevents living people from being categorized as representatives of an earlier evolutionary moment, and thus cast as underdeveloped and inferior.

We might also rethink Jung's treatment of animals. That treatment reflects the science of his day, when animals were believed to have no mind, few feelings, and were guided primarily by a mysterious undefined force known as instinct. In today's world, Jung would have to confront a much more sophisticated body of evidence examining the nature of the animal psyche. There is now considerable evidence that other creatures enjoy an emotional life similar, and perhaps equal, to ours. Given that animals are creatures that demonstrate complex mental processes and possess considerable knowledge of the world, we must change how we conceive of their thought processes and means of communication. Jung would not have hidden behind "instinct" as an explanation for animal behavior. Nor would he have avoided the difficult task of exploring this new understanding of the deeper psyche that allowed all creatures to have a full emotional and intellectual life.*

If we eliminate the traditional assumption that "humans are superior" when describing reality, how might we reframe our questions? Recognition of the parity of other creatures in terms of psychological and spiritual capability was the hallmark of the Sioux understanding of other living things. Hence the belief that the animals could assist humans became a real option for action. This attitude was not a "worshipping" of the animals, as uninformed theologians might say, but rather the adoption of a posture of humility before an aspect of nature that they did not fully understand.

Jung himself, though in a confused way, encourages us to pursue such issues. He once remarked in his Dream Seminar on something he had been told by the Brazilian Indians: "They say that the only difference between themselves and red parrots is that the parrots are birds and they are not; otherwise they are exactly the same." [10] The Brazilians were describing the psychological similarities they shared with parrots, much as the Sioux might have told him that they and the buffalo were the same people. Jung seems to have missed this point, remarking that,

> We would say we are all human beings, but some are English and some are German, showing that we have advanced far enough to discriminate between man and man, but they even fail to notice the difference between man and animal. [11]

---

* Vine Deloria foresaw a time when "Some of us might even contemplate the possibility of a transcendent framework that would incorporate the best insights of each body of knowledge in a new psychology." *Living in the Borderland: The Evolution of Consciousness and the Challenge of Healing Trauma* presents one such framework. What Deloria is describing above is the psychic space in which the Borderland personality lives. They reflect a consciousness that resembles the Sioux psychic experience in many ways but, for most, without the kind of formalized culture and rituals typical of old Sioux culture. They are not Sioux; they are not Indians of any stripe. The Borderland personality represents a new and emergent consciousness—a "new understanding of the deeper psyche," in Deloria's terms—that is co-emergent with the Western psyche's reconnection with its deep roots in nature, from which it was cleaved.

What his comment reveals for us is that while Western thinkers are trained to distinguish between humans and animals on a morphological basis, they have had difficulty conceiving of such similarities in psychological terms, having rejected the concept of animal thought and emotions that would be essential to such a psychological affinity.

Jung thus was led to understand human-animal communications as projections from the emotionally disturbed human to the objects around him. This notion—inherited from Lucien Levy-Bruhl and cast in terms of the "primitive"—never adequately explained why a human being, living in a wholly subjective world, would or could objectify the world and eliminate his intimate subjective apprehension of it. The Sioux stories take us in a more productive direction. Recall, for instance, the medicine man Goose, who, because he had a strong relationship with other creatures and the little stones, petitioned the buffalo, which willingly came and sacrificed itself for him. What do we make of the people who swore that birds could speak their language? Since the messages they received made sense and provided them with information they could not have obtained elsewhere, these experiences may indeed have happened exactly as related. A new psychology must take such possibilities into consideration, rather than forcing them into frames of symbolic analysis inherited from the last century, which have already demonstrated their inability to capture fully the human experience of animals and the world.

The Sioux tradition can also make a major contribution to Jungian thinking regarding the family. Trapped in the European middle class perspective on the family, Jung was not able to see that the individuation process could be nurtured from the very beginning by developing a focus on the child, even before birth, and raising it in an atmosphere where a variety of people of all ages could care for it. Outlining kinship responsibilities meant defining the roles of each person in relation to all others in the family, thereby channeling psychic energy along fruitful paths. In the old days, the Sioux spaced their children because they were always vulnerable to the raids of enemies, and having several small children to care for meant the possibility of losing relatives. The extended family therefore is a concept that might be profitably imported to the Western middle class family, expanding that family to reach the size of a traditional Sioux family and allocating tasks that will relieve the pressures people now feel.

How are we to negotiate the finer intricacies of meaning in an exchange or synthesis between two distinct systems of thought? One of the key areas requiring our attention is that centered on the nature of the symbolic. "Symbol" finds its most precise meaning in the field of communications. It represents an identifiable part of the phenomenal world, whether we view the phenomenon as psychic or material, spiritual or physical. Carl Jung gives the symbol an important role in his psychology because it has, for him, not only a communicative value, but also the ability to represent some cosmic structural reality we can experience but not fully grasp. Andrew Samuels suggests that "Jung's own definition of symbol can be summarized as referring to the best possible formulation of a relatively unknown psychic content that cannot be grasped by consciousness."[12] This generic definition is useful to understand Jung's technical language, but there is considerably more breadth and meaning in the way that Jung sees symbols function. "When man creates a symbol," Jung observed,

> he creates something against and beyond nature, but which nevertheless fits into nature in a special way; and the closer it fits into nature, the longer it will last, the more natural it will be, and the better it will give expression to his instincts.[13]

But symbol creation is not the task of the ordinary human: "Only the passionate yearning of a highly developed mind, for which the traditional symbol is no longer the unified expression of the rational and the irrational, of the highest and the lowest, can create a new symbol."[14] This is so since it is "quite impossible to create a living symbol, i.e., one that is pregnant with meaning, from known associations."[15] It is the person of genius who intuits the symbol as an act of discovery or pioneering.

I emphasize this aspect of the meaning of the symbol because the Sioux radically—and instructively—differ from Western peoples on this subject. Jung claimed that,

> to interpret symbol-formation in terms of instinctual processes is a legitimate scientific attitude, which does not, however, claim to be the only possible one. I readily admit that the creation of symbols could also be explained from the spiritual side, but in order to do so, one would need the hypothesis that the "spirit" is an autonomous reality which commands a specific energy powerful enough to bend the instincts round and constrain them into spiritual forms. This hypothesis has its disadvantages for the scientific mind, even though, in the end, we still know

so little about the nature of the psyche that we can think of no decisive
reason against such an assumption.[16]

Here, the Sioux diverge from the scientific view espoused by Jung. As
we have noted earlier, the Sioux understand that "spirit" *is* in fact autonomous and in some ways distinctly "other."[17] Indeed, without an autonomous spirit, the world would be a machine, which it is not. Western observers present at Indian ceremonies usually misunderstand what is happening,
and the Jungian emphasis on symbols helps us explain why this is so. Western observers often do not listen to the Indian instructions with the extreme
care that is required, being too eager to establish a meaningful connection
between the ceremony and their own understanding of the world. To make
that connection, they look for symbols and symbolism, replacing one aspect
of the ceremony with another (the structure of the sweat lodge, for example,
symbolizes or "stands for" the world). But in Indian ceremonies, there are no
symbols in the Western sense. Most medicine men would not use the words
"symbol" or "symbolize" in their explanation of any part of a ceremony,
ritual or belief. One thing does not stand for another.

The proper word is "represent" and this word has an entirely different meaning in the Sioux context from its meaning in scientific language.
Representation means that there are spiritual presences in attendance in
the same way that people represent an interest group or institution. It does
not mean representation in terms of images or communication. Rather, the
spirits are here—present—ready to participate. Whatever is represented
in a ceremony has nothing to do with the communication of intellectual
concepts. When the medicine man describes the stones used for the sweat
lodge he will say what they represent within his own context of power.
Generally he will talk of the stone people and perhaps even give some of
their names. But stones do not, as a rule, stand for anything other than
themselves. Pledging the pipe to the directions involves an actual calling
of the directional powers to participate in the event. It does not symbolize
anything in particular, for it does not symbolize *at all*.

Thus it is that birds, animals, people, and plants become active participants in the ceremonies. Each is present as the representatives of their
species, of universally existing and applicable personal powers, and of the
spirits. We do not have here an intellectual understanding of the universe,
but an experiential happening of universal significance. Referring back to

the events found in many vision quests, we remember the birds, animals, and spirits that gave the vision questor direct information and assistance. None of these animals or birds were merely symbolic. In the ceremony, a specific energy appeared in particular forms, as birds, animals, and spirits with personal characteristics.

This perspective is strange to Western people, of course, and quite naturally causes consternation to the scientific mind. It suggests to them a primitive magic that can be exercised in the same way that Western man uses his electric dynamos or computers. In the end, whatever power is visible in such ceremonies is often dismissed as being "merely" psychological, having no basis in the world outside of the mind. But it is not magic. Medicine men are wary of magic and know that it is an improper use of medicine powers that do indeed exist outside the world of the mind. People believe that misused powers come directly back to the user in a highly negative and destructive manner. Seeking the death of someone, for example, can result in one's own death or the death of a relative, which in the kinship context is killing a part of one's own self. That the vision quest experience is not symbolic is further suggested by the fact that superior spirits supervise the use of medicine powers and that these powers can be taken away. A symbol in the Western context loses its potency primarily when we become over-familiar with it, and it no longer holds our devotion. We wear symbols out, whereas in the Sioux context a spirit can intervene to remove the power from the ceremony or withhold the representatives of that power.

It is not that Sioux people did not use symbols, but that in this spiritual context, we are talking about real experiences rather than borrowed or transferred meanings. The difference here can be well explained in Jung's own words:

> The naive primitive *doesn't believe, he knows*, because the inner experience rightly means as much to him as the outer. He still has no theology and hasn't yet let himself be befuddled by booby trap concepts. He adjusts his life—of necessity—to outer and inner facts, which he does not—as we do—feel to be discontinuous. He lives in one world, whereas we live in only one half and merely believe in the other or not at all. We have blotted it out with so-called "spiritual development" which means that we live by self-fabricated electric light and—to heighten the comedy—believe or don't believe in the sun. [18]

It seems entirely likely that symbols are necessary to the initial stages of belief, and undoubtedly true that symbolic representations are necessary to knowing. If there is to be adequate and permanent maturation, however, people must come to know in their *experiences*; they remain children if they only believe.

Dreams are the carriers of symbols, and here we find the largest and most intriguing distinctions between Jung and the Sioux. He would no doubt argue that the dreams we have examined were "big dreams," were therefore unusual, and were likely restricted to the principle or spiritual leaders of a community. Yet traditionally, among Sioux people, there were no restrictions on who could have these kinds of dreams. Everyone was expected to open themselves to the greater mystery sometime during adolescence, and few people failed to receive a response of some kind. A dream of any significance had to be acted out in front of the community to ensure its validity. If these dreams were only symbolic descriptions of psychic processes, as Jung felt dreams to be, it would have been hazardous to one's standing in the community to reveal them. Dreams required public performance, and public performance meant the shared experience of manifested power. A "symbolic" dream—in Jungian terms—would not have carried such power, and the dreamer would have been seen as fraudulent. This distinction between dreams with power and dreams that are read in terms of symbolic projection is not meant to denigrate Jungian psychology, but rather to clarify the unique nature of the Sioux experiences. Sioux dreams open up possibilities, for they offer evidence of the existence of a complex, multi-layered universe in which meanings and energies existed that would eventually manifest themselves in physical experiences.

Traditionally, the Sioux symbolized (and here I am indeed speaking of symbolic in the sense of an image "standing in" for a conceptual understanding; this is different from the practice of "representation" described above) human life as two roads bisecting a circle, creating four cardinal directions. A red road runs north to south and a black road runs west to east. These roads represent the good and evil that humans experience. The figure of the roads is useful because it summarizes the moral teachings of the people. Everyone is encouraged to walk the good red road and avoid the black one.* Jungian

---

* Another sharp distinction here is that Jungians would emphasize *bringing to consciousness and integrating* the "dark road"—the shadow, in Jungian parlance—rather than avoiding it. For Indians, the dark road would be as much external as internal, if not more so. From the Jungian

therapy may have, as its own representational equivalent of the red and black roads of the Sioux, the mandala. Common to many cultures, Jung began to give the mandala particular significance when he encountered symbols that occurred frequently in patients' dreams and that seemed to have cosmic significance. Jung had patients draw or paint mandalas, and he looked for mandala symbolism in their dreams as a matter of course. What he found were circles and fours. "The symbols of the circle and the quaternity, the hallmarks of the individuation process," he said, "point back on the one hand, to the original and primitive order of human society, and forward on the other to an inner order of the psyche."[19] If we eliminate the necessity to extend this definition back into "primitive" time to satisfy the needs of a cultural evolutionary framework, we simply arrive at a condition in which the circles and squares of the mandala represent a coming to grips with the goal of wholeness, the bringing together of psyche and matter, space and time, individual and universe.

Joseph L. Henderson suggests as much, noting that,

> The mandala symbol is not an end, but a beginning. It is nothing in itself. Anyone can draw magic circles or squares without significant effect. Only if it provides the initiatory approach to a valid symbol of the Self does the design truly come into its own. It becomes then the individual vehicle of initiation.[20]

Such an analysis holds particularly true if one sees the world as primarily psychic, not always requiring verification in the physical terms laid out by science. The difference, as I see it, is that Jungian patients work toward an understanding of wholeness as represented by the mandala—the mandala's appearance means progress in the therapeutic process; whereas the Sioux place themselves at the center of a kind of cosmic mandala prior to initiating contact with higher spiritual powers. They thus seek balance at the very start.

---

point of view, the (personal) shadow is viewed as primarily internal. There is also a "collective shadow" from the Jungian point of view, but typically this is seen as an external dynamic characteristic of a group or culture. Thus the Indian experiences both simultaneously, while Jungians might say that although individual and collective dynamics can and do exist at the same time, the individual has the choice of avoiding being taken over by either or both through consciousness-raising. (The psychology of the collective—as opposed to "collective psychology"—might be seen as a shadow element of a Jungian psychology that (over)emphasizes the psychology of the individual.)

"The symbol of the mandala," according to Jung,

> has exactly this meaning of a holy place, a *temenos*, to protect the centre.
> And it is a symbol which is one of the most important motifs in the
> objectivation of unconscious images. It is a means of protecting the cen-
> tre of the personality from being drawn out and from being influenced
> from outside.[21]

In addition to being protective, however, this language (when translated
into an indigenous context) might echo closely what a medicine man might
tell his people:

> The definition of the cross or centre as *diopismos*, the "boundary" of
> all things, is exceedingly original, for it suggests that the limits of the
> universe are not to be found in a nonexistent periphery but in its centre.
> There alone lies the possibility of transcending this world. All instability
> culminates in that which is unchanging and quiescent, and in the self all
> disharmonies are resolved in the "harmony of wisdom."[22]

Accordingly, the center, where the red and black roads meet, where the ceremony is performed and focused, is where the transcendence occurs.

Most of the mandalas Jung found in dreams had the quaternity as their
dominant geometric expression. "The use of the comparative method shows
without a doubt," he noted,

> that the quaternity is a more or less direct representation of the God
> who is manifest in his creation. We might, therefore, conclude that the
> symbol spontaneously produced in the dreams of modern people means
> something similar—*the God within*.[23]

But, as might be expected, modern mandalas have generally reflected
the actual psychic content of Western humanity and only hint at the possibility of God. Although they did not use the concept of "God," Sioux
people based all their beliefs on the overwhelming presence of *Wakan Tanka*
in everything. The circle and quaternity of the mandala—if we choose, in
this instance, to universalize—certainly appears in the preparations of a site
for a vision quest, with buffalo robes or prayer feathers set out to represent
the four directions as a physical re-creation of the universe.

In these terms, Jung saw Western religious beliefs as inadequate, declaring,

> I cannot refrain from calling attention to the interesting fact that whereas the central Christian symbolism is a Trinity, the formula presented by the unconscious is a quaternity. In reality the orthodox Christian formula is not quite complete, because the dogmatic aspect of the evil principle is absent from the Trinity and leads a more or less awkward existence on its own as the devil.[24]

Even more curious, however, was his analysis of the Trinity, in which he stated:

> the quaternity has everything to do with human psychology, while the Trinitarian symbol (though equally spontaneous) has become cold, a remote abstraction. Curiously enough, among my collection of mandalas I have only a small number of trinities and triads. They stem one and all from Germans.[25]

If Jung were searching for mandalas, he would certainly have felt at home in a Sioux camp.

In the mandala we find a useful device—comparable, once again, to an x-ray—that can be used in Western psychology as a therapeutic tool. By the same token, however, one might suggest that the use of the four directions in the Sioux pipe ceremony or vision quest is qualitatively different, a living mandala, an invocation or invitation by humans to higher powers to enter into a special kind of event. Since the pipe represents the earth and at the same time the universe, there is no question, in the minds of the people who perform this ceremony, that something powerful and beyond the secular is taking place. M. Esther Harding, following Jung, makes an interesting observation on this point:

> While occasionally one of the conventional Christian symbols occupies the centre in mandalas drawn by modern persons, it is more usual to find a figure that has no formal religious significance, such as a flower, a crystal, or a star. These symbols arise directly from the unconscious and so are still plastic and capable of holding the living meaning that flows into them from the awakened life springs within.[26]

That may be. I suggest that these mandalas demonstrate the power of the universal directions that move individuals forward to a new understanding of nature and away from their collectivity. The Sioux understanding of these particular things would suggest that even more is happening. A thoughtful universe is simultaneously the psyche, and mandalas may offer some flash of recognition of this reality. In our practice, however, the unconscious and the conscious must work simultaneously or we have no possibility of apprehending anything.

In logical terms we posit the prior existence of an unconscious that composes the universe. We then proceed to describe how the unconscious unfolds or manifests itself as an expression of consciousness. Throughout his writings and in his seminars, we see Jung continually distinguishing between the unconscious, which we cannot control, and the conscious, over which we have some influence. The process of therapy involves a sequence in which first the conscious is treated, and as the unconscious responds to the activity in consciousness, it in turn produces something new there, in the conscious mind, which again opens up other areas of the unconscious. With the pendulum moving back and forth, we are able to probe deeper into the unconscious and there we begin to work back down, as Jung phrased it, discovering universal patterns of behavior that transcend whatever memories or emotions we accumulated as individuals during our life experience. Psychotherapy was in itself conceived as a process wherein psyche and matter were brought together.

There is no way, scientifically, to "prove" that Sioux experiences are as I have described and interpreted them. Although the continuing performance of the ceremonies gives evidence that the experience is in some general way repeatable, most Western scientists would suggest that the world they know does not act in the manner in which it does for the Sioux, with openings in time and space, communications with representative animals, calls to vision and vocation, dreams that function in relation to the material world. And yet the most popular Jungian concept today seems to be synchronicity (archetypes having gone out of fashion). Recall Jung's definition: "the simultaneous occurrence of a certain psychic state with one or more external events which appear as meaningful parallels to the momentary subjective state."[27]

I think that the popularity of the synchronicity concept tells us something important. Jung knew he was struggling with a unique phenomenon. "The term explains nothing," he said, "it simply formulates the occurrence of meaningful coincidences which, in themselves, are chance happenings, but are so improbable that we must assume them to be based on some kind of principle, or on some property of the empirical world."[28] The Sioux conception of the great mystery being both energy and personality offers some suggestions for thinking further about the principle or property that is at stake. Synchronistic events for the Sioux are also acausal—at least on the plane of chronology and rationalist materialism—and it is this very lack of causality that distinguishes them from ordinary secular events.

I believe that Jung arrived at the same conclusion, except that he phrased it in terms of a philosophical question, thus relieving himself of the need to take a scientific stand:

> The assumption of a causal relation between psyche and physis leads on the other hand to conclusions which it is difficult to square with experience. Either there are physical processes which cause psychic happenings, or there is a pre-existent psyche which organizes matter.[29]

It should come as no surprise (and indeed, we should read this statement as something of our own analytical payoff) that Jung also postulated that "for the primitive mind synchronicity is a self-evident fact."[30] He intuited, just as many later Jungians have also intuited, connections between this line of thought and the very real practices of the people who have, traditionally, been designated "primitive" by the West.

The best course for the future, in my opinion, would be to explore the philosophical context that Jung proposed, in order to make his discoveries of the psyche even more comprehensible. If, within that context, we can see that the experiences of the Sioux fit reasonably well—and I believe that we have come some distance down this road—then I would feel that we have established a framework within which continued communication can take place. In short, though Jung was a man of his time when it came to developmentalist science, social relations, and colonial histories, new perspectives from contemporary science and psychology allow us to see a number of ways in which his psychology greatly resembles the Sioux traditions. It is worth pursuing this overlap and resemblance, for with almost every topic we have discussed, the Sioux had a broader vision that opens up new questions of both science and psychology. A recounting of Sioux traditions also offers us additional practical physical data to support further inquiry into the philosophical framework offered by Jung. At the same time, we can see from

Jung's insightful comments on a number of subjects, and from his frank admissions about others, that he had glimpsed a different vision of the world than the other thinkers of his time. This vision allows us to look anew at Sioux conceptions as well. In the exchange between Carl Jung and the Sioux traditions, then, we can find new sources of insight, vigorous comparisons, and synthetic opportunities, all of which should be considered vital to a continuing exploration of our world.

NOTES

Frequently Used Abbreviations

The works of C.G. Jung are referred to in the following notes as:

CW   *The Collected Works of C.G. Jung*, Volumes 1 to 18. 2nd edition, trans. R.F.C. Hull, ed. by Sir Herbert Read, Michael Fordham, Gerhard Adler and W. McGuire. Princeton, NJ: Princeton University Press, 1966-1970.

L   *Letters of C.G. Jung*, Volumes 1 and 11. Trans. R.F.C. Hull, sel. and ed. by Gerhard Adler and Aniela Jaffé. Princeton, NJ: Princeton University Press, 1976.

MDR   *Memories, Dreams, Reflections*. UK: Flamingo, 1983.

SDA   *Seminar on Dream Analysis*, Volumes 1 and 2, 4th edition. Zurich, Switzerland: The Psychology Club of Zurich, 1972.

VS   *The Visions Seminars*, Books One and Two. New York: Spring Publications, 1976.

Foreword by Jerome S. Bernstein

1   Deirdre Blair, *Jung: A Biography* (Boston: Little, Brown and Co., 2001), n. 42, p. 762.

2   *L*, Vol. 11, p. 596.

3   *MDR*, pp. 247-248.

4   *CW* 10, § 140.

5   *Ibid.*, § 141.

6   *Ibid.*, § 147.

7   *Ibid.*, "Archaic Man," § 113.

8   *CW* 18, "Healing the Split," pp. 254-255, 258.

9   *CW* 10, "Archaic Man," § 106.

10   *CW* 5, § 38.

11   *CW* 6, § 781.

12   *CW* 10, § 131; *CW* 8, § 516.

13   *CW* 18, pp. 254-255, 258.

14   *CW* 5, § 38; *CW* 10, § 141; *CW* 18, § 593.

Introduction by Vine Deloria, Jr.

1   *The Symbolic Life*, *CW* 18, "The Tavistock Lectures—V," p. 162. He also characterizes religions as therapeutic systems in "The Personification of the Opposites," in *Mysterium Coniunctionis*, *CW* 14, where he noted that "they give a foothold to all those who cannot stand by themselves, and they are in the overwhelming majority," p. 265, raising questions about the equivalence of archetypes and dogmas.

2   *Psychology and Religion, West and East*, *CW* 11, "Psychotherapists or Clergy," p. 3.

3   *Mysterium Coniunctionis*, *CW* 14, "Rex and Regina," p. 326.

4   *Psychology and Alchemy*, *CW* 12, "Introduction to the Religious and Psychological Problems of Alchemy," p. 17.

5   *Mysterium Coniunctionis*, *CW* 14, Editorial Notes, p. vii.

6   *The Symbolic Life*, *CW* 18, "Foreword to Von Koenig-Fachsenfeld: 'Wadlungen des Tramproblems von der Romantik dis zur Gegenwart,'" p. 773.

7   *The Practice of Psychotherapy*, *CW* 16, "Psychotherapy and a Philosophy of Life," p. 79.

8   *Psychological Types*, *CW* 6, "Psychological Types," p. 512.

9   *Aion*, *CW* 9ii, "The Structure of the Self," p. 261.

10   *Ibid.*

11   *Symbols of Transformation*, *CW* 5, "Foreword to the 4th Swiss edition," p. xxiv.

12   *L*, Vol. 1, "To Robert Eisler—25 June 1946," p. 427.

13   *Archetypes and the Collective Unconscious*, *CW* 9i, "Psychological Aspects of the Mother Archetype, On the Concept of the Archetype," p. 79.

14   *The Structure and Dynamics of the Psyche*, *CW* 8, "On the Nature of the Psyche," p. 213.

15   *Psychological Types*, *CW* 6, "X. General description of the Types, 3. The Introverted Type," p. 376.

16   *Symbols of Transformation*, *CW* 5, "The Battle for Deliverance from the Mother," p. 294.

17   *The Structure and Dynamics of the Psyche*, *CW* 8, "On the Nature of the Psyche," p. 205.

18   *The Practice of Psychotherapy*, *CW* 16, "Psychotherapy and a Philosophy of Life," p. 81.

19   *Psychological Types*, *CW* 6, "X. General Description of the Types, Intuition," p. 400.

20   *Ibid.*

21   Jung was not clear on the origin of archetypes, as witness his effort to explain the atom as an archetypal entity. "Concerning the Archetypes and the Anima Concept," in *The Archetypes and the Collective Unconscious*, *CW* 9i, p. 57:

But where did Democritus, or whoever first spoke of minimal constitutive elements, hear of atoms? This notion had its origin in archetypal ideas, that is, in primordial images which were never reflections of physical events but are spontaneous products of the psychic factor.

22 *The Structure and Dynamics of the Psyche*, *CW* 8, "The Structure of the Psyche," p. 152.

23 *Nietzsche's Zarathustra Seminar*, "Lecture V, 15 February 1939," pp. 1528-1529.

Chapter One: Jung and the Indians

1 *MDR*, p. 247.

2 *MDR*, p. 249.

3 *Civilization in Transition*, *CW* 10, "The Complications of American Psychology," p. 514.

4 *MDR*, p. 250.

5 *MDR*, p. 249.

6 *L*, Vol. 1, "To Antonio Mountain Lake—21 October, 1932," p. 101.

7 *Civilization in Transition*, *CW* 10, "Archaic Man," p. 65. Later Jung would discover that a bear had been a part of his family's crest of arms many centuries before, but he did not further reflect on this coincidence.

8 *L*, Vol. 11, "To Miguel Serrano—September 14, 1960," p. 596.

9 *VS*, Book One, Part Seven, p. 242.

10 For a full treatment of such organizations, see Philip Deloria, *Playing Indian* (New Haven, CT: Yale University Press, 1998).

11 This is not to say that others did not adopt the same or similar positions. Indeed, future Commissioner of Indian Affairs John Collier was in Taos at roughly the same time, and he too wrote of Indians possessing the deepest secrets of the human development of personality and community. Mabel Dodge herself probably belongs in this group, as does Mary Austin, Jean Toomer, and many others.

12 *Civilization in Transition*, *CW* 10, "Mind and Earth," p. 48.

13 *Ibid.*, p. 47.

14 *Ibid.*, p. 48.

15 *Civilization in Transition*, *CW*, Vol. 10, "The Role of the Unconscious," p. 13. Strangely, Arnold Toynbee also noted that the invaders of a land had a difficult time adjusting to new lands. In *An Historian's Approach to Religion*, he makes the following statement (p. 35):

> The colonists planted by the Assyrian Government on territory that had been cleared of its previous human occupants by the deportation of the Children of Israel soon found, to their cost, that Israel's undeported god Yahweh had lost none of his local potency; and they had no peace till they took to worshipping this very present local god instead of the gods that they had brought with them from their homelands.

16 Jung remarked, when he arrived in America to receive an honorary degree from Clark University, that there must have been significant intermarriage with Indians to achieve facial and skeletal similarities to Indians.

17 See Vine Deloria, Jr., *God is Red* (Golden, CO: North American Press, 1994), for a more detailed treatment of the relation between land and spirituality.

18 *Ibid.*

19 Barbara Hannah, *Jung, His Life and Work* (New York: Perigee Books, 1976), p. 163.

20 Paul Radin, *The Trickster: A Study in American Indian Mythology, with commentaries by Karl Kerényi and C. G. Jung* (London: Routledge and Paul, 1955).

21 *Archetypes and the Collective Unconscious*, CW 9i, "On the Psychology of the Trickster-Figure," p. 260.

22 *Ibid.*, p. 264.

23 *Ibid.*, p. 263.

24 *Ibid.*, p. 271.

25 *Symbols of Transformation*, CW 5, "The Dual Mother," p. 313.

26 *Nietzsche's Zarathustra*, p. 1282.

Chapter Two: The Negative Primitive

1 *The Structure and Dynamics of the Psyche*, CW 8, p. 104.

2 *SDA*, "Lecture VI—12 December 1928," p. 71.

3 *Ibid.*, p. 70.

4 *Psychological Types*, CW 6, "A Psychological Theory of Types," pp. 540-541.

5 *SDA*, "Lecture I—7 May 1930," p. 584.

6 *Ibid.*, p. 591.

7 *Ibid.*, p. 584.

8 *Psychological Types*, CW 6, "XI—Definitions," p. 463.

9 *Ibid.*, p. 420.

10 *The Archetypes and the Collective Unconscious*, CW 9i, "Psychological Aspects of the Mother Archetype," p. 101.

11 *L*, Vol. 1, "To Marie Ramondt—10 May, 1950," pp. 548-549.

12 *SDA*, "Lecture II—30 January 1929," p. 96.

13 *VS*, Book Two, Part Eight, p. 263.

14 *The Structure and Dynamics of the Psyche*, CW 8, "On the Nature of the Psyche," pp. 182-183.

15 *The Archetypes and the Collective Unconscious*, CW 9i, "The Psychology of Rebirth," p. 119.

16 *The Symbolic Life*, CW 18, "Symbols and the Interpretation of Dreams," p. 241.

17 *Ibid.*, "A Radio Talk in Munich," p. 556.

18 Luther Standing Bear, *Land of the Spotted Eagle* (Lincoln, NB: University of Nebraska Press, 1978; original 1933), p. 69.

19 *The Practice of Psychotherapy*, CW 16, "The Psychology of the Transference," pp. 194-195.

20 *The Structure and Dynamics of the Psyche*, CW 8, "On Psychic Energy," p. 50.

21 *Nietzsche's Zarathustra*, pp. 663-664.

Chapter Three: The Positive Primitive

1   *SDA*, "Lecture IV—12 February 1930," p. 470.

2   *The Symbolic Life*, *CW* 18, "Foreword to Aldrich: "The Primitive Mind and Modern Civilization," p. 562.

3   *Ibid.*, "Symbols and the Interpretation of Dreams," p. 256.

4   *Ibid.*, p. 205.

5   *Psychological Types*, *CW* 6, p. 459.

6   *Mysterium Coniunctionis*, *CW* 14, "III. The Personification of the Opposites, h. The Interpretation and Meaning of Salt," p. 254.

7   *Civilization in Transition*, *CW* 10, "Archaic Man," p. 60.

8   *Ibid.*, p. 59.

9   *Ibid.*, p. 58.

10   *The Symbolic Life*, *CW* 18, "Tavistock Lectures—I," p. 15.

11   *SDA*, "Lecture V—19 February 1930," p. 485.

12   *The Development of Personality*, *CW* 17, "The Significance of the Unconscious in Individual Education," p. 149.

13   *SDA*, "Lecture VII—6 March 1929," p. 152.

14   *The Structure and Dynamics of the Psyche*, *CW* 8, "The Transcendent Function," p. 79.

15   *VS*, Book Two, Part Twelve, p. 438.

16   Joseph Henderson, *Thresholds of Initiation* (Middletown, CT: Wesleyan University Press, 1967), p. 34.

17   *Psychological Types*, *CW* 6, "V. The Type Problem in Poetry, c. The Uniting Symbol as the Principle of Dynamic Regulation," p. 212.

18   *The Development of Personality*, *CW* 17, "Marriage as a Psychological relationship," p. 197.

19   *The Structure and Dynamics of the Psyche*, *CW* 8, "A Review of the Complex Theory," p. 104.

20   Jolande Jacobi, *The Way of Individuation* (New York: Harcourt, Brace & World, Inc., 1965), p. 65.

21   *Ibid.*, p. 67.

22   Joseph Henderson, "Reflections on the History and Practice of Jungian Analysis," in Murray Stein, *Jungian Analysis* (New York: Brunner/Mazel, 1982), pp. 23-24.

23   *Ibid.*, p. 24.

24   *SDA*, "Lecture VI—28 February 1929," p. 142.

Chapter Four: The Jungian Universe

1   *The Structure and Dynamics of the Psyche*, *CW* 8, "Synchronicity: An Acausal Connecting Principle," pp. 435-436.

2   *L*, Vol. 1, "To Laurence J. Bendit—20 April 1946," p. 421.

3   *Ibid.*, "Answers to Rhine's Questions—November 1945," p. 394.

4   *The Structure and Nature of the Psyche, CW* 8, "The Soul and Death," pp. 412-413.

5   *Archetypes and the Collective Unconscious, CW* 9ii, "The Phenomenology of the Spirit in Fairytales," pp. 223-224.

6   *The Structure and Dynamics of the Psyche, CW* 8, "Basic Postulates of Analytical Psychology," p. 348.

7   *VS*, p. 146.

8   *CW* 8, "Synchronicity: An Acausal Connecting Principle," p. 441.

9   *The Spirit in Man, Art, and Literature, CW* 15, "Richard Wilhelm: In Memoriam," p. 56.

10   Aniela Jaffé, *The Myth of Meaning* (New York: G.P. Putnam's Sons, for the C G. Jung Foundation for Analytical Psychology, 1971), p. 153.

11   *The Structure and Dynamics of the Psyche, CW* 8, "Synchronicity: An Acausal Connecting Principle," p. 518.

12   *Ibid.*, p. 506.

13   *Ibid.*, p. 511.

14   *Ibid.*, p. 513.

15   *SDA*, "Lecture IX—4 December 1929," p. 415.

16   *SDA*, "Lecture VIII, 27 November, 1929," p. 410.

17   *The Structure and Dynamics of the Psyche, CW* 8, "On the Nature of the Psyche," p. 233.

18   *Aion, CW* 9ii, "The Structure and Dynamics of the Self," p. 261.

19   *The Structure and Dynamics of the Psyche, CW* 8, "On the Nature of the Psyche," p. 230.

20   *Archetypes of the Collective Unconscious, CW* 9i, "The Psychology of the Child Archetype," p. 173.

21   *The Structure and Dynamics of the Psyche, CW* 8, "On the Nature of the Psyche," pp. 180-181.

22   Fred Alan Wolf, *The Dreaming Universe* (New York: Simon and Schuster, Inc., First Touchstone Edition, 1995) , p. 206.

23   *Ibid.*, p. 206.

24   William McGuire and R.F.C. Hull (eds.), *C. G. Jung Speaking: Interviews and Encounters*, (Princeton, NJ: Princeton University Press, 1977), p. 303.

25   *The Structure and Dynamics of the Psyche, CW* 8, "Basic Postulates of Analytical Psychology," p. 353.

26   *Ibid.*, "The Structure of the Psychic," p. 207.

Chapter Five: The Sioux Universe

1   *L*, Vol. 2, p. 5.

2   *The Structure and Dynamics of the Psyche, CW* 8, "The Psychological Foundations of Belief in Spirits," p. 303.

3   Esther Harding, *Psychic Energy: Its Source and Goal* (New York: Pantheon Books Inc., 2nd printing, 1950), p. 361.

4   James Walker, *Lakota Belief and Ritual*, ed. Raymond J. DeMallie and Elaine A. Jahner (Lincoln, NB: University of Nebraska Press, 1980), p. 18 and passim. Note: The Oglala were one of the seven bands of the Teton, or Western Sioux and currently reside at the Pine Ridge

reservation in South Dakota. The Teton, in turn, were the largest of seven divisions of Sioux people spread from Minnesota west to Montana.

5   Frances Densmore, *Teton Sioux Music*, Bureau of American Ethnology Bulletin 61 (Washington, DC: Government Printing Office, 1918; Lincoln, NB: University of Nebraska Press, reprint 1992), p. 185.

6   *Ibid.*, p. 177.

7   *Ibid.*, p. 93.

8   John Fire Lame Deer and Richard Erdoes, *Lame Deer: Seeker of Visions* (New York: Simon and Schuster, 1972), p. 204.

9   William Powers, *Sacred Language: The Nature of Supernatural Discourse in Lakota* (Norman, OK: University of Oklahoma Press, 1992), p. 102.

10   John G. Neihardt, *Black Elk Speaks: Being the Life Story of a Holy Man of the Oglala Sioux* (Lincoln, NB: University of Nebraska Press, 2004; original publication, 1932), p. 85.*

11   *Ibid.*, p. 21.

12   *Ibid.*, p. 180.

13   *Ibid.*, p. 30.

14   Densmore, *Teton Sioux Music*, p. 175.

15   Plenty Coups and Frank Bird Linderman, *Plenty Coups: Chief of the Crows* (Lincoln, NB: University of Nebraska Press, 2002), p. 65.

16   Powers, p. 96.

17   Densmore, p. 208.

18   Aaron McGaffey (A. McG.) Beede, "Western Sioux Cosmology and Letting Go the Ghost," August 29, 1919 (Chicago, IL: Edward Ayer Collection, Newberry Library), p. 3.

19   Densmore, *Teton Sioux Music*, p. 205.

20   Beede, "Western Sioux Cosmology," pp. 4-5.

21   Densmore, *Teton Sioux Music*, p. 210.

22   *Ibid.*

23   *Ibid.*, p. 235.

24   In the manner of non-Indian scholars, Densmore felt she had to have a stone and almost caused the death of an elder, Chased-by-Bears. "The stone," according to Densmore, "had been in the possession of Chased-by-Bear 40 years, and during that time he had faithfully fulfilled its requirements of character and action. Chased-by-Bears was 64 years old when he gave this information and seemed to be in perfect health." Densmore insisted on having his stone to photograph and to hear his stone songs, but when Chased-by-Bears gave it to her,

> he warned the writer [Densmore] that the stone was still subject to a summons from White Shield. After a few weeks the writer on returning to the reservation was informed that Chased-by-Bears had suffered a stroke of paralysis, which was attributed to his sale of the sacred stone and its song. Mr. Higheagle was requested to visit Chased-by-Bears and ascertain whether the report were true. It was found that Chased-by-Bears seemed to be in danger of death.

---

*   *Black Elk Speaks* should always be read in tandem with *The Sixth Grandfather: Black Elk's Teachings Given to John G. Neihardt*, ed. Raymond J. DeMallie (Lincoln, NB: University of Nebraska Press, 1984).

Chased-by-Bears' recovery took a long time and involved further revelations by him of an herb that he used for healing. "When the writer left the reservation a few weeks later he had almost regained his strength, and a year afterwards he appeared to be in his usual health." Unfortunately he died several years later. See Densmore, *Teton Sioux Music*, p. 235.

25   Frank McLynn, *Carl Gustav Jung* (New York: St. Martin's Press, 1997), p. 270.

26   *Ibid.*, p. 271.

27   *Civilization in Transition*, *CW* 10, "Archaic Man," p. 69.

28   *SDA*, "Lecture X—11 December 1929," p. 429.

Chapter Six: Jung and the Animals

1   *The Archetypes and the Collective Unconscious*, *CW* 9i, "Psychological Aspects of the Mother Archetype," p. 78.

2   *L*, Vol. I, "To Robert Eisler—25 June 1946," p. 427.

3   *Alchemical Studies*, *CW* 13, "Commentary on 'The Secret of the Golden Flower'," p. 12.

4   *The Structure and Dynamics of the Psyche*, *CW* 8, "The Structure and Dynamics of the Psyche," p. 152.

5   *VS*, Book One, Part One, p. 187.

6   *Ibid.*, Book Two, Part Eight, p. 295.

7   *The Symbolic Life*, *CW* 18, "Symbols and the Interpretation of Dreams," p. 234.

8   *VS*, Book One, Part Two, p. 70.

9   *Ibid.*, p. 40.

10 *SDA*, "Lecture III—29 November 1928," p. 37.

11 Jolande Jacobi, *Complex Archetype Symbol in the Psychology of C.G. Jung* (Princeton, NJ: Princeton University Press, 1959), p. 42.

12 *The Symbolic Life*, *CW* 18, "Foreword to Allenby: 'A Psychological Study of the Origins of Monotheism'," p. 657.

13 *The Symbolic Life*, *CW* 18, "Symbols and the Interpretation of Dreams," p. 235.

14 *Psychological Types*, *CW* 6, p. 376.

15 *L*, Vol. 1, "To Pastor Arz—10 April 1933," p. 119.

16 *The Symbolic Life*, *CW* 18, "Foreword to Bertine's 'Human Relationships'," p. 535.

17 *The Structure and Dynamics of the Psyche*, *CW* 8, "Basic Postulates of Analytical Psychology," p. 349.

18 John Yaukey, "Animal Intellect Gaining Respect," *Denver Post* (Sunday, September 19, 1999): 6A.

19 *Ibid.*: 2A.

20 Dimitia Smith, "Can animals think? Parrot seems to say yes," *Denver Post* (Saturday, October 16, 1999): 32A.*

---

* Here, the long gestation period for this manuscript becomes visible. In the midst of editorial revisions in fall 2007, Alex the parrot passed away, having acquired as many as fifty additional words since the 1999 report. See Benedict Carey, "Alex, A Parrot Who had a Way With Words, Dies," *New York Times* (September 10, 2007).

21   *L*, Vol. 1, "Answers to J. B. Rhine's Questions—November 1945," p. 395.

22   See Rupert Sheldrake, "The Case of the Telepathic Pets," *New Age Journal* (September/October, 1995): 99-103.

23   Douglas Burch, "Complex language found in prairie dogs," *Boulder Camera* (Sunday, September 29, 1991): 12A. See other studies: Adam Frank, "Quantum Honey Bees," *Discover* (September 1997): 80-86, on the language of bees; Peter M. Narins, "Frog Communication," *Scientific American* (August 1995): 79-83, on frog language; and Maria Ujhelyi, "Is There Any Intermediate Stage Between Animal Communication and Language?" *Journal of Theoretical Biology* Vol. 180 (1996): 71-76, for a general examination of the issue.

24   *Symbols of Transformation, CW* 5, "The Origin of the Hero," p. 176.

25   *Aion, CW* 9ii, "Gnostic Symbols of the Self," p. 186.

26   *Ibid.*, "The Structure and Dynamics of the Self," p. 226.

27   *Symbols of Transformation, CW* 5, "The Dual Mother," p. 328.

28   *Mysterium Coniunctionis, CW* 14, "Rex and Regina," p. 310.

29   *SDA*, "Lecture VI—12 December 1928," p. 70.

30   *Ibid.*, "Lecture IX—19 March 1930," pp. 538-539.

31   Donald G. McNeil, Jr. "From Many Imaginations, One Fearsome Creature," *New York Times/Science Times* (Tuesday, April 29, 2003). See David E. Jones, *An Instinct for Dragons* (New York: Routledge, 2002).

32   Jerry Paul Macdonald, in *Behold the Behemoth* (Las Cruces, NM: PaleoGenesis Press, 1999), makes a strong argument that behemoth and leviathan, prominent creatures in the Book of Job, were actual dinosaurs. Even more puzzling is a news release from the *Elyria Weekly Republican*, of Elyria, Ohio, November 8, 1877, entitled "Discovery of a Monster containing the Remains of a Human Being":

> Mr. Henry Woodard owns a stock ranch in the Indian Territory, in that Peoria Nation, on which is situated a big sulphur spring. The spring is surrounded by a quagmire, which is very deep and "slushy," and so soft that it will not bear any considerable weight. Mr. W. lately undertook to curb up the spring in order to get water more easily, and while working on the mire came upon what appeared to be an enormous bone. He at once began an examination, which disclosed the startling fact that it was the head of some mammoth beast. His curiosity was amused, and, with the assistance of three other men, he began the work of excavation. For four days they worked, but did not succeed in bringing the monster to the surface. They threw off the marl, but could not lift the head of this golithic giant. They found the skeleton well preserved and the immense teeth still in the jaws. The jaws were both in place, and the spinal column attached to the cranium. The earth was thrown off from the body to the length of twenty feet, but still the gigantic skeleton remained beneath. Three of the front ribs were forced out, and proved by measurement to be each eight feet in length. The dirt was removed from the inside of the osseous structure, and there lay a skeleton of a human being, with 102 flint arrow-points and fifteen flint knives. The cranium indicated that it was the skeleton of an Indian. It would have been impossible for the man to have been inside the animal without having been swallowed by him, and this theory is substantiated by the fact that the bones of the right side of the skeleton, were broken and mashed, apparently by force.*

---

*   The footnote reflects Vine Deloria's simultaneous openness to unexpected historical possibilities and his skeptical stance toward uniformitarian geology and evolution.

33   *The Practice of Psychotherapy*, *CW* 16, "Fundamental Questions of Psychotherapy," p. 124.

34   *VS*, Book One, Part One, p. 3.

Chapter Seven: Animals and the Sioux

1   Powers, *Sacred Language*, p. 154.

2   John Fire and Erdoes, *Lame Deer*, p. 162.

3   Charles Alexander Eastman, *Indian Boyhood* (Lincoln: University of Nebraska Press, 1991; original edition 1902), p. 63.

4   Luther Standing Bear, *My Indian Boyhood* (Lincoln, NB: University of Nebraska Press, 1988; original publication 1931), pp. 56-57.

5   *Ibid.*, p. 57.

6   Densmore, *Teton Sioux Music*, p. 251.

7   Standing Bear, *My Indian Boyhood*, p. 51.

8   *Ibid.*, p. 63.

9   Standing Bear, *Land of the Spotted Eagle*, p. 46.

10   Densmore, *Teton Sioux Music*, pp. 188-189.

11   Eastman, *Indian Boyhood*, pp. 67-68.

12   Standing Bear, *Land of the Spotted Eagle*, p. 76.

13   *Ibid.*, p. 158.

14   Standing Bear, *My Indian Boyhood*, p. 62.

15   *Ibid.*, p. 65.

16   Powers, *Sacred Language*, p. 152.

17   *VS*, Book One, Part One, p. 3.

18   *L*, Vol. II, "To A.D. Cornell—9 February, 1960," p. 542.

19   Standing Bear, *Land of the Spotted Eagle*, p. 215.

20   Standing Bear, *My Indian Boyhood*, p. 52.

21   Standing Bear, *Land of the Spotted Eagle*, p. 204.

22   Standing Bear, *My Indian Boyhood*, p. 103.

23   Standing Bear, *Land of the Spotted Eagle*, p. 58.

24   *Ibid.*, p. 52.

25   Standing Bear, *My Indian Boyhood*, p. 70.

26   Paul Radin, *The World of Primitive Man* (New York : Henry Schuman, 1953), p. 51.

27   Jerome S. Bernstein, *Living in the Borderland: The Evolution of Consciousness and the Challenge of Healing Trauma* (London, UK: Routledge: 2005), offers a contemporary Jungian perspective.

Chapter Eight: The Individual and Kinship

1   *SDA*, "Seminar 1928, Winter Term, part 1929—Lecture III, 23 October, 1929," p. 320.

2   *The Development of Personality*, *CW* 17, "Introduction to Wickes' 'Analsye Der Kinderseele'," p. 44.

3   *Ibid.* Note Jung's explanation given in his seminar on Zarathustra (*Nietzsche's Zarathustra*, pp. 1267-1268):

> … the original condition of the personality is an absolutely irrational conglomeration of inherited units. A part is from the grandfather on the mother's side, another from the grandfather on the father's side; the nose comes from 1759 and the ears from 1640, and so on. And it is the same with your different qualities, a certain artistic quality for instance, or a mental quality. All that is in the family tree, but unfortunately we do not have careful records of our ancestors, but only occasional portraits or perhaps some letter or old tales which allow us a certain insight. The grandmother may have said that one child was like her own grandmother, and so we reach back some generations.

4   *VS*, Book Two, Part Twelve, p. 453.

5   *SDA,* "Seminar 1928—Winter Term, Second Part, 1930, 29 January 1930," p. 453.

6   *MDR*, p. 233.

7   *Ibid.*

8   *The Development of Personality*, *CW* 17, "Analytical Psychology and Education," p. 85.

9   *Symbols of Transformation*, *CW* 5, "Part Two, VIII, The Sacrifice," p. 414.

10   *The Structure and Dynamics of the Psyche*, *CW* 8, "On Psychic Energy," p. 25.

11   Charles Alexander Eastman, *The Soul of the Indian* (Boston, MA: Houghton Mifflin, 1911), pp. 28-29.

12   *The Development of Personality*, *CW* 17, "Child Development and Education," p. 53.

13   Standing Bear, *Land of the Spotted Eagle*, pp. 202-203.

14   John Neihardt, *When the Tree Flowered: The Story of Eagle Voice, a Sioux Indian* (Lincoln, NB: University of Nebraska Press, 1991), p. 206.

15   Standing Bear, *Land of the Spotted Eagle*, p. 70.

16   *Ibid.*, p. 32.

17   *Ibid.*, p. 37.

18   John Fire and Erdoes, *Lame Deer*, p. 151.

19   *Ibid.*, p. 203.

20   *MDR*, p. 237.

21   Thayer Greene, "Group Therapy and Analysis," in Stein, *Jungian Analysis*, pp. 225-226.

22   Edward C. Whitmont, "Recent Influence on the Practice of Jungian Analysis," in Stein, *Jungian Analysis*, p. 337.

23   *Ibid.*, p. 339.

24   *Ibid.*, p. 340.

Chapter Nine: The Voice and the Vision

1   *The Development of Personality*, *CW* 17, "The Development of Personality," pp. 175, 176.

2   *Ibid.*, p. 175.

3   *Ibid.*, p. 176.

4   *Ibid.*, p. 183.

5   *VS*, Book Two, p. 297.

6   *Civilization in Transition*, *CW* 10, "The Meaning of Self-Knowledge," p. 303.

7   Densmore, *Teton Sioux Music*, pp. 184-185, 187-188.

8   *Two Essays in Analytical Psychology*, *CW* 7, "The Relationship Between The Ego and the Unconscious, p. 174.

9   *Ibid.*, "On the Psychology of the Unconscious," p. 116.

10   *The Symbolic Life*, *CW* 18, "Adaptation, Individuation, Collectivity," p. 453.

11   Jacobi, *The Way of Individuation*, pp. 132-133.

12   *Ibid.*, p. 18.

13   Marie-Louise von Franz, *On Divination and Synchronicity* (Toronto, Canada: Inner City Books, December 1980), p. 44.

14   Jacobi, *The Way of Individuation*, p. 92.

15   Neihardt, *Black Elk Speaks*, p. 151.

16   *The Structure and Dynamics of the Psyche*, *CW* 8, "Basic Postulates of Analytical Psychology," p. 354.

17   *Two Essays in Analytical Psychology*, *CW* 7, "The Relations Between the Ego and the Unconscious," pp. 186-187.

18   *The Symbolic Life*, *CW* 18, "Psychology and Spiritualism," p. 313.

19   *VS*, Book Two, p. 438.

20   *Psychology and Alchemy*, *CW* 12, "Individual Dream Symbolism in Relation to Alchemy," p. 212.

Chapter Ten: Dreams and Prophecies

1   Neihardt, *Black Elk Speaks*, p. 50.

2   James Hall, "The Use of Dreams and Dream Interpretation in Psychological Analysis," in Stein, *Jungian Analysis*, p. 128.

3   *The Structure and Dynamics of the Psyche*, *CW* 8, "The Psychological Foundations of Belief in Spirits," p. 306.

4   *Ibid.*, "On the Nature of Dreams," p. 282.

5   *MDR*, p. 394.

6   *The Structure and Dynamics of the Psyche*, *CW* 8, "General Aspects of Dream Psychology," p. 248.

6   *Civilization in Transition*, *CW* 10, "The Meaning of Psychology for Modern Man," p. 149.

7   *The Symbolic Life*, *CW* 18, "Depth Psychology," p. 484.

8   *Ibid.*, "Sigmund Freud," p. 362.

9   Hall, "The Use of Dreams," in Stein, *Jungian Analysis*, pp. 135-136.

10   *The Practice of Psychotherapy*, *CW* 16, "The Aims of Psychotherapy," p. 43.

11   *The Symbolic Life*, *CW* 18, "A Radio Talk in Munich," pp. 556-557.

12   Densmore, *Teton Sioux Music*, pp. 173-174.

13   *Ibid.*, pp. 176-177.

14   *Ibid.*, pp. 207-208.

15   *Ibid.*, p. 248.

16   *The Structure and Dynamics of the Psyche*, *CW* 8, "General Aspects of Dream Psychology," p. 255.

17   *The Symbolic Life*, *CW* 18, "Symbols and the Interpretation of Dreams," p. 208.

18   *The Structure and Dynamics of the Psyche*, *CW* 8, "General Aspects of Dream Psychology," p. 263.

19   *The Development of Personality*, *CW* 17, "Analytical Psychology and Education," p. 119.

Conclusion

1   James Jeans, *Physics and Philosophy* (Cambridge, UK: Cambridge University Press, 1942). See also the writings of Fred Alan Wolf (an array of Wolf's papers can be found at http://www.fredalanwolf.com), and especially F. David Peat's *Blackfoot Physics: A Journey into the Native American Worldview* (Newburyport, MA: Phanes Press, 2002).

2   Jeffrey Iverson, in his book *In Search of the Dead* (San Francisco, CA: Harper Collins, 1992), comments:

> One speculation is that the universe might be composed of thought, which could explain how an observer might appear to interact with his experiment. If matter is a "frozen thought" in a universe composed of "mind-stuff" then almost anything is possible …

3   *The Archetypes and the Collective Unconscious*, *CW* 9i, "The Psychology of the Child Archetype," p. 173.

4   *The Development of Personality*, *CW* 17, "Analytical Psychology and Education," p. 89.

5   *The Structure and Dynamics of the Psyche*, *CW* 8, "On the Nature of the Psyche," p. 215.

6   *Ibid.*

7   *Ibid.*, "Basic Postulates of Analytical Psychology," p. 384.

8   *Ibid.*, "The Soul and Death," p. 414. Jung continually approached the boundaries of the universe conceived as a physical entity, and gave hints of a superior form of existence coincident with ours. See "Spirit and Life," an essay in *The Structure and Dynamics of the Psyche*, *CW* 8, p. 335. When talking about spirit, he observed:

> If we are to do justice to the essence of the thing we call spirit, we should really speak of a "higher" consciousness rather than of the unconscious, because the concept of spirit is such that we are bound to connect it with the idea of superiority over the ego-consciousness.

9   *The Archetypes and the Collective Unconscious*, *CW* 9i, p. 173.

10   *SDA*, "Winter Term—2nd part, 1930, Lecture VIII—12 March 1930," pp. 528-529.

11   *Ibid.*

12   Andrew Samuels, *Jung and the Post-Jungians* (London, UK: Routledge & Kegan Paul, 1985), p. 94.

13   *VS*, Book Two, Part Ten, p. 363.

14   *Psychological Types*, *CW* 6, "XL. Definitions," p. 478.

15   *Ibid.*, p. 475.

16   *Symbols of Transformation, CW* 5, "Symbols of the Mother and of Rebirth," p. 228.

17   Here we need a strong dose of Karl Barth's theology.

18   *L*, Vol. 2, "To Heinrich Boltze—13 February, 1951," p. 5.

19   *The Practice of Psychotherapy, CW* 16, "The Psychology of the Transference," p. 323.

20   Joseph Henderson, *Thresholds of Initiation*, p. 220.

21   *The Symbolic Life, CW* 18, "The Tavistock Lectures—V," pp. 178-179.

22   *Psychology and Religion: West and East, CW* 11, "Transformation Symbolism in the Mass," p. 325.

23   *Ibid.*, "Psychology and Religion," p. 58.

24   *Ibid.*, p. 59.

25   *The Symbolic Life, CW* 18, "Jung and Religious Belief," pp. 714-715.

26   Harding, *Psychic Energy*, p. 414.

27   *The Structure and Dynamics of the Psyche, CW* 8, "Synchronicity: An Acausal Connecting Principle," p. 441.

28   *Ibid.*, p. 531.

29   *Ibid.*, pp. 505-506.

30   *Ibid.*, p. 501.

THE AUTHOR

Vine Deloria Jr., an enrolled member of the Standing Rock Sioux Tribe, was born March 26, 1933 in Martin, South Dakota. His father, Vine Deloria, Sr., and grandfather, Philip J. Deloria, were Dakota Sioux Episcopalian clergymen, and they laid the groundwork for Deloria's subsequent interest in religion and politics, as well as his willingness to mediate and to challenge both Indian and non-Indian peoples. He served in the U.S. Marine Corps from 1954-1956, and graduated from Iowa State University in 1958, the Lutheran School of Theology in 1963, and the University of Colorado School of Law in 1970. Deloria taught at Western Washington University, UCLA, the Pacific School of Religion, and Colorado College before accepting a position as Professor of Law and Political Science at the University of Arizona in 1978. At Arizona, Deloria helped create an M.A. in American Indian Studies and formed the nucleus for what remains one of the nation's best American Indian Studies programs. In 1990, he moved to the University of Colorado, where he held appointments in American Indian Studies, Law, History, Religious Studies, and Political Science.

In 1969, Deloria exploded the generally black-white terrain of American race politics with a bestselling book, *Custer Died For Your Sins: An Indian Manifesto*. In it, he laid out in biting and witty prose the social and political contexts underpinning an American Indian cultural politics. That politics, he argued, was not simply a reflection of African American or other ethnic political movements of the period, but was in fact rooted in the distinct history and political status of Native peoples. Deloria followed *Custer* with a rapid burst of writing and editing in the early 1970s, producing the books *We Talk, You Listen* (1970), *God is Red: A Native View of Religion* (1972), and *Behind the Trail of Broken Treaties* (1974), as well as the edited Volumes *Red Man in the New World Drama Revisited* (1971) and *Of Utmost Good Faith* (1971). In these works, Deloria insisted that treaty rights—codified in hundreds of legal agreements and recognized in the U.S. constitution—must be the guiding principle in relations between the United States and Native American people.

Deloria always wrote with American Indian concerns in mind, but his works moved in other directions as well. In 1974, the editors of six prominent journals of religion collectively named him a "Theological Superstar of the Future," one of eleven "shapers and shakers of the Christian faith." *God is Red* was a highly influential piece of theological writing, and he followed it with a sustained engagement with theology and philosophy, producing works such as *The Metaphysics of Modern Existence* (1979), *Evolution, Creationism, and Other Modern Myths* (2002), and a large number of essays, later collected in *For This Land* (1999) and *Spirit and Reason* (1999). In these works, he insisted upon new approaches to metaphysics, arguing that spiritual traditions were tied as much to land as to mobile religious traditions, and that modern spirituality ought to invest in a specifically American perception of land, one that would bring tribal and non-tribal peoples into the same orbit. This optimistic reading of the possibilities stemmed, in large part, from his willingness to engage European philosophers and theologians deeply, but it also reflected a growing skepticism concerning science and its often instrumentalist uses, which he saw both in terms of Indian people (expressed in his 1995 polemic *Red Earth, White Lies*) and the earth itself. *C.G. Jung and the Sioux Traditions*, his last work, offers an apt culmination of all these intellectual traditions.

THE EDITORS

Jerome S. Bernstein is a Jungian Analyst in private practice in Santa Fe, New Mexico. His book, *Living in the Borderland: The Evolution of Consciousness and the Challenge of Healing Trauma* (Routledge 2005), asserts that a primary issue in Western culture is its disconnection from a living relationship with nature. This dissociation is too often missed in Western clinical models, and Bernstein's book addresses this problem as well as presenting ways of adapting our clinical models to include nature as a living and essential dimension of psyche. He has been in private practice for over thirty years and has had a deep relationship with the Navajo and Hopi cultures over the past forty years. He works collaboratively with a Navajo medicine man, with whom he also gives bi-cultural seminars and clinical presentations. His website is: www.borderlanders.com.

Philip J. Deloria (Ph.D. Yale 1994) is professor in the Department of History and the Program in American Culture at the University of Michigan. His 1998 book *Playing Indian*, which deals with American appropriations of real and imagined forms of Indianness, was the winner of a Gustavus Myers outstanding book award from the Gustavus Myers Program for the study of Bigotry and Human Rights in North America. In 2004, he published *Indians in Unexpected Places*, which examines the ideologies surrounding Indian people at the turn of the twentieth century and the ways Native Americans challenged those ideologies through world travel, film and theater, sports, automobility, and musical performance. Deloria is the author of numerous articles and essays, was a co-author of *The Native Americans* (Turner, 1993), co-editor of the *Blackwell Companion to American Indian History*, and is past president of the American Studies Association. He is the eldest son of Vine Deloria, Jr.

THE ARTIST

Mary Sully (Susan Deloria, 1896–1963) was a Dakota Sioux artist active between the late 1920s and the mid-1950s. In her most distinct project, which she named the "Personality Prints," Sully sought to represent the characteristic elements of individuals prominent in American popular culture. She framed these images in the form of triptychs, each of which followed a similar format that blended together modernist abstraction, symbolic play, and the abstract geometries found in Dakota women's artistic traditions, including parfleche painting, quillwork, beading, and quilting. For more, see Philip J. Deloria, *Becoming Mary Sully: Toward an American Indian Abstract* (2019).

INDEX